Studies in Logic
Volume 23

The Logic of Fiction

Volume 13
Knowledge in Flux. Modeling the Dynamics of Epistemic States
Peter Gärdenfors. With a foreword by David Makinson

Volume 14
New Approaches to Classes and Concepts
Klaus Robering, editor

Volume 15
Logic, Navya-Nyāya and Applications. Homage to Bimal Krishna Matilal
Mihir K. Chakraborti, Benedikt Löwe, Madhabendra Nath Mitra and Sundar Sarukkai, eds.

Volume 16
Foundations of the Formal Sciences VI. Probabilistic Reasoning and Reasoning with Probabilities.
Benedikt Löwe, Eric Pacuit and Jan-Willem Romejin, eds.

Volume 17
Reasoning in Simple Type Theory. Festschrift in Honour of Peter B. Andrews on His 70th Birthday.
Christoph Benzmüller, Chad E. Brown and Jörg Siekmann, eds.

Volume 18
Classification Theory for Abstract Elementary Classes
Saharon Shelah

Volume 19
The Foundations of Mathematics
Kenneth Kunen

Volume 20
Classification Theory for Abstract Elementary Classes, Volume 2
Saharon Shelah

Volume 21
The Many Sides of Logic
Walter Carnielli, Marcelo E. Coniglio, Itala M. Loffredo D'Ottaviano, eds.

Volume 22
The Axiom of Choice
John L. Bell

Volume 23
The Logic of Fiction
John Woods, with a Foreword by Nicholas Griffin

Studies in Logic Series Editor
Dov Gabbay   dov.gabbay@kcl.a

The Logic of Fiction

John Woods
with a foreword by Nicholas Griffin

© Individual author and College Publications 2009. All rights reserved.

ISBN 978-1-904987-99-4

College Publications
Scientific Director: Dov Gabbay
Managing Director: Jane Spurr
Department of Computer Science
King's College London, Strand, London WC2R 2LS, UK

http://www.collegepublications.co.uk

Original cover design by orchid creative   www.orchidcreative.cc
Printed by Lightning Source, Milton Keynes, UK

All rights reserved. No part of this publication may be reproduced, stored in a retrieval system or transmitted in any form, or by any means, electronic, mechanical, photocopying, recording or otherwise without prior permission, in writing, from the publisher.

FOREWORD

NICHOLAS GRIFFIN

It is surprising, on looking back, to discover how little was written on the semantics of fiction before John Woods' *The Logic of Fiction* was published in 1974. The surprise is the greater because Woods' book appeared after almost a quarter century of fierce philosophical debate about reference in which two of the dominant issues were whether singular referential expressions (in particular, names and descriptions) carried ontological commitment and whether the standard theories of such expressions (in particular, Russell's theory of descriptions) were adequate to account for the full range of their uses in natural language. Surely, one would think, the theory of fiction would form an important part of such a debate. Fictional discourse, after all, is one important way in which names and descriptions are used and, more importantly, one notable way in which they are used (apparently) without the ontological commitments which theories like Russell's theory of descriptions take to be standard. Fictional discourse, one would have thought, would be an important testing ground for philosophical theories of referential expressions and one, moreover, in which the standard theories would likely be tested to destruction.

Nonetheless, a lively debate about the semantics of fiction was not part of the lively debate about definite descriptions and proper names which took off after the publication of Strawson's 'On Referring' in 1950. It is true that the two great founding fathers of the modern theory of reference - Frege and Russell - had both mentioned the use of referring expressions in fiction. In 'On *Sinn* and *Bedeutung*', Frege devotes a paragraph to 'Odysseus was set ashore at Ithaca while sound asleep' (Frege [1892], p. 157) in which he concludes that, since the subject expression lacks a reference, so, too, does the sentence in which it occurs; that is, the sentence lacks a truth-value. Frege excuses this by claiming that in fiction 'we are interested only in the sense of the sentences and the images and feelings thereby aroused'; the question of truth is not involved in a work of art, but only in scientific investigation.

But this is hardly satisfactory for at least three reasons: (1) There are many cases, even within 'scientific investigations', where referential expressions apparently lack reference. Frege himself notes 'divergent infinite series' as an example ([1892], p. 163) and proposes, in that case, to assign it a conventional or stipulative reference, e.g., the number 0. This, as Russell mildly says, 'is plainly artificial, and does not give an exact analysis of the matter' (Russell [1905], p. 420) - it is surely open to stronger complaints than that (cf. Gallie [1973]). Moreover, it leaves Frege with two theories of reference the applicability of which depends, apparently, on whether the context is artistic or scientific.[1] (2) While there are cases in 'scientific' prose where putatively referring expressions lack a reference, there are also cases in fiction where referring expressions do have a reference, and not a merely stipulative one. Is it true or false that Napoleon, on being told in 1812 that Moscow had been abandoned, scowled and called for his carriage, as Tolstoy says in *War and Peace*? Maybe, in reality, Napoleon cursed and called for his chief of staff; maybe he just stood dumbfounded. If he did either of those things, then what Tolstoy says would seem to be false. Yet it is not that Tolstoy simply got it wrong; if Tolstoy made a mistake, it was not at all the same sort of mistake that a historian would have made if she'd said what Tolstoy did. We are not entitled, for example, simply to dismiss from the novel any consequences which depended upon this action. If, on the other hand, Tolstoy got it right, this might be because of his meticulous study of contemporary memoirs, but it need not. It seems, rather, that whether Napoleon *actually* did what Tolstoy said is irrelevant to the novel; what is relevant to the novel is what Tolstoy said he did. It seems, therefore, as if we've reached a conclusion sympathetic to Frege's: questions of truth-value are irrelevant in fiction. But if Tolstoy's sentence is neither true nor false, it is not because any of the referring expressions that occur in it lack a reference. And, on Fregean semantic principles, if all the expressions which make up Tolstoy's sentence have a reference, then so too does the sentence itself, i.e., in Fregean terms, it has a truth-value. (3) However, finally and most importantly for the semantics of fiction, it is surely wrong to think that truth-values are of no concern in fiction. In following a narrative, for example, we are concerned with more than just the sense of the sentences: we have to take the descriptions of what has happened previously as true in order to understand the description of what happens next. Unless we take it as true that Odysseus was put ashore sound asleep, we cannot understand why he does not at first realize that he is back at home. Moreover, how, without attaching truth-values to the sentences involved, are we to understand inferences such as the following stereotypical example : 'Either the maid did it or the butler did it. And the maid didn't do it. Therefore, the butler did'?

In 'On Denoting', Russell says even less about fiction. He recommends replacing fictional names by definite descriptions and, by applying his theory of scope, he does acknowledge that fictional sentences in which the description has secondary scope may be true. However, in all cases where it has primary scope, the sentence will be false (Russell [1905], p. 425). Thus it will be false that Odysseus was set ashore while sound asleep. He defends this position at greater

---

[1] Frege gives no account as to when each theory should be applied; and, to complicate matters further, there is a third theory that can be identified in his work. See Pelletier and Linsky [2009].

length in *An Introduction to Mathematical Philosophy* ([1919], pp. 169-70). But Russell's approach, on which all declarative fictional sentences get truth values, is hardly more satisfactory than Frege's. It is correct to say that Sherlock Holmes was a detective and incorrect to say he was a carpenter. On Russell's theory both alike are false. Although Russell is far from specific about the details, it seems clear that he would want to distinguish between the two by meta-fictional means, by saying, for example, that while it was true that Conan Doyle had said (in the Sherlock Holmes stories) that Holmes was a detective, it was false that he had said that he was a carpenter. There is good reason why Russell is not specific about the details, for sentential operators like 'Conan Doyle said in the Sherlock Holmes stories that' are highly intensional and their behaviour was not at all well-understood in Russell's day. A crude initial attempt is to cash out ' Conan Doyle in the Sherlock Holmes stories said that Sherlock Holmes was a detective' as 'The texts written by Conan Doyle that comprise the Sherlock Holmes stories contain the sentence "Sherlock Holmes is a detective"'. But this hardly does justice to the case. In fact, it may well be false. 'Sherlock Holmes is a detective' may well be a sentence which does not occur in any of the Sherlock Holmes stories, nor need the stories contain any sentence which has the same meaning as 'Sherlock Holmes is a detective'.[2] That Holmes was a detective may well be something that the reader is expected to infer from other sentences in the stories. Now it doesn't matter that most of the sentences from which the inference is drawn will, on Russell's account, be false – for 'Sherlock Holmes is a detective' will also be false on that account. But about what are we to draw the inference? The inference should be of the form: $\underline{Fa}$, $(\forall \underline{x})(\underline{Fx} \rightarrow \underline{Gx})$ ∴ $\underline{Ga}$, but on Russell's theory this is not possible, for Sherlock Holmes is not an admissible instantiation for '$\underline{a}$'.

It is, in fact, very difficult to see how either theory could deal with these problems, though my brief remarks here will hardly suffice to convince anyone that they are insuperable. In Frege's and Russell's defence, it has to be acknowledged that a theory of the semantics of fiction was very far from their main concerns; both were concerned much more with the philosophy of mathematics than the philosophy of language and it is more remarkable that they

---

[2] Equally, the sentence (or some equivalent of it) might occur in the stories and be false. After all, Conan Doyle's story 'The Final Problem' contains sentences which state plainly that Holmes is dead; in subsequent stories this proves to be false. There are in fact two separate issues which come together in this particular case: the omniscience of the narrator (Watson) and the omniscience of the author (Doyle). Famously, Doyle (no less than Watson) thought that Holmes was dead at the end of 'The Final Problem', but had to revise the narrative to meet the demands of his readership. The omniscience of the author is usually to be relied upon; that of the narrator much less so.

considered fiction at all than that they failed to develop and adequate theory of it. This excuse, however, hardly applies to the generation of philosophers, starting with Strawson in 1950, who were concerned with the problems of reference. These were primarily philosophers of language and many of them were especially concerned with ways in which Russell's theory (which by then dominated the field) failed to provide an adequate account of how definite descriptions were used in ordinary language – something which, incidentally, it was never Russell's intention to supply. Strawson, in 'On Referring', says even less about fictional uses of definite descriptions than Frege and Russell, and what he says is both less clear and less satisfactory. He acknowledges that the statements in *Pickwick Papers* are about Mr Pickwick, but only in some special (and unexplained) sense of 'about'.[3] Otherwise, in the original publication of the paper, he described fictional uses of referring expressions as 'spurious', though in later reprints he withdrew that word, preferring to call them '"secondary"' (Strawson [1950], p. 35n) – thereby appropriating Russell's terminology but none of his subtlety. And there, sad to relate, the theory of fiction more or less stuck until Woods. Between 1950 and 1974 a whole library of papers appeared on reference, on names and descriptions, on the logic of existence, on ontological commitment – but virtually nothing on fiction. Routley's two bibliographies in *Exploring Meinong's Jungle and Beyond*, which were intended to be comprehensive up to publication in 1980, lists eight items explicitly about fiction, all from the period 1974-79 - nothing prior.[4]

Now there was in fact an author writing in the early years of the twentieth century who had a good basis on which to build a plausible theory of fiction, but who didn't actually build one, and this was Alexius Meinong with his theory of objects. Meinong, of course, was as much a psychologist as a philosopher and his main concern was with the contents of mental acts, in particular with the content of assumptions. He was not greatly concerned with the philosophy of language in general or with the semantics of fiction in particular. In his most important work, the second edition of *On Assumptions* [1910], there are a few brief comments on fiction in the relevant sense[5] but in all

---

[3] Special and unexplained senses were a hallmark of Strawson's paper: most famously there was a special and unexplained sense of 'imply' in which 'The present King of France is bald' was said to imply (but not to entail) 'The present King of France exists'.

[4] In fact, Routley overlooks one earlier paper, namely Woods' own 'Fictionality and the Logic of Relations' [1969]. Routley was certainly aware of it, since Woods reports discussing it with him in 1971 (Peacock and Irvine (eds.) [2005], p. 105). A slightly earlier but widely distributed 'selective bibliography' (Peacocke and Scott [1979]) lists only Woods [1974].

[5] Meinong uses 'fiction' in a technical sense to refer to assumptions for which factual verification has been renounced ([1910], p. 82).

of them he is concerned with the psychological state of either the writer or the audience ([1910], pp. 34, 86, 96, 115-6). There is no discussion of the semantics of fiction, for which Meinong's theory of objects would have provided a very good beginning. The fact that the closest we had come to an adequate theory of fiction before 1974 was Meinong's theory of objects, serves to emphasize the difficulty of the task. For Meinong's theory of objects was thought to be totally discredited, demolished by a battery of devastating arguments due to Russell.

What made Meinong's theory of objects a good starting point for a theory of fiction was its admission of non-existent objects; objects which had properties and identity conditions, and which could be quantified over, but which did not exist. It was this feature of Meinong's theory that was thought to have been most thoroughly discredited, but on the face of it, this was exactly what was needed for the theory of fiction. For fictions, it would seem, are populated with objects which have properties, which are distinct from one another, and which can be quantified over, but which (in most cases) do not exist. This gives us what Woods in Chapter II calls 'the naive approach' to fiction. On this approach 'there are vastly many statements about all manner of fictional persons, places and things, some of which are true and others of which are false' (p. 24). Thus it is true that Holmes is a detective and that Moriarty a villain. Moreover, it is true that Holmes is the same person, not just from beginning to end of a single story, but through all of them, and that he is not the same person as Watson in any of them; and that, if Holmes detests Moriarty, then there is someone whom Holmes detests. In *The Logic of Fiction*, we have for the first time a systematic account of a theory which acknowledges all these points (and the difficulties which attend them[6]) and which avoids all the problems, mentioned above, which attend Frege's and Russell's theories.

Woods, however, unlike Routley who was working around the same time, was not attempting to revive Meinong's theory.[7] The prevailing wisdom at the time Woods was writing was that Meinong's theory was past reviving. While Woods acknowledges the force of the pre-philosophical intuitions which comprise the naive approach, unlike Meinong, he is not prepared to make them, unamended, the basis for his theory. But there are other important divergences between Woods' theory and Meinong's, divergences which do not in themselves require a modification of the naive approach to fiction. Meinong conceived of objects very generally indeed, much more generally than is necessary for a theory of fiction. On Meinong's theory, for every description there is an object

---

[6] Chapter II gives an excellent survey of the problems involved in providing a theory of fiction, most of them are still in contention.
[7] While Woods makes occasional references to Meinong, his direct debts to Meinong are few: none of Meinong's works is cited in his bibliography.

described. Woods wanted to limit his concern to fictional objects. Accordingly, he makes an important distinction between these and what he calls 'nonesuches'. The latter are the purported referents of 'bare' descriptions, the sort of description that occurs mainly as an example in a logic paper; famous examples include 'the present king of France', 'the round square', and 'the golden mountain'. For Meinong, such descriptions refer to genuine (but incomplete) objects; for Woods, they do not refer at all: the objects to which they appear to refer are nonesuches. Elsewhere, arguing from a more Meinongian point of view, I have complained that it is not as clear as it might be how to draw the distinction between fictional objects and nonesuches (Griffin [2005]). But be that as it may, it is hard to deny that making the distinction served Woods very well in isolating the sort of case he was interested in. Prior to Woods, almost all the discussion of non-referring names and descriptions (which had grown very elaborate by 1974) had dealt with nonesuches, with remarks about fictional objects confined, as we have seen, to asides or footnotes in which they were give a treatment that was essentially parasitic upon that provided for nonesuches. Yet fictional discourse presents different, and in many ways more difficult, semantic problems than those presented by bare descriptions like 'the present king of France'. By separating nonesuches from fictional objects and focussing his attention entirely on the latter, Woods was able to set aside almost all the intractable disputes that had bedevilled the theory of reference over the previous two decades. Whatever the ultimate tenability of the distinction, making it in the first place was a brilliant methodological move.

Although making the distinction between nonesuches and fictional objects gave Woods a clear run at the theory of fiction, he was still faced by a dauntingly difficult task, for fictional objects pose far more difficulties than nonesuches. This is partly due to the fact that they have, or at least seem to have, many more properties. Nonesuches, if they have any properties at all, have only those conveyed by the descriptions which refer to them (or, at most, only those and any further properties which they entail). Fictional objects, by contrast, seem to come, not only with the often vast descriptions provided explicitly by the works of fiction in which they appear, but with even vaster descriptions implicit in the story; for no novelist, however painstaking, could possibly say all, or even most, of what must be assumed about even the most thoroughly-described character. This is what Woods calls the 'fill-question' (pp. 63-5). That characters are subject to the laws of physics, that they have a biology appropriate to human beings, and that not all of their doings are chronicled (that things happen to them off stage as it were), are matters that are taken for granted in most fiction. And yet it is quite possible to write fiction in which characters do not obey the laws of physics (e.g., Wells' *The Man Who Could Work Miracles*) or do not have a standard human biology (e.g., Woolf's Orlando). As Woods notes (p. 64), the reader assumes that all such departures from normalcy will be signalled by the author. But fiction is never quite straight-forward: whose standards of normalcy are to be assumed? It matters greatly when it comes to filling out the plays of Jonson, for example, that Jonson was learned in contemporary alchemical lore, just as it matters, in filling out Shakespeare's history plays, which contemporary historical works he was familiar with. But equally, it matters whether an author is playing to (or playing with) the ignorance of his audience, whether he is making in-jokes above the audience's head, or whether he is aiming to instruct his audience. It is entirely possible for a single piece of fiction to be filled out in two different ways: allegory, for example, depends upon on it.

At a first approximation, one may think of filling out a work of fiction as closing it under the principles of some body of belief – sixteenth century alchemy or nineteenth century forensic science or, in a worst case scenario, the crackpot fantasies of the author – the identification of which is the work of the literary historian rather than the logician. Nonetheless, closure is a matter for the logician, even though the logical relation involved will rarely be entailment, for most of the inferences involved in filling out a fictional work will be defeasible.[8] The logician, in fact, will not be able to assume as an invariable rule that even logical principles hold in all fiction. It is possible – indeed, it is easy – to write fiction in which the laws of logic are violated: imagine a fiction in which a character squares the circle or discovers four integers which refute Fermat's last theorem.[9] The only requirement is that the author be suitably inexplicit about the method used or the numbers discovered.

To my knowledge, Woods was the first philosopher to take on board the possibility of fiction which encompasses the impossible. It adds greatly to the difficulty of devising an adequate theory of fiction, for it requires that, if fictional objects are to be countenanced, they must be permitted to have inconsistent properties. This in turn would require some emendation of the base logic, in order to save any work of fiction which admits such an object from triviality. Classically, the 'detonation principle', $(\varphi \wedge \neg \varphi) \to \psi$, holds for any ψ, so that (assuming that fictions are closed under classical inference principles) every sentence will be true in any fiction that countenances an inconsistency. This is hardly news to Woods, who wrote his doctoral thesis on the paradoxes of strict implication. In my view, it shows the need for a paraconsistent base logic, e.g. a relevant logic, where such dangerous classical principles fail. Woods, however, offers a rather more *ad hoc* proposal in the form of a restriction on $(\varphi \wedge \neg \varphi) \to \psi$ (p. 51; where, alas, it is misprinted in the original edition). It may be that he still prefers this modest proposal (or some variant of it) to the more

---

[8] There is, in fact, a sizeable body of fiction which gains its effect by encouraging the reader to fill out the story by making defeasible inferences, only to have those inferences defeated in the thrilling conclusion.

[9] For an example, see Priest [1997], where two characters discover an impossible box.

wholesale revisions of logic required by a paraconsistency programme.[10]

What causes the difficulty here is that whatever is the case in a work of fiction obviously depends upon what the author says - and the author might say anything, so that anything at all might be the case in some work of fiction or other. In fiction, it would seem, anything goes and the hope of devising a logic of fiction might seem doomed to disappointment. The problem is seen most sharply if we take (as Woods ultimately does not) the claims made in fiction to be true. Since such truths depend on the author's say-so, if the author says that the circle was squared then it is true that the circle was squared – logic to the contrary notwithstanding. It may seem as if these are unusual, pathological cases to be dealt with by some monster-barring device. But this is hardly the right approach: many perfectly ordinary stories (think in particular of old stories and legends) involve things or events which are in some sense impossible. Moreover, even if the cases were pathological, how are they to be avoided? Very little, if anything, can be prohibited in fiction. Literary licence should be unconstrained – at least semantically.

The upshot for the logic of fiction should not be to try and scale back its claims until they are so minimal that every fiction whatsoever must accept them. There is, I contend, no such minimalist position that the logic of fiction can adopt. To propose one is simply to invite a writer to devise a fiction which violates it – in all probability, such a fiction is already written. But to acknowledge this is not to admit defeat for a logic of fiction. More or less every fiction has its logic (though there may be dadaist exceptions even to this), it's just that one logic (however minimal) does not fit all fictions. 'The' logic of fiction needs sufficient flexibility to acknowledge this. In particular, the logic of fiction must not be confined only to possible objects. Now it is no part of Woods' project to devise a possibilia logic for fiction, but this is not merely because fiction can so readily accommodate impossibilia. It is part of Woods' position that fictional objects, however consistently they may be described, are *never* possible but non-actual objects. Woods holds that it is not possible for fictional objects to exist, even if their descriptions ascribe to them no impossible properties (pp. 76-79). I'm not entirely sure of Woods' argument here. On the one hand, he seems to argue that as fictional objects, it is essential to their nature not to exist. But, on the other, he has an argument that, for it to be possible for an object to exist, it must be a constituent of some world which could be actualized, and the worlds of fictional objects could never be actualized. For my own part, I do not feel compelled by either line of argument. But he also offers a

---

[10] In later writings Woods uses a 'cost benefit' analysis to help decide such matters. In Peacock and Irvine [2005, p. 324] he seems pessimistic about the advantages of relevant logics (he emphasizes their 'mammoth computational cost'), but elsewhere he acknowledges some advantages (Woods [2003, pp. 169-170]).

third argument which I believe requires more consideration: for any fictional object, x, it is *possible* that x is an inconsistent object, for the author might have ascribed inconsistent properties to x. So for any fictional x, though x may not have the property of being F and ¬F, x does have the property of being possibly F and ¬F, and this is surely bad enough (p. 78). I do think that it is possible for a sufficiently developed theory of non-existent objects to overcome this problem that allows fictional objects to be possible objects, but I am not sure that any of the standard neo-Meinongian theories have the resources to do this.

This, however, does not exhaust our concern with objects which are inconsistently described in fiction. For we need to distinguish cases in which an author deliberately describes objects in inconsistent ways from cases where this happens inadvertently. Just because an author explicitly asserts both F(a) and ¬F(a) in the same story does not mean that she envisages a as an inconsistent object: the inconsistent descriptions of it may just be a mistake. Nor need the mistake be as explicit as the one just described.. Dr Watson, as is well known, has an old war wound. I am reliably informed that in some stories it is located in his leg and in others in his arm. Doyle evidently did not intend to portray him as having two war wounds, nor as having one wound which was in two different places. Woods (p. 49) distinguishes these cases of authorial error from those in which an impossibility such as circle-squaring is deliberately included in the fiction (though the author, thinking perhaps that circle-squaring is possible, may not realize that what had been included is inconsistent). It is only the latter cases which pose problems for the logic of fiction. Cases of inadvertent inconsistency cause different problems for the interpretation of fiction. Somehow, such lapses have to be cleared up in a way which does least damage to the story.[11] The sayso semantics does have its limitations. Nor are its limitations confined to implicit or explicit contradictions: authors may make all sorts of mistakes. In *The Antiquary*, for example, Scott has the sun set into the sea while Arthur Wardour and his daughter are trapped by the rising tide on the *east* coast of Scotland. No inconsistency is involved, it is just a mistake of the sort that is typically corrected by readers silently employing the principle of charity.

The most serious challenge to sayso semantics, however, is much more pervasive and banal than either deliberately engineered inconsistency or even author error: it arises from the inevitable use of relations in fiction. Fictional characters have relations to one another, and also to the things which make up

---

[11] Essays by John Sutherland (1996; 1997]) give many fascinating examples, not all of them are easily disposed of. More difficult still, as Sutherland makes clear, what might at first sight seem to be mere carelessness on an author's part may, when more carefully (or perhaps just differently) viewed, be seen as unsuspected subtleties in the text. How such matters affect the semantic analysis of fiction is an unresolved (and largely unstudied) problem.

their fictional world. More problematically, they very typically have relations to items in the real world. It didn't actually happen, but it would certainly have been possible for Conan Doyle to write a Sherlock Holmes story in which Holmes had tea with Gladstone. Even without such specific events, novels are typically set in actual places, at actual times. Most fiction takes place on earth and most of that which doesn't, takes place within our galaxy or, at very least, within our universe. This simple fact leads to serious problems for the say-so semantics. Suppose Conan Doyle had written the story just envisaged, then by the say-so semantics it would be true of Holmes that he had tea with Gladstone and thus, by the symmetry of the relation, it would be true of Gladstone that he had tea with Holmes. But Gladstone never had tea with Holmes. This is certainly one of the most difficult problems facing a theory of fiction. So far as I know, Woods was the first to notice it. He presents it in Chapter II, §5 (pp. 41-2), but it appeared earlier in his 'Fictionality and the Logic of Relations' (Woods [1969]).

The problem also affects Meinongian theories,[12] and has been extensively studied by those hoping to rehabilitate Meinong. Routley, for example, deals with it by distinguishing between 'entire' and 'reduced' relations ([1980], pp. 268-9, 577-90). Only the former have the full range of logical entailments one expects from the relation in question, but they hold only when all the terms of the relation exist or none of them does. When some terms exist and others don't, the relation is always reduced and the usual entailments cannot be relied upon. Thus even, if it were true that Holmes had tea with Gladstone, we cannot infer that Gladstone had tea with Holmes for the relation involved is reduced. More elegantly, Parsons ([1980], pp. 26-27, 59-60, 75-77) introduces a device of 'plugging up' relations in one or more of their argument places to make monadic properties. Thus from the fact that Holmes has the plugged up relation $\lambda \underline{x}(\underline{x} \text{hadteawith Gladstone})$ we cannot infer that Gladstone has the plugged up relation $\lambda \underline{x}(\text{Holmes had tea with } \underline{x})$. Neither of these policies seem to me to work very well.[13]

Woods' earlier solution was actually an improvement on these. Woods distinguishes between fictionalizations and history-constitutive descriptions of an object (pp. 42-7). What the author says of a fictional object of his own

---

[12] There it arises from two Meinongian principles, corresponding respectively to the principle of unconstrained literary licence and the say-so semantics in the theory of fiction. These are Meinong's principle of freedom of assumption, which allows one to characterize an object in any way one wants, and what Routley calls the characterization postulate, according to which an object has the properties by which it is characterized.

[13] I have criticized them in Griffin [2009], pp. 216-19.

creation is, by the say-so semantics, history-constitutive of that object; what the author says of actually existing objects is a fictionalization of them. Thus, if Doyle wrote the Holmes story we have been imagining, it would be history-constitutive of Holmes that he had tea with Gladstone, but a fictionalization of Gladstone that he had tea with Holmes. By contrast, the biographical facts about Gladstone, e.g., that he championed Irish Home Rule and enjoyed chopping down trees, are history-constitutive of him. Although the distinction was introduced in order to solve problems caused by the use of relations in fiction, it is not confined to relations: if Gladstone, during his fictionalized tea with Holmes, has a coughing fit (a monadic event, we may suppose), that, too, is a fictionalization of Gladstone. Woods' treatment extends niftily to deal with other complexities to be found in fiction, especially in the Holmes stories where Conan Doyle's canon has been extended by many other authors. In Randall Collins' *The Case of the Philosophers' Ring* (Collins [1978]), Holmes is hired by Bertrand Russell to solve the theft of Wittgenstein's mind. Here, Holmes's being hired by Russell is a fictionalization of both Russell and Holmes: Doyle's say-so extends only to his own creations, though other authors may fictionalize as they please. This is certainly desirable, though iterated fictionalizations can make it difficult to determine who is fictionalizing what (see Woods' discussion of Faust, pp. 45-6).

Woods' distinction is not a distinction between different kinds of properties and relations. This is a complaint that might fairly be urged against Routley's distinction between entire and reduced relations, where it does seem as if two different relations (with distinct logical properties) share only a form of words in common. In Woods' theory *sentences* are fictionalizing or history-constitutive, depending on how they are used; but the predicates and relational expressions in them have exactly the same semantic value whichever way they are used. As Woods sets up the distinction (especially on p. 44) it seems to be a distinction between different kinds of truth or, rather, between different ways in which a sentence may be made true. Fictionalizations, of both real and fictional entities, are made true by the author's sayso; in the case of fictionalizations of fictional entities, the author whose sayso makes the sentence true is not the author who created the entity. History-constitutive sentences are true by author's sayso when they are about a fictional entity; but the truth or falsity of history-constitutive sentences about real entities does not depend on author's sayso at all.

Somewhat later in Chapter II, Woods does introduce an explicit contrast between 'true-in-reality' and 'true-in-fiction' and he offers a partial recursive definition of the latter (pp. 61-63). As Woods notes (p. 61), any attempt to amalgamate the two would require a 'compliantly nonstandard' treatment of consistency. So, too, would any attempt to treat truth-in-fiction as a single body of truths; for fictional characters (and real ones) are fictionalized in different ways. Georg Benda's operatic version of *Romeo and Juliet* has a happy ending. But even with a paraconsistent logic to help us, there seems little point in attempting to amalgamate the truth about Benda's Romeo with the truth about Shakespeare's. What is really needed is a notion of the truths of particular fictions or groups of fictions, this would largely obviate the need for paraconsistency except in the case of those fictions which explicitly countenance inconsistencies. Such a project, of course, adds further complexities both to the semantics of fiction (because of the multiplicity of fictional truth-predicates) and to its interpretation (since decisions have to be made about which works can be combined to support a single truth-predicate and which cannot).

These difficulties, however, are avoided on Woods' account. Despite a long discussion (pp. 71-81) of Routley's neutral quantification logics (as presented in Routley [1966]) designed specifically for the rehabilitation of a Meinongian theory of objects, Woods moves on to consider a free logic approach, thereby retaining quantifiers with serious existential import. Now it might seem natural (though I confess that my Meinongian upbringing may have given me a distorted sense of what is natural) in pursuing a free logic approach to fiction to embrace a dual-domain semantics (of the type adumbrated by Leblanc and Thomason [1968]), in which the outer domain, over which the quantifiers do not range, contained fictional objects. Once again, Woods does not take this approach. I am not exactly sure why, but the issues mentioned in the previous paragraph may be part of the answer. The complexities of fiction place severe demands on the outer domain: one needs either special identity conditions on the elements of the outer domain, so that objects can be distinguished from their fictionalizations (Benda's Romeo from Shakespeare's, and so on), or else, and perhaps more plausibly, different outer domains for different literary works. Woods may well feel that the gains which might thereby be achieved are not worth the additional complexity involved.

Instead, Woods returns to the notion of bet-sensitivity that he introduced early in the book (pp. 13-14). Statements purportedly about fictional objects are neither true nor false, but they are bet-sensitive. If I bet that Sherlock Holmes is a detective and you bet that he is a carpenter, I win and you lose. But the claim with which I win, we learn in Chapter IV, does not win because it is true, nor because your claim is false. It wins because it is right to affirm it, even though it is not true (p. 92). It is, Woods maintains, true-by-convention, whereas your claim is false-by-convention. Woods gives a counter-factual account of truth (and falsity) by convention: An atomic sentence φ is true (false) by convention iff φ is neither true nor false but if it were either true or false it would be true (false) (p. 94). [14] Woods leaves it open whether the semantics of the base logic

---

[14] Sentences about nonesuches, e.g., 'The present king of France is bald', also lack a truth-value, but are neither true nor false by convention, since, if they were true or

assigns truth-value gaps or third values to some sentences or whether the valuation function is simply undefined for them (p. 95). One untoward result of this, noted by Woods on p. 92, is that one cannot *know* that Holmes is a detective unless one rejects truth as a necessary condition for knowledge. On the other hand, the proposal has numerous advantages, which Woods lists on pp. 92-4. Nonetheless, Woods argues that the counterfactual definition of truth-by-convention requires the use of possible worlds semantics and yet fictional worlds are not to be identified with possible worlds. The latter claim strikes me as undeniable (possible worlds, as Woods points out, satisfy completeness conditions which fictional worlds lack), though the former seems open to question; indeed, there is reason to believe that possible world semantics is not entirely satisfactory as a semantics for counterfactuals (cf., e.g. Fine [1975]; Mares [2004], pp. 13-14).

Be that as it may, barring some enormous elaboration of the conventions by means of which fictional sentences are rendered true-by-convention, Woods' approach does not so far yield a great deal of traction as regards the problem of conflicting fictionalizations. Woods takes this up in his final chapter (pp. 117ff). After considering an eight-valued system which he quickly finds wanting, Woods turns to his final proposal: the modal olim-operator, **O**, read: 'in fiction it is the case that'. Since, on Woods' account, fictional sentences lack truth-values and fictional names lack referents, the semantics of the **O**-operator are largely substitutional, and based on the say-so condition: '**O**(φ)' meets the say-so condition iff either 'φ' represents a sentence that occurs in a work of fiction (base condition) or is a logical consequence of some consistent sentence ψ which meets the say-so condition (p. 133). Once fictional sentences are protected by the **O**-operator, truth-values can be assigned - '**O**(φ)' is true iff **O**(φ) – and many of the problems of fictional discourse noted above can be avoided. For example, '**O**(Holmes had tea with Gladstone)' and '¬(Holmes had tea with Gladstone)' may both be true, as may '**O**(φ)' and '**O**(¬φ)': in fiction Romeo both lived happily ever after and did not. It might be argued that this last does less than full justice to case, for it is only in different fictions that Romeo lived happily ever after and did not: no one (to date) has envisaged him doing both in the same work. Yet the operator approach to fiction may readily be extended to cover such complexities (though Woods himself does not consider the possibility) by introducing different olim-operators for different works of fiction. Thus (using obvious abbreviations) '**O**$_B$(Romeo lived happily ever after)' and '**O**$_S$(Romeo died tragically)' are both true, while '**O**$_B$(Romeo died tragically)' and '**O**$_S$(Romeo lived happily ever after)' are both false. The say-so conditions are easily adjusted for such a development; though, of course, the problem of identifying which works (or groups of works) require their own olim-operator

---

false, there is no saying which they would be: they are not bet-sensitive.

replaces the earlier one of identifying which required their own fictional-truth predicate (with no reduction of difficulty, it might be added).

Nonetheless, there are, I believe, problems with this account. Woods' claims it as a success that 'Someone admires James Bond' (which stems from an earlier example: 'Kingsley Amis admires James Bond') can be represented as '$(\exists \underline{v})O(A(\underline{v},b))$', thereby showing that 'a real object may enter into something like intentional relations with the fictional' (p. 135). But existential instantiation gives us '$O(A(\underline{a},b))$', rather than the original example. Indeed, '$O(A(\underline{a},b))$' is surely false: for 'Amis admires Bond' is not (one supposes) a sentence which occurs in any work of fiction, nor does it express a logical consequence of any sentence which does so occur. On the other hand, Woods' use of substitutional quantification does allow him to instantiate fictional names for variables in quantified formulae, despite the lack of fictional objects for the quantifiers to range over: something that was precluded in his earlier free logic approach.

Other problems have to do with the modal character of the olim-operator. In his axiom-set for **O**, Woods includes the problematic Axiom 3, $\Box\varphi \rightarrow \mathbf{O}\varphi$ (p. 141), which makes all logical truths fictional truths. With a classical view of logical consequence this is required by the say-so condition, for every logical truth is a (classical) logical consequence of any sentence. Having only one olim-operator may seem to help here, but the help is only illusory. With one olim-operator, **O**φ satisfies the say-so condition iff 'φ' represents a sentence (or a logical consequence of a sentence) which occurs in *some* work of fiction. No doubt many logical truths are represented in some fiction or other, but one only gets all of them by taking the consequence condition classically. The trouble is that if we take the consequence condition classically, we get all of them in *every* work of fiction. Yet, as we have seen, it is easy to conceive works of fiction in which some logical truths are explicitly denied. Let φ be such a truth and ψ some arbitrary consistent sentence in the same work. Then we have **O**¬φ, by the base condition, and **O**φ from ψ → φ, by the classical consequence condition. Moreover, the result holds even if we index the olim-operator to a specific work. There is, of course, no contradiction in asserting '**O**¬φ ∧ **O**φ', even if **O** is indexed, yet the result seems to do less than justice to the sort of fiction envisaged. Moreover, worse yet follows. From '**O**¬φ ∧ **O**φ' we get '**O**(¬φ ∧ φ)', by Woods' Axiom 4. But logical equivalents are intersubstitutable, so from '**O**(¬φ ∧ φ)' we get, for any sentence ψ, '**O**(¬ψ ∧ ψ)', whence, again by Axiom 4 (and ∧-elimination), we get '**O**ψ', for arbitrarily chosen ψ. Thus in fiction everything is the case. If we relativize the olim-operator to individual works of fiction, we get the even more unpalatable result that everything is the case in every work of fiction. The obvious options are either to proscribe authored inconsistencies (as distinct from accidental ones) in fiction (which is surely draconian) or adopt a paraconsistent base logic (which is surely preferable).

These problems notwithstanding, there seems to me to be much mileage left in the olim-approach to fiction, especially with an multiplicity of olim-operators and a paraconsistent base logic. Equally, there is scope for development of Woods' free logic proposal and (even more so, in view of the quantificational problems mentioned in the last paragraph but one) in a more Meinongian approach which countenances fictional objects. One of the great merits of Woods' book is that it takes seriously the wide-ranging demands that fiction imposes on logic and semantics, and does not try to force fiction into some pre-conceived logical mould. It offers an open-ended inquiry into a variety of ways in which logic might tackle the semantics of fiction. We still do not have an adequate logic of fiction, but thanks to Woods' pioneering efforts, we are much closer to one now than we were when he set out to write his book. His book was not the last word on the logic of fiction; it was much more important: it was very nearly the first.

References

Collins, Randall [1978], *The Case of the Philosophers' Ring* (New York: Crown).

Fine, Kit [1975], Review of David Lewis, Counterfactuals, *Mind*, 84, pp. 451-458.

Frege, Gottlob, [1892], 'On *Sinn* and *Bedeutung*', transl. by Max Black, in Michael Beaney (ed.), *The Frege Reader*, (Oxford: Blackwell, 1997), pp. 151-171.

Gallie, R.D. [1973], 'On a Special Stipulation of Frege', *Mind*, 82, pp. 445-9.

Griffin, Nicholas [2005], 'Through the Woods to Meinong's Jungle', in Peacock and Irvine (eds.) [2005], pp. 15-32.

Griffin, Nicholas and Jacquette, Dale (eds.) [2009], *Russell vs. Meinong. The Legacy of "On Denoting"* (New York and London: Routledge).

Leblanc, Hugues and Thomason, Richmond [1968], 'Completeness Theorems for Some Presupposition-Free Logics', *Fundamenta Mathematicae*, 62, pp. 125-64.

Mares, Edwin D. [2004], *Relevant Logic. A Philosophical Introduction*, (Cambridge: Cambridge University Press)

Meinong, Alexius [1910], *On Assumptions*, transl. by James Heanue, (Berkeley: University of California Press, 1983).

Peacock, Kent A. and Irvine, Andrew D. (eds.) [2005], *Mistakes of Reason: Essays in Honour of John Woods* (Toronto: Toronto University Press).

Peacocke, C.A.B, and Scott, Dana [1979], *A Selective Bibliography of Philosophical Logic* (Oxford: Sub-Faculty of Philosophy; 3rd edn.)

Pelletier, Francis Jeffry and Linsky, Bernard [2009], 'Russell vs. Frege on Definite Descriptions as Singular Terms', in Griffin and Jacquette (eds.) [2009], pp. 40-64.

Priest, Graham [1997], 'Sylvan's Box', *Notre Dame Journal of Formal Logic*, 38, pp. 573-82.

Routley, Richard [1966], 'Some Things Do Not Exist', *Notre Dame Journal of Formal Logic*, 7, pp. 251-276.

Routley, Richard [1980], *Exploring Meinong's Jungle and Beyond* (Canberra: Research School of Social Sciences, Australian National University)

Russell, Bertrand [1905], 'On Denoting' in *The Collected Papers of Bertrand Russell*, vol. 4, *The Foundations of Logic, 1903-05*, edited by Alasdair Urquhart, (London and New York: Routledge, 1994), pp. 415-427.

Russell, Bertrand [1919], *An Introduction to Mathematical Philosophy* (London: Allen and Unwin, 1967)

Strawson, P.F. [1950], 'On Referring', *Mind*, 59, pp. 320-44; reprinted in A. Flew (ed.) *Essays in Conceptual Analysis* (London: Macmillan, 1966), pp. 21-52.

Sutherland, John [1996], *Is Heathcliffe a Murderer? Puzzles in 19th Century Fiction* (Oxford: Oxford University Press)

Sutherland, John [1997], *Can Jane Eyre be Happy? More Puzzles in Classic Fiction* (Oxford: Oxford University Press)

Woods, John [1969], 'Fictionality and the Logic of Relations', *Southern Journal of Philosophy*, 7, pp. 51-63.

Woods, John [2003], *Paradox and Paraconsistency: Conflict Resolution in the Abstract Sciences*, (Cambridge: Cambridge University Press, 2003).

ANALYTICAL TABLE OF CONTENTS

Preface 7

Introduction 11

I. Logical Reconstructions
   §1. Rational bets 13
   §2. Base logics 14
   §3. Logical structure: Reconstruction and regimentation. 18
   §4. Deviant logics 21

II. Non-entities and Nonesuches
   §1. The naive approach. 24
   §2. Non-existent, non-intentional objects 29
   §3. Fictional existence 31
   §4. Ellipses 34
   §5. Mixed modes of being 41
   §6. History constitutiveness 42
   §7. The Law of Non-Contradiction 47
   §8. Non-refuting deviation 48
   §9. An essential property 54
   §10. History 55
   §11. Truth-value gaps 57
   §12. The say-so semantics 60
   §13. The fill-question 63
   §14. The quantificational problem. The modal problem 65

III. Free Logic and Facts
 §1. Free logics. 68
 §2. Neutral logics 71
 §3. Impossibilia logics 74
 §4. Possibilia 75
 §5. Narrowly free e-logics 80
 §6. Facts 83
 §7. The substitutional interpretation of quantification   88

IV. Truth-by-Convention
 §1. The value c 92
 §2. Truth-by-convention 94
 §3. Conditionals. 95
 §4. Possible worlds. 101

V. Many-valued and Modal Logics
 §1. The system $\mathscr{L}^3$. 109
 §2. The system $\mathscr{L}^4$. 113
 §3. Dimensions 117
 §4. The composition system $\mathscr{L}^8$ 119
 §5. Ambiguity. 127
 §6. The olim modality 131
 §7. Quantification 134
 §8. Quantified modal logic 141

Bibliography of Cited Works. 145
Index 148

INTRODUCTION

There is a very natural question of how to interpret the sentences of fiction, both those that actually occur in a story or follow from those that do, as well as those we ourselves use in recording our thoughts about fictional beings. It is, however, for all its naturalness, a question which is not accorded much attention by philosophers of language. It may be that part of the reason why this is so is that fictional discourse is not, really, all that important a component of language, and so may be presumed safely left to one side until harder and more basic concerns are disposed of. I would prefer to say not that the structure of fictional discourse is not all that important, but rather that it is not all that obscure, that its theory need not be despaired of. It is, in any event, undesirable to mistake the import of the fact that, when compared with this world's daily goings-on, what Sherlock Holmes did can never rival in importance what my local Hospital Board may do; only the former sort of event can cost me money or a kidney, or help restore my children's health, or give employment to a distant cousin. On no account, however, is it fair or allowable automatically to transfer such a verdict of unimportance for these goings-on to questions of the *structure of the language* in which the goings-on are recorded and discussed. True, it may be silly for a philosopher to dwell very long upon Sherlock, but a philosopher of language must be ready with opinions of 'Sherlock'.

Part of one, rather abrupt, explanation of the relative lack of interest in 'Sherlock' is that there is nothing especially distinctive or problematic about fictional discourse, for it is, all of it, false.

A somewhat less severe explanation could claim, with some justice, that the structure of fictional discourse is just that of any language whose grammatical rules tolerate sentences some of whose singular terms are empty. As such, it might be said, the structure of fictional discourse has already been given, for it is but that of FREE LOGIC.

It shall be a central theme of this essay that such positions are very much mistaken. Our objective shall be a sketch of an adequate SEMANTICAL THEORY for sets of fictional sentences of English. Now it is true that much of what is distinctive about fictional discourse is the distinctive manner in which it is produced and the distinctive context in which it may be supposed embedded. In pursuing a semantics for fiction we mean to adopt the view that those pragmatic parameters that deeply touch upon the question of how to understand the structure language of fiction are those for which it is possible to find, at appropriate levels of abstraction, semantic analogues.

Questions of the semantic structure of fictional discourse are not so undifficult as not to make welcome guidelines for keeping the main project in manageable focus. In particular, nowhere in this essay has it been thought advisable to deal with such additional, and difficult, topics as allegory, irony, and satire. Neither do we stray beyond representational, naturalistic fiction in the directions of poetry, painting, or the plastic and theatrical arts. Ours is a semantical project, not an aesthetic one. All the same, there is, I think, some reason to hope that, once the first is done, the second may be undertaken with an improved understanding.

I

LOGICAL RECONSTRUCTIONS

§1. *Rational bets.* – There exists in English, and in every civilized tongue, a sizeable set of sentences that exhibit a peculiar and much ignored property. It is that, although they may contain names and variables (or pronouns) that are empty or have no values – in the precise sense that what those names purport to name and what those variables purport to range over do not exist – these sentences are nonetheless BET-SENSITIVE. As an example, if you say that Sherlock Holmes lived in Baker Street I may wager that you are mistaken. Suppose that I venture a case of '66 Chambolle-Musigny in support of the counterclaim that Holmes lived on Berczy Street. Then, as we all very well know, what you say wins the bet; what I say loses it. Even if I were careful to hedge my bet, by counter-claiming only that Holmes did not live in Baker Street, what you say wins: what I say loses. It is an interesting and important curiosity of the affair that a certain kind of semantic defense of my hedged counterclaim – namely that Holmes could not have lived in Baker Street because he could not have lived anywhere, he being but fictional – is not automatically, or always, if *ever*, deemed a satisfactory endorsement of my claim at the expense of yours. The bet is still yours.

Not every class of sentences containing empty singular terms is bet-sensitive. As between "The present king of France is bald" and "The present king of France is vigorously hirsute" there is no rational wager to make. And as between "The present king of

France is bald" and "It is not the case that the present king of France is bald" a rational bet, of sorts, can be conceived, but, unlike the previous case, the dissenting opinion wins it.

We may classify a sentence containing empty singular terms as bet-sensitive if a bet, that so-and-so did such-and-such, can be won or lost according as the sentence "so-and-so did such and such" or a contrary of it is rightly assented to, yet not lost even given that "So-and-so does not exist" is rightly assented to. "Sherlock Holmes lived in Baker Street" is bet-sensitive; "The present king of France is bald" is not.

Our question is: shall the concept of bet-sensitivity be supposed semantically significant? I assume that an affirmative verdict would warrant the hypothesis that bet-sensitive sentences differ from bet-insensitive sentences by virtue of a difference in logical structure. If that should prove to be so, then an important semantical question, for certain classes of English sentences, is: what is the logical structure of bet-sensitivity?

§2. *Base logics.* – One way to approach a question of the logical structure of $\mathscr{E}$, a certain class of sentences, is to attempt to state what sort of theory of language would be adequate for sentences of that class or kind. In stating, or sketching, a theory of language for $\mathscr{E}$, it is not uncommon to observe something like the following procedures.

A base logic, **BL**, is postulated to underly $\mathscr{E}$. It need not (yet) be decided whether **BL** is an entirely standard logic, either in the sense that its syntax is first order (perhaps augmented by individual constants) or in the sense that its formal semantics involves only set theoretic entities and the usual functions from the language, L, of **BL** into them.

Also assumed is a SEMANTIC METALANGUAGE, SML, for the formal language, L, of **BL**. SML, customarily, is some or other natural language enriched by needed auxiliary symbols. It is the job of SML to provide a notion of a STRUCTURE for L. A structure for L consists of a non-empty set, called the DOMAIN D; the elements of D are said to be INDIVIDUALS. By "individuals" no ontological position is intended; an individual, currently conceived, is any object whatever over which our theory quantifies.

The formal language L is presumed to contain a supply of n-ARY FUNCTORS; and SML provides that for each such expression there is a function from D^n to D, that is, from the set of ordered n-tuples of the elements of D into D itself. It is also supposed that for each n-ARY PREDICATE of L, there is an n-ary relation, R, such that $R \subseteq D^n$; that is to say, R is taken to be a subset of the set of n-tuples of elements of D, where n is the degree of our predicate.

It is usual to expect from SML an account of what a MODEL of **BL** might be. To that end, a distinction is admitted between logical and nonlogical concepts, and, correspondingly, between the logical and nonlogical axioms for **BL**. It is not crucial that the distinction answer to everyone's intuitions of the relevant differences: in fact, not everyone agrees on what those differences are (witness one's concern over how to classify the standard identity axioms). To demand that SML settle this question, before moving on to the business of models is tantamount to insisting on a theory of logical truth. But it is to such an objective (among others) that the notion of a model is introduced.

A distinction between logical and non-logical axioms is useful in other ways. We shall want to consider the REPRESENTATION QUESTION for $\langle \mathscr{E} \cdot \mathbf{BL} \rangle$. That is the question of by what formal sentences of the language of **BL** it is illuminating to represent the English sentences of $\mathscr{E}$. It is supposed that there exist, or anyhow that it is desirable that there exist, mapping of sentences in $\mathscr{E}$ into L, such that the truths of $\mathscr{E}$ are represented in some distinctive way in L. Since some of the truths of $\mathscr{E}$ are bet-sensitive sentences having the *look* of contingency ("Sherlock Holmes lived in Baker Street") it may be that we shall elect to represent such truths by some of the nonlogical axioms of **BL**, for they, too, will have the look of contingency.

A logical axiom is true in every structure for L irrespective of the peculiarities of those structures. Nonlogical axioms, however, hold in a structure because of peculiarities of that structure.

A *model* of **BL** can be understood as a structure for L in which all the nonlogical axioms are true. And a formula of L will be said to be *valid* in **BL** if it is true in every model of **BL**.

In pursuing the question of the logical structure of bet-sensitive sentences of *&*, we do not assume a standard semantic for **BL**. Neither do we assume a nonstandard semantics. Our position at present is neutral with respect to standardness. When we speak of a nonstandard semantics for **BL**, a set-theoretical nonstandardness is usually intended. By a set-theoretically nonstandard object we understand an object, x, that is not a set, not a truth value, and not an object that is definable in terms of these. It is plain to see, that set theoretically nonstandard objects need not be nonstandard in other ways – philosophically, for example. People are not philosophically nonstandard, but they probably are set-theoretically nonstandard. 'Nonstandardness' is not necessarily a term of disparagement.

It is not wisely presumed that the mere recognition of facts, for example, commits a semantics to nonstandardness; for it is not clear that facts, whatever the philosophic odour in which they languish, cannot be defined or construed via sets and sequences. Even the Meinongean gesture of welcoming non-existent objects is not necessarily fatal. In one semantics non-existent objects might all be identified with the null set; and in another they might be admitted into classes that are virtual in something like Quine's sense,[1] whereupon the question of their nonstandardness would await a more general verdict concerning the nonstandardness of virtual classes. Likewise, not every non-classical truth value is set theoretically nonstandard. Some non-classical truth values can be construed as sequences of the classical truthvalues, and so are not, in our sense, nonstandard objects.

However, a semantics is not guaranteed to be standard if it recognizes none but set theoretically standard objects. A semantics would be nonstandard if it assigned to any sentence of L a non-classical truth value, even where that value is definable as in the paragraph above.

[1] W. V. Quine, *Set Theory and Its Logic*, revised edition (Cambridge, Mass: The Belknap Press, 1963), 15 ff.

A theory of language for $\mathscr{E}$ that recognized the entelechies could be said to be a philosophically nonstandard theory, and a silly one. A theory for $\mathscr{E}$ that countenanced phlogiston would be a physically nonstandard theory, and a silly one. A theory for $\mathscr{E}$ that welcomed animal spirits or monads would probably, too, be nonstandard, in some or other way; but none of these, on their face, would be required to have a nonstandard formal semantics. A theory whose formal semantics is set theoretically standard is not therefore, just so, spared the ignominy of preposterousness.

Without presuming to define nonstandardness for formal systems, we note that a theory is nonstandard if it recognizes set theoretically nonstandard objects, if it countenances many-sorted quantification, if it does not preserve the Laws of Excluded Middle and Non-Contradiction, if it recognizes a non-paraphraseable existence predicate, and if it countenances modal operators. The formal language L is assumed to contain at least:

(a) a neededly non-zero supply of formal names (individual constants), and, similarly, individual variables.
(b) similarly, n-ary functors and n-ary predicates.
(c) the classical quantifiers, '∃' and '∀'.
(d) the atomic sentences of the sentential calculus.
(e) an unlimited supply of atomic singular sentences.
(f) the connectives.

We remark, again, that L may later be supposed to number one or other of several varieties of item not here displayed.

SML is English, with the following auxiliary symbols:

(i) an assortment of variables 'ϕ', 'ψ', 'χ', etc., with or without indices, asterisks or accents, ranging over the sentences (open or closed) either of L or of $\mathscr{E}$, and over predicates of $\mathscr{E}$ or L as well.
(ii) a supply of variables 'v_0', ..., 'v_n', 'v', varying through the individual variables and constants of L.
(iii) the variables 'a_0', ..., 'a_n', 'a', ranging over the constants of L and the names of $\mathscr{E}$.

(iv) the letter S, with or without indices, asterisks and accents, as a variable over the sentences of $\mathscr{E}$.
(v) Quine corners, '⌜' and '⌝'.

§3. *Logical structure. Reconstruction and regimentation.* – Our purpose is to penetrate to the logical structure of bet-sensitive sentences of $\mathscr{E}$. Since bet-sensitive sentences, or their empty parts, seem readily to combine with certain English constructions to form other bet-sensitive sentences (e.g. "Freud psychoanalyzed Gradiva", "A distinguished European philosopher is in love with Molly Jeavons", "Kingsley Amis admires James Bond") we shall suppose $\mathscr{E}$ to contain a generous assortment of other kinds of sentences of our everyday involvements. In pursuing the question of an adequate theory of language for $\mathscr{E}$, it is assumed that the logical structure of bet-sensitive sentences will be disclosed, along the way, as it were. And since we fancy a contrast between bet-sensitives such as "Holmes solved the Case of the Speckled Band" and bet-insensitives such as "The present king of France is wise", we do not preclude the presence in $\mathscr{E}$ of sentences of the latter sort, if only that we might better understand that contrast.

Since our wish is to reveal the logical structure of bet-sensitives by way of saying something about an adequate theory of language for $\mathscr{E}$, it is assumed that we have reasonably solid intuitions concerning which of the sentences of $\mathscr{E}$ require our assent, which our dissent, which our uncertainty, and about which are the logical consequences of these. Our intuitions are thought to be reasonably solid when those fluent in $\mathscr{E}$ can agree in most specific cases when to assent to, dissent from or withold a sentence of $\mathscr{E}$, and when to reckon a sentence as a logical consequence of a sentence of $\mathscr{E}$. In speaking of such consensuses, we use the words 'intuition' and 'intuitive' to convey that these verdicts regarding $\mathscr{E}$ are not normally supported by appeal to explicit criteria. They are prereflections of our semantic dawn.

In representing $\mathscr{E}$ in L, we seek a perspicuous mode of exhibiting our intuitive judgements concerning $\mathscr{E}$. The theory of how to represent $\mathscr{E}$ in L is sometimes called a RATIONAL (OR LOGICAL)

RECONSTRUCTION of the body of our intuitions concerning $\mathscr{E}$ (or, more briefly, of our intuitive theory of $\mathscr{E}$). It is desirable, indeed mandatory, that a logical reconstruction accord with our intuitive theory, but it should also seek to encode the intuitive theory systematically. The general pattern of systematic representation is appealed to with a view to deciding special cases left slack by the intuitive theory. In that way the logical reconstruction can actually enhance our store of intuitions.

Sometimes it happens that one essays a semantical analysis of a linguistic corpus such as $\mathscr{E}$ without recourse to a formal language wherewith canonically to represent the sentences of the corpus. In such a case one might seek for functions from $\mathscr{E}$ into a proper subset $\rho(\mathscr{E})$ of $\mathscr{E}$, with $\mathscr{E}$-$\rho(\mathscr{E})$ now regarded as sentences that are at best structurally misleading, due to orthography, grammar or such like; regarded, that is to say, as a structurally misleading abbreviation for logically perspicious sentences of $\rho(\mathscr{E})$. (Thus "No one can outskate Hull" might get mapped onto "It is not the case that at least one person exists who can outskate Hull"; "Zachary exists" might be taken to "There exists an object to which Zachary is identical"; and "Constance believes Ted to be boring" might be taken into "There is a state of mind, x, of Constance, and x is a believing and x is a Ted-is-boring".)

The language $\rho(\mathscr{E})$ usually will contain the English idioms for the truth functional connectives, for the quantifiers, and will contain an assortment of dummy letters. In this way it is possible to produce sentences whose structure is truth functional and quantificational, without having to move, beyond $\mathscr{E}$, to a representing formal language, such as L. Sentences in $\mathscr{E}$ are said to be CANONICALLY REPRESENTED in $\rho(\mathscr{E})$; yet some sentences could be supposed to have a null canonical form in $\rho(\mathscr{E})$, and so be dispensed with as inessential to any serious scientific purport ("Nothing noths"?). A well-known example of this method – called regimentation – is the procedure whereby singular definite descriptions are contextually eliminated in favour of the idioms of quantification and identity.

According to the logical reconstructionist approach, the representation function takes the sentences of 𝒮 into the sentences of a semi-interpreted formal language, L; and so, takes the sentences of 𝒮 outside of 𝒮. It is in the language L of such a base logic **BL** that the logical relations among sentences of 𝒮 are represented by the logical relations, in **BL**, among the formal representatives of 𝒮. Decisions as to what kinds of formal sentences are selected to represent what kinds of 𝒮-sentences, augmented by information concerning what logical relations hold in **BL**, jointly disclose the logical structure of 𝒮.

These two approaches, although directed to common goals, are structurally and methodologically dissimilar. They can also suggest differing philosophical prejudices. A fanatical antiplatonist may disdain logical reconstruction for regimentation for want of a toleration of abstract entities. A less driven foe of platonism may allow himself the method of reconstruction only after persuading himself of its ontological neutrality; he may, that is to say, accept it as a heuristically useful *façon de parler*, expungeable, on demand, for empirically better-mannered equivalents.

It is not here intended that subscription to a semantic method either commits us to or reflects any substantive philosophic dogma. Philosophic dogma, where there is any, will be conveyed more directly, either as conclusions of arguments or as confessions of assumption. Nor do we here entirely favour the one approach over the other. In fact, SML is assumed to be an appropriately regimented language. To give a (contentious) example, nowhere in SML is it the case that quotations are contexts for occurrences. Thus, if we encounter in SML

(1) 'Cicero' has six letters

and

(2) Tully = Cicero

there is no question of inferring

(3) 'Tully' has six letters,

since the word formed by concatenating left to right occurrences of uppercase See, followed in order by Eye, See, Ee, Ar and Oh, is not presumed to occur in (1).

As we have said, the principal target of this study is the logical structure of bet-sensitive sentences; in particular, of sentences concerning fictional beings and fictional goings-on. But there is a tangential purpose, as well. It is disclosed in the subtitle.

§4. *Deviant logics.* – A formal theory, nonstandard in the sense of §2, will more likely than not include a DEVIANT LOGIC. 'Deviant', I believe, originates with Quine.[2] It is offered by Quine pejoratively, but with a correct descriptive connotation: a logical theory is deviant when it deviates from what is reckoned standard and good. It would amply justify the pejoration if deviation from what is good (and standard) compelled acceptance of something bad or less good. But that is not obviously so in the case of logic; it is obviously not so elsewhere. A logic is not to be disparaged just because it fails to preserve a theorem or axiom of old or current veneration. Deviant logics are made objects of disparagement, or at least of suspicion, when their departures are badly motivated; or when their metamathematical structures are only imperfectly understood; or when there is, or seems to be, no reasonable or consistent interpretation of its axioms and theorems. Sometimes a deviant logic is rejected just on the grounds that classical logic is immutably correct. But no serious student of logic advances such an argument (nor should he).

Three-valued logic is often decried because of a silly motivation, such as that occasioned by recognition of borderline cases, of empirical inexactness, open-texture, or what not. If that were the only motivation for a departure from classical negation, three-valued logic would probably make no serious claims on our attention. Three-valued logic is sometimes shied away from because its metamathematical properties are not very deeply known:

Yes, yes, I can hear the objections being shouted from all corners. If one is going to use undefined terms why not undefined truth values? Is not that more natural? Maybe so, but I have yet to see a reasonably workable three-valued logic. I know it can be defined, and at least four times a year

---

[2] W. V. Quine, *The Philosophy of Logic*, (Englewood Cliffs: Prentice-Hall, 1970), 80ff.

someone comes up with the idea anew, but it has *not* really been developed to the point where we could say it is pleasant to work with. Maybe the day will come, but I have yet to be convinced. So my advice is to continue with the two-valued approach because it is easy to understand ...[3]

Of course to counsel caution toward a given system of deviant logic is compatible with vigorous endorsement of others. There is, in fact, nothing in Scott's remark that precludes his agreeing that it is important "to frame philosophically interesting systems of non-standard logic and to prove metatheorems about them".[4]

Systems of quantified modal logic, under their intended interpretations, are attacked for being not coherently interpretable. Quine so alleges in several places.[5] It may be that Quine's skepticism has been answered by Kripke. Kripke has provided a formal semantics for several systems of quantified modal logic, and has proved such systems consistent and complete under specified interpretations.[6] When a logician complains that a logical system cannot coherently be interpreted, and another logician responds by providing a formal semantics that is provably consistent and complete, and consonant with deep intuitions concerning the meaning of its logical notions, that normally is taken to dispatch the complaint. If the first logician perseveres with his objections, that may mean that, from the beginning, he was intending to say some such thing as that such systems do not usefully represent needed portions of English. It may not mean that, of course. It is not clear, in fact, what it would mean.

[3] Dana Scott, "Advice on Modal Logic", *Philosophical Problems in Logic*, ed. Karel Lambert (Amsterdam: North-Holland, 1970), 153.
[4] Geoffrey Hunter, *Metalogic*, (London: Macmillan, 1971), xiii. In fact, Hunter goes so far as to say, "... I believe that the logician's most urgent tasks lie at present in the field of non-standard logic." I don't say that this is a sentiment that Scott would share.
[5] See for example, W. V. Quine, "Three Grades of Modal Involvement", *The Ways of Paradox*, ed. by W. V. Quine (New York: Random House, 1966), 156-174.
[6] Saul Kripke, "Semantical Analysis of Modal Logic I", *Zeitschrift für Mathematische Logik und Grundlagen der Mathematik*, 9, 67-96; and Saul Kripke, "Semantical Analysis of Modal Logic II", *The Theory of Models*, ed. by J. W. Addison, L. Henkin, and A. Tarski (Amsterdam: North-Holland, 1965), 206-220.

Nonstandard, or deviant logics, exist, in plentiful numbers,[7] and several are known to be consistent and complete. Some are supposed, and reasonably so, to deepen our understanding of philosophically perplexing issues. Certain logicians, of conservative resolve, still advise caution towards such systems. It is hard to avoid the thought that, apart from sentiments of taste, behind such advice lie concealed philosophical theories and prejudices. There is nothing wrong with a theory just because it is a philosophical theory; and it is difficult to see how one could altogether avoid philosophical prejudice. However, when it is a philosophical position that determines so severe a posture towards deviance, it is well that we be allowed to know this to be the case.

Very many subtle formal questions and doubts attend the development of any nonstandard system. Such questions call for technical expertise that lies beyond our province. It is, therefore, no part of our purpose here to venture solutions to logical problems. These pages would wrongly be read as offering any, save the most indirect, contribution to logical theory. Rather, our goal is to suggest philosophic problems that may find happy solution in one or other deviant base logic. The reasoning that occasions such a hope is entirely elementary: bet-sensitive sentences do not go easily into standard first order logic; yet they have a non-trivial structure; hence some or other deviant base logic may be needed for their adequate representation.

Our problem is to penetrate the logical structure of bet-sensitive sentences; secondarily, it is to inquire whether there is philosophic motivation enough to justify the adventuresomeness of Hunter's exhortation, noted above. The second problem is pursued by seeking suggestions of how to solve the first in a variety of nonstandard systems.

For all the talk of logic, it will be clear that our enterprise here is metaphysical.

---

[7] And growing numbers. Witness the recent contributions to the various 'Recent Work' conferences in logic, such as the Irvine Meetings of 1968, the Buffalo Meetings of 1969, the Toronto Meetings of 1970, and the Victoria Conference on Formal Ontology of 1972.

II

NON-ENTITIES AND NONESUCHES

§1. *The naive approach.* – There is, I think, something that might be called "the naive concept of fictionality". It is embedded in pre-philosophical discourse about fictional persons and their goings-on, and it embraces a whole range of more or less sophisticated practices, from schoolboy agitations concerning the moral character of Tom Sawyer's Aunt Polly to Mr. Leavis' rhapsodies of Lawrence. The naive concept seems to fill out, in the direction of theory, somewhat as follows. Sherlock Holmes lived in Baker Street; he did not live on Berczy Street. So by one half of what has come to be known as the Tarski-condition "Holmes lived in Baker Street" is true and "Holmes lived in Berczy Street" is false. We know where Holmes lived, whence, by classical epistemology, by which S knows that ϕ only if that ϕ is true, it is true that Holmes lives in Baker Street. Generalizing, it will be plain that there are vastly many statements about all manner of fictional persons, places and things, some of which are true and others of which are false. The conventional wisdom has it that the condition of truth for such matters is the author's sayso and whatever can legitimately be inferred from statements true in virtue of the author's sayso.[1] What establishes

---

[1] As it stands, this will not quite do, for it does not provide such truths as that Freud psychoanalyzed Gradiva. Thus in the sentence footnoted, we need to insert, after 'sayso', 'or imply or presuppose such'. Hereafter, where needed, the qualification is understood. Given the qualification we have the means of distinguishing fictional truths, such as that Holmes lived in Baker Street, which originate solely in Doyle's stories, from such truths as that Holmes is revered by some members of the Baker Street Irregulars, which, although they do not originate in fiction, depend on truths that do. These latter we call 'parasite fictional truths'.

the truth of my statement that Holmes lived in Baker street is an appeal to Doyle's stories, and what establishes the truth, if indeed it be true, of the statement that Hamlet was unworldly and philosophical are certain familiar strategies of inference, principles and laws, in application to what we think we know of Hamlet non-inferentially, directly from Shakespeare's play.[2]

Assuming sentences of fiction to fall into a subset $\mathscr{E}$, of English, it rather looks as if the conventional wisdom proposes a semantics for the sentences $\phi \in \mathscr{E}$ that record or purport to record fictional goings-on. This semantics would probably include a function from $\mathscr{E}$ into the set $\{T, F\}$ of the classical truth values; it is a function V, such that for atomic ϕ, $V(\phi) = T$ if ϕ occurs in an author's work (or good translation of it)[3] and $V(\phi) = F$ if $\ulcorner \neg \phi \urcorner$ occurs in an author's work. Even at this elementary level, there are problems. For, ϕ can occur in one author's work and $\ulcorner \neg \phi \urcorner$ in another's. Then, too, we shall have to be wary of any clause in such a semantics that provides that if $V(\phi) = T$ and if ψ is a logical consequence of ϕ, then $V(\psi) = T$. If the truths of fiction (if one can call them that) are closed under the consequence relation, then, unless we are

---

[2] Recall, for example, Freud's psychoanalytic study of Wilhelm Jensen's novella, *Gradiva: A Pompeian Fantasy*. If psychoanalytic theory is a good (enough) theory, then some of the true statements about the characters in Gradiva may have been unearthed by Freud. Roughly, the convention pertaining to inferences from fictional sentences is that, unless the author indicates otherwise, standard inference procedures are retained.

Perhaps it should be mentioned that by "true in virtue of the author's sayso" I mean "true in virtue of the content of the story written by the author"; I do not mean "accords with what the author told me over drinks last summer in Venice". Authors can misremember and misinterpret their own works – sometimes notoriously. We should also remark that the sayso condition of truth is quite a different matter from the 'self-guaranteeing' character of a certain class of token-reflexive sentences. Thus "I can construct an English sentence" is true in virtue of its utter's sayso, but not in virtue of what I am calling the sayso condition.

[3] Translation is the subject of much anxiety and little theory. I do not really suppose that we can say what are the truth conditions of "x is a good translation of y". There may even be problems in fixing the domain and counter domains of a respectable translation relation. I here invoke the notion of a translation only to be a little more specific about the membership of $\mathscr{E}$. Thus I assume $\mathscr{E}$ to include Dorothy Sayers' translation of *The Divine Comedy*, whether or not it is rightly called a 'translation' according to theories yet to be proclaimed.

careful, we shall have it that every logical truth is likewise a truth of fiction. I do not think that, on that score, our intuitions incline us very definitely, one way or the other, and it may be premature so early in the proceedings to build such a clause into the naivist's semantics.

While speaking of true fictional sentences it would be well to defeat at once a possible confusion. A fictional sentence is not required to be used only to report fictional goings-on. Some of the time they are used, as by authors, to bring it about that there be those fictional goings on for the rest of us to report on. Thus when Sir Arthur Conan Doyle first penned a chronicle of Holmes, he can hardly be supposed to have used the sentence-tokens descriptive of Holmes to report the truth about Holmes. He used them rather to tell a story, to create a character, to endow him with (the beginnings of) a history. Doyle's venture was not *bound*[4] by the sayso condition of truth (as we might call it) since Doyle's venture was not *reportage*. Doyle was not reporting established episodes in the life of Sherlock Holmes; he was establishing those episodes. If the creative venture succeeds, then, of course, the rest of us, and Doyle too, have something to report in respect of which the sayso condition of truth must be honoured.[5]

This, for better or worse, is the kernel of our ordinary, pre-reflective view of such matters, and it easily expands into a fairly detailed overview: we denote, refer to, describe, and count fictional objects; we know who they are and some of what they did and suffered; we see that they are identified and individuated by certain constellations of their properties, fixed by what about them is true

---

[4] This needs qualification. Doyle is bound by his own sayso in certain ways, for example, in the sense that later parts of the story must, in certain respects, 'accord' with earlier parts. Doyle must not violate Holmes' identity criteria (whatever they are) on pain of the story's ceasing to be about Holmes. This is, in a way, a restriction on the sayso criterion. Further restrictions will be discussed later.

[5] There are syntactic intimations of the current distinction. A story can contain sentences in the continuous present tense, yet those are truths that for the rest of us are most naturally conveyed in the past tense. Some form, to be sure, of the continuous present is available to us, but it functions smoothly only with a modifier such as "At this stage in the story ..." understood.

and what is false. Subject to a *caveat*, they are strikingly accessible to "the whole distinctively objectificatory apparatus of our language: articles, pronouns and the idioms of identity, plurality and predication, or in canonical notation, quantification theory".[6] All of this stands in marked contrast to the semantic behaviour of such constructions as 'the present king of France' and 'Mrs. Sherlock Holmes', to say nothing of terms for such MEINONGE as the round square. On the naive view, therefore, it is not at all clear that we would be right to call fictional objects INTENTIONAL.[7] The *caveat* is that fictional objects do not exist, hence cannot, without deviation, be reckoned to fall within the range of variables bound by the standard quantifiers, and so (it can be objected) are not, after all, accessible to the objectificatory apparatus of our language.

Yet this is a view of quantification and existence that is simply not reflected by our ordinary unregimented linguistic practices. "There are some things that do not exist" is a truth of English not preserved under a regimentation whereby the English "*a* exists" is systematically canonically represented by '$(\exists x)(x = a)$', yet not by a sentence in the form '$F(a)$'. Supposing "Some things do not exist" to be a member of $\mathscr{E}$, the intuitive verdict of its truth suggests that the base logic **BL** for $\mathscr{E}$ cannot be exactly the first order predicate calculus. The suggestion only suggests; it does not prove. But it does alert us to the possibility of a deviant logic for the rational reconstruction of some of $\mathscr{E}$.

The equation of existence and quantifiability does not exactly serve the intuitive theory of fictionality. That being so, we shall renounce, for the time being, the standard interpretations of existence and quantification. In addition to the standard quantifier '$\exists$' we introduce into L a quantifier 'Σ'. '$\Sigma x(x$ exists)' is read "there are things that exist;" its contrary, "there are things that do not exist". Provided that it has an identity-predicate it is not necessary

[6] W. V. Quine, *Word and Object* (New York: Wiley, 1960), 236.
[7] For a characterization of intentionality it may be useful to consult Anscombe, "The Intentionality of Sensation", *Analytical Philosophy*, Second Series, ed. by R. J. Butter (Oxford: Blackwell, 1965), 159ff.

that L contain a constant predicate for 'exists', since 'x exists' may be construed, as usual, as '$(\exists y)(x = y)$' and "Some things do not exist" as '$\Sigma x (\forall y)(y \neq x)$'. It is also supposed that L contain a corresponding nonstandard universal quantifier, 'Π', introduced by the definition $\pi = $ df. $\neg \Sigma \neg$. L is now assumed capable of representing "Some things do not exist", and **BL** is assumed to countenance its canonical representative: $\ulcorner \neg \Sigma v$ (v does not exist)$\urcorner$ is not a theorem of **BL**. On its face, such an L makes possible a straightforward representation of our everyday subject-predicate discourse about fictional objects.

It should be remarked that what we say we know of fictional objects plays havoc with any view of existence by which something exists just in case it satisfies (spatio-temporal) predicates. In that event, Holmes would manage not to exist only by failing to satisfy the predicates of Doyle's stories. Yet it is our ordinary pre-reflective understanding, I believe, that some weak version of Meinong's principle of the independence of *Sosein* from *Sein*, is true; in particular, that "is a man" or "lived in London" are predicates that do *not* entail 'exists'. For, to be a little previous, Holmes is a man (or was), and he did live in London, and does not exist and never did. Such, again for what it may be worth, is the heart of the naive theory of fictionality.

The general point is that there is a set of English sentences among which we find, "Holmes does not exist", "Holmes was a friend of Watson", "The Case of the Speckled Band was solved by Holmes", ..., that easily and naturally serve to convey some of what we say we know. They are, then, sentences that under natural-seeming procedures of semantic valuation (the sayso semantics) will be assigned the truth value, truth. This is not yet to say that such sentences must be preserved at all costs. In particular, it was noted that they are not preserved by standard quantification theory; and standard quantification theory might well, for sundry convincing reasons, be accepted as an adequate scheme of canonical representation for English. Whereupon, these English sentences would not be preserved, at all or as they stand, by that theory of English. For now, however, it is enough to see that fluent practitioners of the arts of English do not exhibit a linguistic behaviour that calls out for analysis in ordinary quantification theory. On the face of it, it is not ground enough to disqualify sentences of $\mathscr{E}$ just on account of their discord with first order logic.

§2. *Non-existent, non-intentional objects.* – It would be well, as early in the proceedings as possible, to anticipate and annul a very powerful-looking objection. It is that from the fact that there are pictures of x, sketches of x, caricatures of x, it does not follow that there is someone or something that is x. That is so: it does not follow from the fact that I want x that among all that there is is the thing I want. Neither does it follow from my daydreaming of an elegant woman in Outremont's spring sunshine that someone is she. Such might[8] be intentional objects – 'objects' x that need not exist, in order for "S is thinking about x" to be true, but also, and most important, that do not fit "the objectificatory apparatus of our language: articles, pronouns and the idioms of identity, plurality and predication". What is striking about fictional objects is that, short of non-existence, they fail this test of intentionality. Of Holmes there is no stopping such idioms as "he who did so and so", "the sole solver of the case of the such and such", "an unsympathetic personality", "one and the same with the man who lived at so and so address in Baker Street", "was only one of the persons who attempted to aid the Baskervilles family", and "is ϕ", "is ψ", "is χ", ... for a multitude of everyday predicates ϕ, ψ, and χ .... By most reasonable tests, the present king of France might be an intentional object, but not, certainly, in the way Holmes is. For even though Holmes does not exist, we know who he is. He is a non-entity who is a somebody. The present king of France is a nonesuch. Nonesuches do not fall within the values of Σ-bound variables. There are no nonesuches. So our **BL** is not spared the task of pronouncing on non-referring singular terms. It is rather

[8] The word "might" is a seemly caution, however; I do not assume that we have a sufficiently rich and complete theory of intentionality to make it automatic that the elegant woman of my daydreams be classified one way rather than the other. No doubt the answer would turn on how individuating a stock of truths 'about' her my dreamy imagination has produced.

only that our **BL** and the ordinary first order predicate calculus do not exactly agree on what terms are nonreferring. They agree on the 'present king of France'; they disagree on 'Sherlock Holmes'.

It hardly wants saying that not every object that does not exist is fictional, for there are the objects of mythology (e.g. Zeus). And not every assent-worthy statement that nonetheless reports something that did not 'really' happen is a statement of fiction, for there are statements about legendary figures (*e.g.* Paul Bunyan). Mythological figures can be likened to fictional characters at least in the sense that they are reckoned not to exist by whomsoever recognizes their mythologicality or their fictionality. And mythological statements resemble fictional statements at least insofar as neither kind is thought, by those who recognize them to be mythological or fictional, to describe the real world. But there are differences. Mythology tends to be theology and science fallen into disrepute – what began as serious reports of the nature of the world end up as the cherished or tolerated fantasies or fancies of a tribe or a people viewed as benighted, and usually heathen. Fiction, however, pretends no such literal congress with reality; it is make-believe from the beginning. The most singular difference between the legendary, on the one hand, and the fictional and mythological, on the other, is that the classification of a person as legendary does not compel an affirmation of its non-existence. Neither need it be that all assent-worthy statements about legendary figures fail to record what really occurred. Sometimes people become legends because they did, really, do extraordinary things, in consequence of which a reputation is born and bestowed upon a gullible world eager to augment it, indeed to exaggerate it out of recognizable shape. Thus, Nero, Billy the Kid, and Orson Welles.

The naive concept reflects current English usage, and so provides, concerning Holmes

I *The Axiom of Non-existence*:
    (a) that he does not and never did exist; that he is unreal; that he is merely fictional.

II *A Moderate Version of the Principle of the Independence of Sosein from Sein*:

(b) that notwithstanding his non-existence he is (or was) a man, a male human;

(c) that he was British;

(d) that he resided in Baker Street in London;

and so on.

(We may note that the Axiom is incompatible with the *strong* Independence Principle which says that no predicate satisfied by Holmes entails either his existence or non-existence, exempting 'does not exist' if that should happen to be a predicate.)

And although not recognizably central to the intuitive concept, it would seem to follow from (a)-(d)

(e) that Holmes was a minded object, a being capable of action, passion, and thought;

and

(f) that he was a spatio-temporal being, having a body of such and determinate proportions, a physiology of such and such functions, a series of geographic locations, and a specific temporal history.

On this view, an elemental category-difference between Holmes and ourselves is that Holmes does not whereas we do exist or did. There is however a second, at least as major, such difference which is as odd-seeming as it is unavoidable. It is that

(g) science fiction and fantasy-fiction both being kinds of fiction, Holmes can by his author's sayso, depart from, without by so doing refuting, the laws of nature and of logic. For example, Holmes could have travelled backwards in time and could have squared the circle.[9]

§3. *Fictional existence.* – Regarding theses (a)-(g) one may elect a Parmenidean complaint and protest that it is false that Holmes

---

[9] Of course he did not do these things, in the precise sense that Doyle did not invent such adventures for him. Occasionally, when a point of theory calls for it, I will nonetheless take such liberties with Holmes and will suppose for him adventures that Doyle did not make available to him. In some instances the liberty runs to licence and seems to libel a literary reputation. I hope that I may be forgiven these emendations.

does not exist; that since we *refer* to Holmes it must be that he exists somehow or in some sense. And since we can say that Holmes exists (merely) in fiction, exists (merely) in Doyle's stories, it may be alleged to follow that Holmes exists. Yet the naivist would be right to insist that this does follow.[10] One can say, intelligibly enough, that the average man exists only in statistics and that the perfect woman, under a certain conception of perfection, exists only in a sailor's dreams, but it would not follow from this, nor would it be true, that the average man exists or that the perfect woman exists. To the contrary: one very standard way of saying that the perfect woman does *not* exist, and that the average man does *not* exist is to say that 'they' exist merely in a sailor's dreams or a statistician's fancy. So too with Sherlock. It would be hard to dispute that the intuitive and philosophically unprejudiced gloss upon the proposition that he exists merely in fiction is that he is merely fictional and hence does not exist. "Sherlock Holmes exists" requires special pleading; its negation does not.

On the other hand, although it is intelligible to say that Holmes is a fictional person, a fictional Briton, and so on, it is certainly not open and shut that we gracefully acquiesce in similar-sounding conclusions to the effect that he is therefore not a person, not a Briton, etc. So to do is to embrace for fictional discourse what Quine, somewhere in *Word and Object*, calls "the conniving mode of speech". "Holmes is merely fictional: he doesn't exist" is not misleading, if at all, in *anything* like the way that "Holmes is merely fictional: he is not a person, and not British" is. It is natural to think that if one says *of* something that it does not exist one evokes a range of contraries at least one of which as it happens applies truly to Holmes ('dead', 'extinct', 'unexemplified', 'fictional', 'mythological', etc.). But if one says of something that it is not a person, the range of natural contraries[11] ('a machine', 'a brute', 'a vegetable', etc.) contains no candidate properly applicable

---

[10] Hence the force of 'merely'.
[11] ϕ and ψ are, very roughly speaking, natural contraries if ϕ and ψ are natural-kind predicates (in the sense of John Woods, "Semantic Kinds", *Philosophia* 3) that cannot jointly be satisfied.

to Holmes. So too for 'not a man' and 'not British'; none of their natural alternatives (*e.g.* 'a woman' and 'an Armenian') correctly applies to Holmes. If it is thought that 'is a fictional character' will serve as an appropriate contrary of 'is a man' and 'is British', then Holmes will not be a man and not be British, even though by the sayso condition this is what he most certainly is. And although some locutions descriptive of Holmes are naturally enough prefixed with some such qualifying word as 'fictional', this seems not to be so of descriptions of Holmes' action and passions. It is not easy (though I do not say it is impossible) to understand "Holmes fictionally cogitated about fictional Moriarty, fictionally yearned fictionally to trap him, and fictionally took the following fictional steps to do it ..." To qualify thus Holmes' actions and passions seems either to qualify the sense out of them,[12] or to be a needlessly long-winded way of rendering Holmes' fictionality. In any event, verisimilitude demands that the sentences constitutive of the text of the story not be qualified so; hence at least a very large number of fictional truths appear successfully to resist the qualification.

However, if we grant that among fictional objects there are persons susceptible *simpliciter* of such actions and passions, if we say that Holmes just did and suffered these things, then it follows, surely, from all that he did and from the fact that he did them and suffered them *simpliciter*, that Holmes was a man, was British, and so on.

Parallel considerations seem to attend the contention that statements about the fictional can be true. For suppose one argues that they are not true, on the grounds that they are true merely by appeal to the author's sayso, that they are true merely *in fiction*, and hence that the standard alternative to "true" does in fact apply to statements about Holmes, it being false that Holmes lived in Baker

---

[12] That *a* did so-and-so only fictionally suggests an element of pretense. If I only pretend to mail the letter, and say that I did mail it, it is appropriate to speak of my fictional mailing of the letter. But such cannot fit the case of Holmes; it is not the case that he pretended to do all the things which we're inclined to say he did. For example, he did not pretend to pretend when he pretended to Baskervilles that he was going to London.

Street, and false that he was male ("that he was male"?). Apparently what would establish their falsehood is the truth of "Holmes did not *really* live in Baker Street" and "Holmes was not *really* a male". Yet how is one to understand these? That he did not exactly reside in Baker Street – he only stayed there occasional weekends? That he was not a real male – he was given to cowardice, foppery or a kind of sexual unorthodoxy? No, the intuitive interpretations seem to be these: if I were to go to Baker Street I should never bump into Holmes; how could I, Holmes being merely fictional? And a perfect census of the period could never have turned up Holmes; how could it have, Holmes being merely fictional? It is noteworthy, perhaps even curious, that these interpretations actually reinforce, not refute, the naive view. For they emphasize Holmes' fictionality without in any *obvious* way determining the truth value of these statements which record his sex and his nationality, and, for that matter, his perils and triumphs. It can be made to seem unutterably strange to say of one who asserts that Holmes lived in Baker Street, not in Bleeker Street, that he has said nothing true. What he does say is right, not wrong, correct, not incorrect, why then not true as opposed to false? This being so, could it not be said that one way of being true is to be true-in-fiction, as another way of being true is to be true in a scientific theory, or true in an interpretation of quantification theory? In general, the predicate schema 'true-in-θ', where θ is a theory, can be expected to pick out the theorems of θ. Now, unless θ is a sound theory its theorems will not all be true. And if it is sound and complete, its theorems will all be true. In the latter case 'true-in-θ' is no alternative to "true", for they come to the same thing; and in the latter case, 'true-in-θ' is an undesirable alternative to "true", for it defeats the intuition that the favourably evaluated sentences of θ all be true.

§4. *Ellipses.* – Once we concede that some sentences about the fictional are true, and others false, the observations recorded in (a) to (g) seem unavoidable. In distressed recognition of the point, some philosophers counsel a manoeuvre whereby fictional sentences, ϕ, true by the naive theory, are supposed untrue and are replaced by a true sentence, ψ, with which the original is said to be confused. It is then ventured that the promptings to assent to ϕ are acceptable only for ψ, even though in common, pre-theoretical speech the more relaxed ϕ may go proxy for ψ. Representative, if not typical, of such an approach is an ELLIPSIS THESIS by which "Holmes lived in London" is an ellipsis for, means the same as, some sentence recording the origin or locale of the former.

Confusion concerning meaning is a perpetual philosophical liability. It has tentatively been hazarded here that, for the naive view of fictionality, something like a sayso semantics is adequate and correct. A sayso semantics for a fictional sentence of $\mathscr{E}$ is a semantics for the canonical representative ϕ or $\mathscr{E}$ by which there exists a function, V, from ϕ to $\{T, F\}$ such that $V(\phi) = T$ if ϕ represents S and S occurs in a work of fiction. Thus, there is a sentence of English, stating some fact about the origin or locale of a member of $\mathscr{E}$, that seems to serve in defining a truth-predicate for the canonical representative of our sentences of fiction.[13] Now one fairly respectable notion of sentential meaning is captured in the concept of truth conditions. Such meanings (call them c-meanings) enter into such intuitively uncontroversial pronouncements as that

(1) Holmes lived in London

has as part of its c-meaning the sentence

(2) "Holmes lived in London" is a member of L,

where L is an appropriate member of the sequence, **Lit**, of works of English fiction.

Not to be confused with c-meaning is a notion of meaning that, though lately and severely disparaged, can boast a long pedigree. It is fairly called 't-meaning', after its conceiving meaning to be that in virtue of which sentences translate one another. Here translation is assumed, radically, to be pretty much the kind of sentence-to-sentence performance that one can sample at meetings of such

[13] If only in the interests of a less punishing prose style, we will normally abbreviate such locutions as "semantics for the canonical representatives of the sentences of $\mathscr{E}$" to "semantics for the sentences of $\mathscr{E}$".

multi-linguistic groups as the United Nations. Whatever the difficulties in understanding such a procedure, especially in an intralinguistic setting, it appears entirely certain that (1) does not t-mean (2).

Philosophers do not always honour the appearances, nor should they. The gross form of the ellipsis thesis for fictional sentences is such an example. On this view, sentences like (1) are always ellipses for, always t-mean the same as, sentences like (2). In general, a sentence ϕ can be an ellipsis for a sentence ψ in either of two circumstances. The one is the circumstance in which ϕ and ψ are inessentially orthographically varying tokens of the same sentence type, with ϕ the orthographically slighter token. The other circumstance in which ϕ might be reckoned to be an ellipsis for ψ is when ϕ t-means the same as ψ, with ϕ and ψ tokens of possibly distinct types, and ϕ a relevantly truncated version of ψ.

It will be noticed that ellipticality according to the first condition is ellipticality according to the second, assuming the reflexivity of "t-means the same as". It is natural, therefore, to begin the assessment of the ellipsis thesis by considering the question of the sameness or difference of t-meaning of (1) and (2).

It is initially plausible to suppose that, owing to the presence in it of quotemarks, (2) mentions (1). Assuming quotation to a context, assuming, that is, that in $\ulcorner\phi\urcorner$ ϕ occurs, then we have it that (1) occurs in (2) either with the t-meaning it is said to have by the ellipsis thesis, or not. In the former case, (2) implies

(3) ""Holmes lived in London" occurs in L" occurs in L
But (3) is false.

On the other hand, if (1) does not occur in (2) with the t-meaning it must have should the ellipsis thesis be true, that is tantamount to a refutation of the ellipsis thesis. For, one would have supposed that (1) occurs in (2) with just the t-meaning it has in the text of the story; hence, if, in (2), (1) occurs not t-meaning (2), it occurs that way in the story.

It may be, of course, that some case might be made for saying that (3) is acceptable by virtue of the circumstance that (1) and (2) are inessentially orthographically varying tokens of the same type, and so, from the logical point of view, differ no more relevantly than 'color' differs from 'colour' or 'SALLY' from 'Sally'.

If this should be so, if (1) and (2) are, logically speaking, tokens of the same type, we shall have lost the intuitive support for saying that (2) is a truth condition of (1), – that (2) c-means (1). True, every sentence may be regarded, trivially, as giving its own truth condition; so if (1) and (2) are in all the relevant respects the same sentence, (2) may be regarded, trivially, as a truth condition of (1). But it could no longer be claimed that the circumstance in which (2) is a truth condition of (1) is a circumstance *distinctive* of fictional sentences, for, as we have just seen, that is a circumstance pertaining to all sentences. If (1) and (2) are in all the relevant respects the same sentence, then (2)'s being a truth condition of (1) lapses into a trivial non-sayso semantics for (1), their inessential orthographic differences notwithstanding. This, of course, is not a just complaint against the ellipsist, for it is to accuse him of succeeding at what he set out to do. But it is nonetheless a point of some importance, as we shall soon see.

On the other hand, (1) although mentioned in (2), quote-named in (2), might not *occur* in (2). If the quotation in (2) is not a context,[14] if quote marks do not flank occurrences, then the argument of the preceding paragraph collapses. In that event, (2) would seem to have less logical structure than it shows. But then it becomes thoroughly problematic that the logically dense (2) should warrant our confidence that (2) t-means (1). For, the meaning of (2) cannot now be supposed to be a function of the meanings of (1) and the context ""..." is a member of L". If a philosopher says that "The cat is on the mat" t-means "The dog is in the manger" that alone is not reason enough to believe him.

Suppose, then, that (1) t-means

(4) Holmes resided in London.

By the ellipsis thesis, (4) t-means

---

[14] A view sometimes associated with Quine, though perhaps not with utmost historical fidelity. See David Kaplan, "Quantifying In", *Words and Objections*, ed. by Donald Davidson and Jaakko Hintikka (Dordrecht: Reidel, 1969), 207.

(5) "Holmes resided in London" is a member of L;

whence, given that t-meaning is an equivalence relation, we have it that (2) t-means (5). But now it is quite impossible to believe that (2) and (5) are truth conditions of (1) and (4), yet that (2) is not a truth condition of (5), nor (5) of it. What does it matter that (5) does not occur in (2)? Neither does (1) occur in (2).

A sayso semantics has at most a limited scope; it interprets at most a proper subset of the sentences of a language. One class of sentences, to the semantics of which a man's sayso is relevant, is the class of sentences reporting his sayings. Thus "Zachary said that Tommy Tweed is bearded" may be judged true if Zachary said that Tommy Tweed is bearded. But such a semantics is not distinctive; it is not in our sense a sayso semantics. A sayso semantics is made distinctive by the fact that its truth predicate is governed by a condition of material adequacy

(M) x is true iff p,

putting for 'p' a sentence of the object of language L and for 'x' the structural descriptive name or Gödel-number name of a sentence of L, provided that it *not* name p or a translation of p. And that is tantamount to saying that what is distinctive about a sayso semantics is that (1) and (2) do not t-mean the same. The ellipsis thesis runs, as it must, across the grain of a sayso semantics. It rejects, therefore, the idea that (2) is distinctively a truth condition of (1). But its claim that (1) and (2) t-mean the same is a semantic mystery. Central to the idea of ellipticality is that (1), by being an ellipsis for (2), has a logical structure not all of which it shows, the logical structure, namely, of (2). The ellipsis thesis cannot be interesting until that structure is proclaimed, and this the ellipsist has yet to do.

It need hardly be said that adequacy condition (M) is not a generally adequate condition. Where it is adequate, if at all, it is natural to expect the sentences, whose truth predicate it constrains, to reflect a semantically discriminable feature that (M) can recognize. The fact is that the sentences of fiction normally do not appear to be structurally distinctive, and that is not altogether surprising. For, they could not all display a semantically distinctive structure without, almost certainly, wreaking havoc with verisimilitude. (Recall our complaints, just above, concerning the adverb "fictionally".) On the other hand, if they are not semantically distinctive, if they do not structurally differ from other sentences of daily life, it is a mystery why they should be subject to (M).

Of course, in actual practice it is easy to convey what is semantically distinctive about fictional sentences – for they have a fictional subject matter. A theory of fictional sentences will therefore need to reflect a semantic counterpart of this pragmatic feature of their use: fictional sentences are used to tell stories and to chat about storied goings on.

To this end it is supposed, for the time being, that what is semantically distinctive of fictional sentences is that they are modified by a sentence operator. We denote this operator by '**O**', after the Latin *olim* for 'once upon a time'. In general, we surmise that a fictional sentence S of $\mathscr{E}$ is to be represented in L by a sentence $\ulcorner\mathbf{O}(\phi)\urcorner$. The represented sentence is assumed to have the logical structure of the representing sentence but not a like orthography. From the logical point of view most fictional sentences are misspelt. Only thus do they serve the needs of verisimilitude. By these lights, the worries of the previous section concerning the adverb "fictionally" are recognized; but they are also annulled by recognition of a category of logically lazy orthography.

It now becomes possible to venture an explanation of the distinctive applicability of (M) to sentences of fiction. It is that (M) applies only to sentences in the form $\ulcorner\mathbf{O}(\phi)\urcorner$. And it also becomes a little clearer why one could be tempted by an ellipsis thesis. For, we have it now that the sentence of fiction $\ulcorner\mathbf{O}(\phi)\urcorner$ is true if $\ulcorner\mathbf{O}(\phi)\urcorner$ is a member of L; and if the implication went the other way, we could claim truth and membership in L to coincide, equivalently, over the domain of the sentences $\ulcorner\mathbf{O}(\phi)\urcorner$. In particular with (1) and (2) now more revealingly rendered as

(1') **O** (Holmes lived in London)

and

(2′) "**O** (Holmes lived in London)" is a member of L,

we see that the former is an ellipsis for the latter, but only provided that it is an ellipsis, as well, for

(1″) "**O** (Holmes lived in London)" is true.

However, it is discouraging to note that the implication does not reverse itself. The English sentence whose ordinary orthographic form is

(6) Freud psychoanalyzed Gradiva

is thought by the naivist to be true, but it occurs nowhere in fiction. Likewise, stories usually preserve some truths about the world, such as

(7) Caesar crossed the Rubicon,

and yet we may not wish to allow that (7) is modified by the *olim* operator. So the implication might not hold in either direction.

The naivist must also note that the foregoing version of the ellipsis thesis commits him to the position that none of the sentences of a story mean quite what they seem to mean. The *olim* operator, whose presence is not usually disclosed in the text, is so conceived that neither

(8) ⌜**O**(ϕ)⌝ implies ϕ

nor

(9) ϕ implies ⌜**O**(ϕ)⌝

holds true for all ϕ. Although all the sentences of L are reckoned by the ellipsist to have the form ⌜**O**(ϕ)⌝, they in fact look, relatively, to have the form ϕ. They do not, in consequence, mean what they would seem to mean. What, then, do they mean?

I shall not here surmise how the ellipsist would wish to proceed with these questions. It is enough to note that they threaten the naivist no less. In fact, it is in the company of the latter's intentions that we find it natural to pursue them. However, the *olim* operator is too intriguing a device just to be forgotten; we return to it in Chapter Five. Meanwhile, it will suffice to assume some semantically discriminable feature, without here hazarding to identify it, by which fictional sentences may be recognized by the semantic component of a good theory of language for $\mathscr{E}$.

§5. *Mixed modes of being.* – On the assumption that some fictional sentences are true, and their negations false, it is evident that Holmes' repetoire is far from exhausted. Holmes is capable of entering into all sorts of quite ordinary relations with others – *e.g.* friendship with Watson, hostility with Moriarty. The naivist finds it tempting to say that some of the relations, R, in which Holmes stands to x are such that, given that it is Holmes, the fictional being who stands in that relation, and given further that R is the kind of relation it is, it follows from the fact that Holmes bears R to x that x, likewise, is fictional. Such 'relations'[15] seem to include "x kicks y.", "x congratulates (has tea with, hunts, thinks of, speaks to, believes such and such about) y." It also appears that some, but not all, of the relations just mentioned are such that from the fact that a *real* entity bears them to x it follows that x likewise is real. Prime Minister Gladstone, it seems, could hardly have kicked, congratulated, had tea with or spoken to Holmes without Holmes being real; yet he might have thought of, believed something about or admired Holmes without Holmes being real.

Such temptations are better resisted. The author's sayso condition of truth yields a set of perplexities concerning, to put it scholastically, mixed modes of being. That Holmes lived in London is, if a truth at all, a truth equally about Holmes and about London. And if Holmes, on his author's sayso, could have tea with Watson, why could he not have tea with Gladstone? The point is quite general: Holmes could have borne to a real entity any relation intentional or non-intentional, that Holmes is capable of bearing to a fictional entity of a appropriately similar type. Holmes could have dined both with Moriarty and with Gladstone, could and did patronize both Watson and Scotland Yard.[16] Suppose that on

[15] Whether these are relations serving to interpret the standard logic of relations, I leave an open question.
[16] If this is the case, then one commonly suggested difference between so-called intentional and non-intentional verbs, namely that the latter have and the

Doyle's sayso, Holmes did have tea with Gladstone, and did stand to Gladstone in various other such relations. It follows from this, given the symmetry, on one interpretation, of having tea with, that Gladstone (of all people) had tea with Holmes. And from the truth of "Holmes admired (or kicked) Gladstone" (if these verbs abide by the definition, from the logic of relations, of conversity: $(x \, R \, y) = (y \, \breve{R} \, x)$), it emerges that Gladstone was admired (or kicked) by Holmes. On the assumptions made, the naive view does not scruple to admit the truth of both "Holmes had tea with Gladstone" and "Holmes admired Gladstone" (just as it can hardly deny that Holmes resided in London); but it balks very strongly at having to concede the truth of what may be presumed to be the equivalents of these. So an inconsistency dogs the naivist's intuitions.

§6. *History constitutiveness.* – I am reminded however of a view of Cook Wilson, according to which "Zachary loves Sally" is a different statement according as it is 'about' Zachary or Sally. Let us see whether useful sense can be made of this.

It can be said, I think, that one would record our encounter, of the previous section, over tea in an inventory of those events which *constitute the life or the history* of Holmes, but not of Gladstone. We may have in this the beginnings of a reconciliation of our inconsistency. Within the class of true statements about a person, place or things, and about encounters involving them, it seems possible to find a distinction between those statements which contribute to the life or history of the object involved, and those that make no such contribution. For example, if one undertook to catalogue all the episodes in the life of Sherlock Holmes, or anyhow all that one could ever discover, one would be remiss to omit the occasion on which he had tea with Gladstone. Even for Holmes, elementary social congress with the First Minister of the Kingdom is not without importance. On the other hand, if asked to compile a complete inventory of the events in the life of Glad-

---

former do not have existential import, is illusory. And it is, at least by the lights of §1.

stone, it would be quite out of the question to include his having had tea with Holmes. Some recognition, of course, of their meeting is required, but it is achieved by some such sentence as "Doyle fictionalized Gladstone in one of his Holmes-stories and there depicted him as having had tea with Holmes". (We remark, parenthetically, how misleading it would be to say this of Holmes.)

Concerning real persons, the statements which are, as we might say, HISTORY CONSTITUTIVE of that person, are none of them true *simply* in virtue of the author's sayso condition. And among statements which are not history-constitutive of real persons there can be included statements which are true simply in virtue of the sayso condition. These could be called FICTIONALIZATIONS about such persons. They are true, but make no contribution to the person's history. Thus the statement that Gladstone distrusted Disraeli is true and history-constitutive of Gladstone, whereas the statement that Gladstone had tea with Holmes is a true fictionalization about Gladstone. We remark that even had Doyle included in one of his stories the statement that Gladstone distrusted Disraeli, it would not be a fictionalization about Gladstone, nor about Disraeli, because it would not have been made true *simply* by Doyle's sayso.

As for fictional persons, there arises the need to draw a parallel distinction. Just as Gladstone's identity is fixed by some, not necessarily exhaustively specifiable, set of statements history-constitutive of him, and never by fictionalizations, so too is the identity of fictional persons fixed by (some part of) *their* histories. Who Holmes is and what he did is fixed by Holmes' author's sayso, by Doyle, and by none other. It is Doyle alone[17] who confers upon Holmes his identity and history. Yet, as Doyle could borrow Gladstone for a guest appearance, so too can he borrow a fictional person, Sybil say, for a guest appearance. Sybil *can* appear in a Holmes-story, but if it is Sybil who appears (as opposed to

---

[17] This requires qualification. In certain cases authorship (usually by legal means) is transferrable. E.g. Although Jimmy Hatlo is dead, the persons he created still thrive. Henry Tremblechin and Little Iodine continue to enjoy the fruits of statements history-constitutive of them, even though they are not made true by Hatlo's sayso, but rather by the persons to whom Hatlo transferred authorship, by the persons who go proxy for Hatlo.

someone else called "Sybil"), she appears as the person she is, with a fixed identiy conferred not by Doyle, but by Disraeli. Disraeli's descriptions of Sybil are history-constitutive of her, whereas Doyle's contributions to Sybil, true simply in virtue of his sayso, are true fictionalizations about her.

In the Holmes-stories, Sybil and Gladstone can be depicted as doing such and such, but not Holmes. Holmes is not *depicted* as having solved the case of the speckled band – rather he just solved it. Similarly, Gladstone, occurring, as it were, in *his* history is not, by the true statements about him, depicted as having been Prime Minister of Great Britain – he just was. The language of depiction, therefore, in at least one of its natural employments, is the proper adjunct of fictionalizations but not of history-constitutive statements.

Thus we might imagine SML to contain the appropriate dyadic predicates together with something like the following characterizations.

1) ϕ is HISTORY-CONSTITUTIVE of a real entity, x, *only if* ϕ is true, ϕ is about x, and it is not the case that ϕ is true simply by the author's sayso criterion.
2) ϕ is a FICTIONALIZATION about a real entity, x, *if and only if* ϕ is true, ϕ is about x, and ϕ is true simply by the author's sayso.
3) ϕ is HISTORY-CONSTITUTIVE of a fictional entity, x, *if and only if* ϕ is true, is about x, ϕ is true simply by the author's sayso condition, and the author whose sayso makes ϕ true is the *creator* of x.
4) ϕ is a FICTIONALIZATION about a fictional entity, x *if and only if* ϕ is true, ϕ is about x, ϕ is true simply by the author's sayso criterion, and the author whose sayso makes ϕ true is not the creator of x.[18]

---

[18] This is too strong a condition if it is possible for the creator of x to borrow x for other stories by the creator of x, in which x plays a non-self-history-contributing role. Could Holmes have shown up in *The White Company*? I do not know. If he could have done, then Doyle would have been fictionalizing his own creation, in violation of (4).

It is immediate that these two predicates are not one another's contradic-

These ideas have epistemological implications that should here be emphasized. For example one does not always *refute* a claim by establishing the truth of its negation. One does not always *prove* a claim simply by validly deducing it from a set of true premisses. And therein lies the foundation for not less than a methodological complaint: if, in order to deal with Sherlock, it is necessary to augment our stock of expressions of semantic evaluation by recognition of two new primitives, susceptible of co-application with 'true', or with 'false', then no semantic or epistemic expression previously defined via 'true' and 'false' is spared the need to be redefined. And that, it can justly be argued, is simply too much work for so little gain.

It can also be objected that conditions (3) and (4) take the concept of fictionality too far from literary experience for it to count any longer as the ordinary intuitive concept. For one thing, there is the vexing problem of the ubiquity of Faust. We have Marlowe's Faust, Lessing's Faust, Goethe's, Klinger's, Chamisso's, Grabbe's, Lenau's, and Mann's. Goethe's Faust alone has inspired operatic, symphonic or oratorio elaborations from Berlioz, Gounod, Schumann, Liszt and Boito. Conditions (3) and (4) require Faust to have had a unique literary creator, C,[19] and that, once launched, the authored truths about Faust not authored by C be construed as fictionalizations about the original. Usually, the test of paternity is a quite straightforward one – he whose stories of x occur earlier than all the other is the creator of x. But is it not just a bit off-colour that the great Goethe should stand less of a chance than Lessing in a test of Faust's literary paternity? Even

---

tories; they are contraries. Suppose that Gladstone, on the basis of his faithful reading of the Holmes-stories, comes to admire Holmes, much as Kingsley Amis seems to admire James Bond. Then the statement that Holmes was admired by Gladstone is true and history-constitutive of Gladstone, but not necessarily of Holmes; nor need it be a fictionalization about Holmes. Similarly, let us suppose that the late Mr. Gregorias Smashington, a modest grocer in Gutherie, admired Gladstone. Is this part of Gladstone's history? I am inclined to doubt it, in spite of the fact that it is unquestionably part of Smashington's. If this is so, here is a statement which is with respect to Gladstone neither history-constitutive nor a fictionalization.

[19] C, of course, could be a *set* of co-authors.

Marlowe's Faust which, more likely than not, would win the case, is incomparably less well known than Goethe's and Mann's too, for that matter. For the vast majority of educated people who are not literary scholars, Faust just *is* Goethe's Faust.

Neither does it accord very well with our everyday understanding to argue that there are at least as many different and distinct Fausts as there are different and distinct Faust-authors. Ours is a problem regarding the identity of Faust. Conditions (3) and (4) presuppose that there are sane and reliable means of settling questions of literary paternity, hence of identity; but that seems not to be true of Faust. If there is but one Faust, there is the difficult question of whether to choose the earliest author or the best known or the best; and if there is no doubt whatever about whom to select (*viz.* every author of a Faust story), then we have far, far too many Fausts. The problem posed by Faust is ubiquity, not multiplicity.

Happily for the particular case of Faust, the issue of literary paternity is quickly settled by drawing out a few details of Faust's history. As it happens, none of our contender's can win the suit. Faust did not have a literary birth at all. One need only mark the distinction[20] between legendary figures and fictional characters, to find one's way to this conclusion. Faust was a real person, a 16th century German doctor, and something of an itinerant magician. He was the subject of legendary tales celebrating Faust's magical powers and his consort with Satan. The legends proved popular, and Faust was made the subject of uncounted folktales, most of them no doubt libellous. Faust's exploits apparently did not see print until the late 16th century when they were chronicled in Speirs' *Wolksbuch* of 1587.

Faust, then, was already prominently in eminent domain long before his acknowledgement by Literature. And since Faust is not a fictional character in the first place, no Faust-author was his creator. And no Faust-story contains any authored-truth about him that is not a fictionalization.

Although Faust is not in fact a good example of the kinds of

[20] Noted in §2 above.

identity problems not explicitly solved by condition (3) and (4), it is clear that some other entirely literary creation *could* exhibit a Faustian ubiquity and so prompt the very identity crises that we have been discussing. Its settlement, I suspect, is under-determined by the ordinary concept of fictionality. Probably the least jarring recommendation is that we adopt the chronological solution to the problem of uniquity. Thus: C is the creator of fictional object x if C authors the x-stories and no stories by authors other than C, in which x's identity criteria are honoured, antedates C's x-stories. Needless to say, the *general* notion of identity criteria is a perplexing one, but since it does not create a special problem for an account of fictionality, the naivist may reasonably enough let it lie.

§7. *The Law of Non-Contradiction.* – Aside from its methodological turgidity, by the current device the inconsistency is extirpated, and one might imagine a supporter of it urging that it is true both that Holmes had tea with Gladstone and that Gladstone had tea with Holmes. Though true (he might say), they are, with respect to Gladstone, fictionalizations. Our temptation to reject "Gladstone had tea with Holmes" is explained as resulting from a confusion between what it is that is rejected, a sentence's truth or its history constitutiveness.

Consider, too, the situation in which, by the author's sayso, Gladstone had tea a time t_0 with Holmes in Baker Street, yet, by the correspondence theory of truth, Gladstone was at t_0 dead or in Abyssinia. Needed premisses assumed, we have a violation of the classical Law of Non-Contradiction. At so serious a juncture, the notion of history constitutiveness is something of a life-saver for the naivist. For, he is enabled (emboldened, some would say) to fall into step with Meinong and to charge the classical Law with an undisclosed metaphysical bias in favour of real objects, and to recommend its restriction to sentences that agree on points of history constitutiveness. Thus restricted, one would not be justified to infer, from a true fictionalization about x, the falsehood of its negation when taken as history-constitutive of x; neither could one infer from the truth of a statement history-constitutive of x

the falsehood of its negation if taken as a fictionalization about x. (As, *somewhat* similarly, one cannot always infer from the truth of ϕ in theoretical physics the falsehood of ⌜not-ϕ⌝ in applied physics.[21])

It is nothing if not heroic to rebuke the classical Law for its metaphysical favouritism, and then to clip its wings, in order that we might be allowed to retain some intuitions concerning Sherlock Holmes. Lest his light be thought utterly unworthy of the candle, the naivist must say more than he has so far done about his Meinongean liberties with the Law. Some amendment, to be sure, of the network of respectable beliefs needs be undertaken in order to safeguard sentences, such as that Gladstone had tea with Holmes, that go contrary to the facts. But is the intuitive conviction that they are true to outrank the classical Law?

It is of some importance to see how radical the naive theory is. By its central semantic precept, that an author's sayso implies the truth of what he says, not only are we driven to a certain churlishness toward Non-Contradiction, but we commit ourselves to accepting that fictional beings may exhibit behaviour that deviates from, without annulling, not only the contingent episodes of this world's history, but its canons of nature and logic, as well. For how else are we to characterize Holmes' behaviour in a time machine and how shall we understand Holmes' having squared the circle? If the former does not crush Relativity Theory, the latter does not vindicate Hobbes. The naivist regards these as abnormal truths, as truths about Holmes – not as truths about Reality. And that is tantamount to saying that, for the naivist, fictional truths can be history-constitutive only of objects that are not real; that a truth that, by its customary syntactic and semantic profile trivially should refute a law, but does not, is but a fictionalization of Reality, as it were. A base logic in which that distinction is honoured might be a multi-sorted theory, with one stock of variables for

[21] For example, the model of a scientific theory might differ in logical type from the distinguished model of the experiment with which it is to be linked by co-ordinating definitions; the model of the theory might contain continuous functions and infinite sequences, yet the data in canonical form (i.e. the model of the experiment) might be discrete and finististic.

sentences representing fictionalizations about objects x and another available only to sentences representing sentences history constitutive of objects y. Not, of course, a usual sort of multi-sorted quantification theory, since the real object/unreal object distinction cuts across that between fictionalizations and history-constitutives. A similar objective might better be achieved by dropping the multi-sorted approach in favour of a single-sorted theory augmented by needed predicates. One such, '$\mathscr{F}$', might be introduced, the extension of which contains just those objects whose behaviour could deviate from, without refuting, natural and logical laws, as well as the contingent facts. The effect of such a predicate would be to moderate the usual axioms and inference rules of standard quantification so as to reflect that special part of the theory of fictionality in which standard inferences do not go through owing to the unreality of their subject matter. It would be natural then, that our extension of ordinary logic would be one in which the standard thesis

(1) $\forall v_0 (\phi v_0 \to \phi v_1)$

is replaced by

(2) $\forall v_0 (\phi v_0 \to (\neg \mathscr{F} v_1 \to \phi v_1))$[22],

in which '$\neg \mathscr{F}$' receives the intuitive reading 'is real'. An $\mathscr{F}$-logic is kith and kin of a free logic, with whose special predicate constant '$\mathscr{E}!$', for 'exist', '$\neg \mathscr{F}$' might be extensionally equivalent. Free logics are discussed in Chapter Three.

Not that an $\mathscr{F}$-logic, (or a MEINONG-LOGIC as we might call it) meets every problem concerning self-contradiction. One would still need a policy by which to deal with a distinction between self-contradictions occasioned by slips of the pen or lapses of an author's memory, and those deliberately, and known to be self-contradictory, woven into the fanciful fabric of the story. Our actual literate practice in such situations is, in certain ways, to ignore the contradiction; and so our representation relation, between the

[22] Or (1′) by (2′), where these differ from (1) and (2) only by having the neutral quantifier 'Π' where they have '$\forall$'.

fictional sentences of $\mathscr{E}$ and the formal sentences of **BL**, might provide that the mutually inconsistent fictional sentences of $\mathscr{E}$ be represented by logically independent sentences of **BL**.

However, these and other relatively minor difficulties pale before a very major one. It is that, on the author's sayso, we are required to contradict *ourselves* when, as upon occasion we must, we attach to fictional goings-on self-contradictory descriptions. For, if I am obliged to say, of a fiction object x, something of the form $\ulcorner \phi$ & $\neg \phi \urcorner$ then, thanks to a simple proof due to Lewis,[23] I am obliged to count everything as true. From $\ulcorner \phi$ & $\neg \phi \urcorner$ we have both ϕ and $\ulcorner \neg \phi \urcorner$ by two applications of simplification; and from ϕ we have $\ulcorner \phi \vee \psi \urcorner$, by addition; yet adjoining this with $\ulcorner \neg \phi \urcorner$ we have ψ, by disjunctive syllogism, for any ψ one wishers to choose. Thus, if we were to imagine our story represented in a formal language θ, all the story's constitutive sentences being represented as θ's non-logical axioms, and the other sentences of the story, true by the remaining clauses of the author's sayso semantics, as its non-logical theorems, then θ would be absolutely inconsistent: its every sentence would be a theorem.

Assuming our **BL**, θ, to contain Lewis' S2, and supposing ϕ to be some fiction-theorem in the form $\ulcorner \psi$ & $\neg \psi \urcorner$, it is easy to show that θ is Post-inconsistent. Let χ be some atomic sentence of S2 that is also a sentence of θ. Then from ϕ we obtain ψ; and from ψ $\ulcorner \psi \vee \chi \urcorner$. From ϕ again, we also have $\ulcorner \neg \psi \urcorner$. Adjoining we have χ, by disjunctive syllogism. Since χ is an atom that is a θ-theorem, θ is Post-inconsistent.[24] Ordinary substitution into χ gives the theoremhood of every sentence of θ.

This bodes ill for the naivist, but it need not wholly dispatch him. It is always open to him to seek some further amendment of his **BL**, for example, to write in a rule designed to staunch a contra-

---

[23] C. J. Lewis and C. H. Langford, *Symbolic Logic* (New York: Dover, 1932), 250.

[24] Of course, if we decided to represent, say, the sentences that constitute the text of the story by the non-logical axioms of **BL**, at least one of which is atomic, Post-inconsistency ensues. It would then be necessary to confine substitution to the logical theorems of **BL**.

diction's logical flow. Thus he might propose a rule for '$\mathscr{F}$' as follows:

⌜$\mathscr{F}^3$⌝ is a theorem only if

(a) ⌜ϕ & ¬ϕ⌝ can be a theorem, for some ϕ.

(b) ⌜(ϕ & ¬ϕ) ⊰ ϕ⌝ is a theorem only if ψ is ϕ or ψ is ⌜¬ϕ⌝ or ψ is derivable from ϕ [respectively ⌜¬ϕ⌝] without the use of [respectively ⌜ϕ⌝] as premiss.

By this rule, if ψ were neither ϕ nor ⌜¬ϕ⌝, there would be no χ such that χ is assertable solely upon the grounds that ⌜(ϕ & ¬ϕ) ⊰ χ⌝ is logically valid according to S2 or that ϕ and ⌜¬ϕ⌝ are theorems. This should guarantee that ψ, distinct from ϕ and ⌜¬ϕ⌝ is deducible from ⌜ϕ & ¬ϕ⌝ only in conjunction with Δ, where Δ is a set of theorems, such that ψ is not deducible from it alone and is presumed to be restricted thus: if its members are about x they are history-constitutive of x, then x does not exist; otherwise its members are fictionalizations about x.

By this strategy, we would, of course, expect to be permitted the inference to that Holmes squared something with a ruler and compass, and that this came as a surprise to the London Mathematical Society, from such premisses as that Holmes squared the circle with ruler and compass and that thus squaring the circle would come as a surprise to the London Mathematical Society if they were to learn of it, and they did learn of it from Watson.

Now, the need of the naive concept of fictionality for some such inference-inhibiting device as the special predicate '$\mathscr{F}$' may be thought to expose it, unequivocally, as the unstable notion we should long ago have recognized it to be. But the naivist would be right to insist that that is not a conclusion that is warrantedly drawn from the *ad hoc* role of the '$\mathscr{F}$'; for it can be argued that it is not *ad hoc*. In fact, it is a reflection of as central an aspect as any of the intuitive concept of fictionality that fictional characters are objects that exhibit so radical a difference from others (after all, they are objects that don't exist) that to lose sight of it is almost automatically to fall into confusion and paradox. And they are in fact so construed: for the naivist will understand that fictional persons do not disturb Reality even when they depart Reality's strictest and most primordial governances. He realizes that a fictional character can square the circle without making every statement true. It is plausible therefore to think that fictional goings on *cannot* correctly be reasoned about in the ordinary way, that the concept of fictionality contains built-in exceptions to the classical logics that attend our standard conceptions of reality. In a word, the logic of the naive theory of fictionality is expressly a non-standard one. Far from being an *ad hoc* contrivance, guiltily sneaked into the theory to save it from assorted howling grotesqueries, the predicate '$\mathscr{F}$' can, with some justice, be said to capture one of the deepest aspects of how we construe fictional objects.

There may be something good to be said in behalf of this refusal of non-*ad hoc*ness. But it is doubtful that the rule for '$\mathscr{F}$' is tolerable, on general methodological grounds. For, we have it, straightaway, that anything in the extension of '$\mathscr{F}$' can, short of absolute inconsistency, satisfy truth-functionally self-contradictory predicates. Such predicates thus applied do not mean what they seem to mean. They deviate from, without disclosure, the standard meaning of 'and' or 'not' or even both. What, then, do such predicates so applied mean? And does the policy whereby they do not mean what they seem to mean need to be implemented by so cumbersome a contrivance as the rule for '$\mathscr{F}$'?

One means, certainly, of accommodating the abnormality of ratiocination concerning the fictional is to tamper with the rules of inference of the **BL** of $\mathscr{E}$.[25] Whence the inference-inhibitor '$\mathscr{F}$'. Another option, and a better one perhaps, is to tamper elsewhere, with, for example, the representation relation from $\mathscr{E}$ into the language L of the **BL**. In particular, the representation relation could so be defined as to take fictional sentences in the form $\ulcorner \phi \,\&\, \neg\phi \urcorner$ into the atomic formulas of L, or anyhow into its logically independent sentences. And thereby is honoured our

---

[25] Needless to say that inference could not usefully be represented in a **BL** comprising merely S2, the rule for '$\mathscr{F}$', and a generous assortment of fiction axioms. It would need axioms for quantifiers, certainly; perhaps also for adverbs and epistemic operators.

practice of just not believing that the nomological misdeeds of fictional beings makes our every sentence a theorem. We do not in fact see such sentences as self-contradictory; or rather, we construe them as self-contradictory only, so to speak, from the dramatic, not the logical, point of view.

Both devices come to much the same thing; each attempts to codify one and the same feature of our actual literate practice. By the first approach of invoking the rule for '$\mathscr{F}$', the representation relation is kept standard with respect to fictional sentences in the form $\ulcorner \phi \mathbin{\&} \neg \phi \urcorner$ and our theory of inference, and ultimately our theory of meaning for the connectives, is made non-standard; by the second, the reverse is true. Not that there is nothing to choose between them. Both approaches however compel the conclusion that in those fictional self-contradictions that are true either 'not' or 'and' is non-truth-functional. So fictional self-contradictions would not mean what they must appear to mean for them to have the desired effect on plot and action. So conceived, the self-contradictoriness of fictional sentences $\ulcorner \phi \mathbin{\&} \neg \phi \urcorner$ is a property of a logically misleading orthography. They are, on the first approach, non-standard conjunctions or standard conjunctions of a sentence and its nonstandard negation; on the second they are, say, logically atomic. The non-standard molecularity and the atomicity of 'orthographic self-contradictions' are but another side of an earlier conception of the logical structure of fictional sentences. We proposed in §4 the quite general hypothesis that orthography is an especially bad guide to the logical form of fictional sentences for want of a natural-seeming English counterpart of the olim-operator **O**. Our complaint there was that orthography under-reflects logical structure; our complaint now is that it can also over-reflect it.

Perhaps the simplest, and a good enough, method of dispatching the problem of self-contradictory fictional truths is to refuse the sayso condition of truth licence to verify sentences in the form $\ulcorner \phi \mathbin{\&} \neg \phi \urcorner$; that is, we might amend the sayso semantics for $\mathscr{E}$ in such a way that all sentences in the form $\ulcorner \phi \mathbin{\&} \neg \phi \urcorner$ are mapped onto falsity. But, then, doubts about the adequacy of a sayso semantics threaten to be contagious. In particular, it becomes harder to justify a verifying verdict for *any* fictional sentence that, by a correspondence theory of truth, is false.

§9. *An essential property.* – It is an axiom of the naive theory that, being fictional, Holmes does not exist. Yet Doyle might have had Moriarty seriously wonder whether there really existed such a person as Holmes, and upon investigation Moriarty could discover, could come to *know* that Holmes existed. If, then, Moriarty knows that Holmes exists, as well he could by the author's sayso, it follows, by classical epistemology, that Holmes does exist, in violation of the axiom. But the question is, *could* Moriarty know that Holmes exists? Our naivist must answer that he could not. As was suggested at the close of the preceding section the sayso criterion need not be deemed exceptionless. And it is as natural a constraint on it as can be that an author cannot make true any statement about a fictional being which affirms or entails its existence. So to rule may seem *ad hoc*; but it is not unsupportably so. For it amounts to saying that even the author's sayso cannot withold a defining categorical or essential predicate from Holmes. One feels the presence, if not the need, of a 'transcendental argument', to the effect that nonexistence provides the very possibility of there being an author's sayso criterion. But charity alone commands forbearance.[26] This is not to say that such statements as "at last Moriarty knew with fearful certainty that Holmes did actually exist" play no important role in the story; it is just that they do not and cannot have existential import. (The best Moriarty could do is to make the discovery that *there is* such a person as Holmes. By the decision of §1, not everything there is need exist.) With nonexistence assumed to be an essential property of fictional beings, we may have solved one problem and embrace another. The problem solved is how, naturally and without *ad hoc*ness, to

---

[26] See for example, Barry Stroud, "Transcendental Arguments", *Journal of Philosophy*, 65, 241-256. But see also Jaakko Hintikka, "Transcendental Arguments", *Noûs*, 6, 274-280.

constrain the author's sayso. The problem embraced is that of giving sense to essentialism.[27]

But is it really convincing to say that, although an author's sayso can make it true that a fictional being violates the Law of Non-Contradiction, the author's sayso cannot make it true that a fictional being survives a substantial change? And if we are to refuse the sayso condition licence to provide for the latter circumstance, why should we not equally refuse it licence to provide for the former (and nastily problematic) circumstance? And, if we feel it necessary, or appropriate, to accord, on the author's sayso some semantically favourable recognition to such sentences as "Holmes really did exist", would it not be enough to allow for their truth yet not for their history-constitutiveness? True, here is a suggestion not wholly without merit; but it still does not solve the contradiction problem. Even so, it does serve to drive home the point that the naivist's preservation of the axiom of non-existence, even at the expense of the sayso condition, is somewhat *ad hoc*.

§10. *History*. – Even assuming tolerable provision for fictional truths in the form $\ulcorner \phi \,\&\, \neg \phi \urcorner$ and for unwanted authored affirmative existentials, the naive theorist is left with an impressively full plate. He still has need of a restricted Law of Non-Contradiction with which to accommodate fictional truths that contradict the facts. That, in turn, places great weight upon the semantic component of the theory which relies upon the difficult notion of historicality.

Some statements, we said, are neither fictionalizations nor history-constitutive; these make no contribution to the history of what they are about. How are we to tell what contributes to an individual's history? Taking Gladstone as example, imagine that the person who is to keep a complete inventory of the events constitutive of Gladstone's history is Gladstone himself. Imagine,

---

[27] This is essayed, for example, in John Woods, "Essentialism, Self-Identity and Quantifying In", *Identity and Individuation*, ed. by Milton K. Munitz (New York: New York University Press, 1971), 165-198, and also in John Woods, "Description, Essences and Quantified Modal Logic", *Journal of Philosophical Logic*, 2, 304-321.

further, that Gladstone *qua* investigator satisfies the following conditions:

i) at any given time t_i of his life, he has perfect and comprehensive observational powers with respect to his own personal experience – perceptual, introspective, epistemic, doxastic, optative. He knows at t_i what he is doing, thinking, wishing and hoping; what he wants, plans to do, what is happening to him (subject only to the restriction that he be able to tell from what he knows on the basis of what is now before his eyes, in his soul or on the basis of recollections of such) and what is befalling others currently within his purview;
ii) that, at t_i, all consequences involving himself available to him on the basis of information collected under i) are consequences he draws;
iii) that, in order to avoid something like Tristram Shandy's troubles,[28] Gladstone, *qua* investigator, ignores the knowledge he has of his own investigative activities.

The class of hoped-for statements would then be those yielded by a perfect exercise, over every t_i, of those powers. The history of Gladstone would be the complete and perfect *auto*biography of his personal experiences.

It will be objected that ours is far from a tight test of historicality. For one thing, it extrudes from a person's history welcome periods of deep sleep.[29] Then, too, there is the point that the question of what inferences are allowably made by a fictional being from information regarding himself is no less vexing than that of what

---

[28] "Tristram Shandy, as we know, used up two years in chronicling the first two days of his life, and lamented that, at this rate, material would accumulate faster than he could deal with it" (Bertrand Russell, *Mysticism and Logic* [London: George Allen & Unwin, 1917], 90). Russell, of course, demurs from like lamentation, his thoughts being of Shandy at the logically allowable "ripe old age of denumerable infinity" (in a charming phrase of, I believe, Carnap).

[29] I owe this point to Martyn Estall, in conversation To take account of it, it may be necessary to free the subject from autobiographical responsibilities and to transfer the job to his Guardian Angel, or his mother.

inferences, from such data, *we* are entitled to. And that, as we shall see, is enough of a problem for clause ii) not to be of much help.

§11. *Truth-value gaps.* – Did Holmes have a mole on his back or did he not? Doyle did not say. It would appear, given that Doyle is dead and that, for this question, the sayso condition (whatever we may now think of it) is unavailable, that the matter is necessarily insusceptible of settlement. Until now, we have been reading the sayso semantics as asserting the equivalence: ϕ is true (relative to work fiction Γ) if and only if ϕ occurs in Γ or follows from or presupposes sentences that do. But let the sentence "Holmes has a mole" not occur in Γ, then it would seem that, if fictional statements are always either true or false, that Holmes had a mole is false. That, in turn, *suggests* that with respect to all such properties (attributed to Holmes in statements that are in this way false) Holmes is, as Meinong would have it, an *incomplete object*. Whether or not this is the naive view of fictionality I cannot say with any real confidence. But, naive or not, Meinongean incompleteness creates problems. For, let a Holmes story be represented in a formal theory. Let its nonlogical axioms include the sentences of the text, let its theorems be its axioms as well as the sentences arising therefrom by some suitable set of inference procedures, and let it also happen that among its theorems are the negations of those sentences about Holmes (and the other objects of the story) that are not true by the author's sayso. Under these assumptions we may have it both that "Holmes is hirsute" is true and a theorem but that, for want of the author's sayso no sentences, "Holmes has i-hairs" ($i \geq 1$) and "Holmes has no hair" are theorems. Then provided that our **BL** contains elementary number theory, it looks as if our story-theory involves a paradox suggestive of ω-inconsistency: although it is a theorem that there is some number that numbers Holmes' hairs, no particular number numbers them, and yet it is not a theorem that no number numbers them.[30]

[30] Let ϕ be an arithmetic predicate of a language L*, strong enough to express arithmetic, then L* is ω-*inconsistent* if it is provable in L* that some number satisfies ϕ and also provable in L* that each member of the sequence 0, 1, 2, ..., n ... does not satisfy ϕ, and not provable in L* that no number satisfies ϕ.

In fact, however, in these circumstances the story finds itself in even worse logical shape; for, if it is our policy to make theorems out of the negations of those Holmes-sentences, ϕ, such that ϕ does not occur in the text or follow from those that do, then since neither "Holmes has 8, 013 hairs" and "It is not the case that Holmes has 8,013 hairs" enjoys the backing of the author's sayso, the negation of each is a theorem, and they being contradictories, the story-theory is not ω-, but *absolutely* inconsistent.

Doubtless this argues the need for a different policy concerning incompleteness. One alternative, would be to replace the extreme decision to regard as false sentences not authenticated by the author's sayso or not consequences of those that are, with the proposal that they be reckoned neither true nor false. So regarded, stories are not liable to an automatic and inescapable charge of absolute inconsistency; but, what is more, non-truth-valuedness seems an intuitively more satisfactory counterpart of Meinongean incompleteness.

Perhaps, on the other hand, it is not particularly useful to render the incompleteness of fictional beings in terms that imply the failure of the classical Law of Excluded Middle.[31] It is always open to us to understand Meinongean incompleteness epistemically, and to replace the ontological notion of indeterminacy with the epistemological one of unknowability. By these means, all sentences about the fictional are bivalent (*i.e.* true or false), though some of them present for our knowledge a rather trivial class of insolubilia.

It is not hard to see that those who would find perplexing the epistemological rendering of indeterminacy probably will not have attended to the following distinction: If a reader knows that Sherlock Holmes has some hair on his head, and claims nonetheless that it is not the case that he possesses any particular number of them, that is because he makes the (bad) inference from

(1) K(Holmes has a number of hairs on his head)

to

---

[31] The adjective "classical" does not present to utmost historical fidelity: it denotes what is sometimes called the Law of Bivalence, and it provides for every sentence of L exactly one of the truth values truth and falsehood.

(2) $\Sigma x((x$ is a number) & K(Holmes has x hairs on his head)),
in which the conclusion is in a form *de re* (putting 'K' for 'It is known that').

In any event, it is easy enough to prove that fictional beings are not *by nature* ontologically or epistemically incomplete. It is always possible that the story provides for a Wise Man who, for each character of it, knows that he is a "bivalent being" and who knows, moreover, which predicates he satisfies and which he does not, for all predicates ϕ.

Of course, if one drew the inference to the conclusion *de dicto*

(3) K($\Sigma x(x$ is a number) & Holmes has x hairs on his head).
there would not be the slightest good reason to doubt that Holmes had some fixed number of hairs, even though in the manner of (2), we might never know what that number was.

Still, it needs to be recognized how unlikely it would be to get an easy consensus on incompleteness. For one thing, it can be made to sound rather inviting that what is truly distinctive about fictional objects is their ontological indeterminacy. And whatever precisely might be intended by "ontological indeterminacy", it could reasonably be proposed that it be semantically acknowledged by truth value gaps. In fact, a decision whereby author-inexplicitness makes for the failure of Bivalence suggests that one commit the base logic of the theory of fiction into intuitionistic hands.

If we were to associate truth-by-the-author's-sayso with INTUITIONISTIC PROVABILITY and falsity-by-the-author's-sayso with INTUITIONISTIC DISPROVABILITY, then that a Holmes-sentence is neither true nor false might reflect the intuitionistic circumstance of being neither provable nor disprovable and might therefore provide an interpretation of the failure, in such logics, of Excluded Middle. In intuitionistic systems, such as that of Heyting,[32] the provability of a formula consists in there being a construction or a general method of construction that renders that formula assertable; and in such systems it is not in general the case that for every formula, ϕ, $\ulcorner \phi v \neg \phi \urcorner$ is provable, since there is no general method of the appropriate sort that, for any formula ϕ, results in a proof of

[32] Arend Heyting, *Intuitionism* (Amsterdam: North-Holland, 1956).

ϕ or a proof of $\ulcorner\neg\phi\urcorner$. In a rough and ready way, therefore, provability – or there being a general method of constructing a verification – of a formula can be likened to truth in virtue of the author's sayso; and as the author's sayso does not, in general, afford a method, for every Holmes-sentence ϕ, of verifying ϕ or of verifying $\ulcorner\neg\phi\urcorner$, the purported failure of Excluded Middle for fictional sentences can be seen in an intuitionistic light.

Further parallels can be drawn. In intuitionistic systems a negated formula $\ulcorner\neg\phi\urcorner$ can be asserted exactly if there is a construction that begets a contradiction on the assumption of ϕ.[33] And in fiction $\ulcorner\neg\phi$ (Holmes)$\urcorner$ is assertable when the author's sayso takes one to a formula ψ that is incompatible with $\ulcorner\phi$ (Holmes)$\urcorner$ and yet not to $\ulcorner\phi$ (Holmes)$\urcorner$ itself, for on the assumption of $\ulcorner\phi$ (Holmes)$\urcorner$, and given the rule that if χ is assertable and χ' is assertable then $\ulcorner\chi \,\&\, \chi'\urcorner$ is assertable, we would have the (author unwanted) contradiction $\ulcorner\psi \,\&\, \phi$ (Holmes)$\urcorner$.

But the fit between the structure of fiction and that of intuitionism is not as tight as one might like it to be. In particular, in the system of Heyting, no formula $\ulcorner\phi \,\&\, \neg\phi\urcorner$ is assertable. Yet if we were to modify Heyting's system so as to allow for procedures of verification for certain sentences, $\ulcorner\phi \,\&\, \neg\phi\urcorner$, so as to reflect the occasional nomological misdeeds of fictional beings, we should also have to make room for restrictions on the inference-potential of such sentences. Since Heyting's system contains theorems that are analogues of classical simplification, addition and disjunctive syllogism, then, without that amendment, from a self-contradiction every sentence intuitionistically follows.

§12. *The sayso semantics.* – The primary semantical task of the naive theory of fictionality is the articulation of a sayso semantics for fictional sentences. It may not be entirely clear what exactly would count as an adequate sayso semantics, but it is reasonable to look for settlements of such issues as: (1) whether the consequences of fictional truths are likewise fictional truths, i.e.

---

[33] Intuitionistic contradiction is taken as primitive, and takes in more than merely formal truth-functional contradictions, $\ulcorner\phi \,\&\, \neg\phi\urcorner$.

whether the property of being a truth of fiction is closed under consequence; (2) whether any facts about the world, and whether any laws of nature, may ordinarily be presumed to hold in fiction; (3) whether 'indeterminate' fictional sentences shall be allowed truth value gaps; (4) whether there are manageable conditions on such mixed parasitic fictional sentences of "Freud psycholanalyzed Gradiva".

One such articulation of a sayso semantics for fiction might involve the introduction into our SML of a predicate 'true-in-fiction'. Thus SML would have at least two truth predicates, 'true-in-reality' and 'true-in-fiction, each collecting different, but not necessarily disjoint, sets of sentences naively presumed to be true. The general theory of truth might be reckoned to be the union of the theory for 'true-in-reality' and the theory for 'true-in-fiction'. The former theory might proceed along standard model theoretic lines; how the latter would proceed we have yet to say. One thing is clear, however; clear and problematic. It is that, in the face of the severe logical difficulties lately discussed, such a union could be endorsed only under compliantly nonstandard treatments of consistency.

A full definition of "true-in-fiction" is probably much too much to hope for. Even so, it ought to be possible to state some of its more likely seeming conditions and to suggest the general pattern that the full account could be expected to exhibit.

The definition, no doubt, will be inductive. Its basis is probably best generated as follows. Let ϕ be a sentence, and let Γ be an appropriately specified literary corpus; then let us say that ϕ is ELEMENTARILY TRUE-IN-FICTION iff ϕ is a member of Γ.

The inductive conditions might then include:

(1) If ϕ is elementarily true-in-fiction, ϕ is true-in-fiction (or 'FICTRUE', for short).

(2) If ϕ is fictrue and ψ is an appropriate past tensification of ϕ, ψ is fictrue as well.

(3) If ϕ does not occur in Γ, i.e. if ϕ is not elementarily fictrue, ϕ is about an object x of kind K, and ϕ is an instance of ψ, where

ψ is a theorem of an adequate theory of K-objects, then ϕ is fictrue, provided that $\ulcorner \neg \phi \urcorner$ does not occur in Γ.

(4) If ϕ is a logical consequence of ψ and ψ is fictrue and consistent, then ϕ is fictrue, provided that $\ulcorner \neg \phi \urcorner$ does not occur in Γ.

So far, the definition decides our questions as follows. Every author-uncontradicted logical truth is fictrue; fiction preserves all this world's facts and laws except for when it provides for an explicit departure; indeterminate fictional sentences need not be supposed to have truth value gaps, but there is also room for a contrary policy. Not every author-indifferent sentence, by any means, would rightly be said to be gappy, even if gappiness were an available verdict in some such cases. For examples, "Holmes had an alimentary canal" is, on this definition, fictrue – by clause (3) and the gastro-intestinal theory of humans. Still, if we wished to close all the gaps, this is easily enough done by a condition to the effect that $V(\phi) = T$ iff $V(\neg \phi) = F$, for all fictional sentences ϕ and all valuations V.

Even as things stand, our definition invites the methodological complaint that it invokes concepts that are not, many of them, less in need of ventilation than the notion of fictruth itself. Condition (1), it will be objected, obliges us to come forth with an appropriately controlled treatment of "is a sentence of fiction", and that, in its turn, calls for not less then a theory of English sentencehood. Condition (3) places most of its weight on the unexplicated locution, "adequate theory of objects of kind K", which in at least two places is known to be intractable.

Still to come is an answer to the question of how to evaluate such mixed parasitic sentences as "Freud psychoanalyzed Gradiva". The purport of such a claim, so the naivist will claim, is that there *is* something x to which Freud bore the appropriate psychoanalytic relations (house-calls excluded) – something in the form:

(i) $\Sigma x(x = $ Gradiva & Freud psychoanalyzed x).

When is '$\Sigma x(x = $ Gradiva)' true? And when, and how, of that x, can "Freud psychoanalyzed x" be true?

Our definition needs to contain two further clauses, one dealing with parasitic relational sentences such as "Freud psycholalyzed Gradiva", in which the first term denotes a real entity, and the other a fictional being; and the second dealing with quantifiers. Thus we might consider a condition

(5) If ϕ does not occur in fiction and ϕ is $\ulcorner\psi^n(a_1, a_2, ..., a_n)\urcorner$ then ϕ is fictrue if $\ulcorner\exists v(a_1 = v)\urcorner$ and $\ulcorner\Sigma v(a_2 = v)\urcorner$ and ... and $\ulcorner\Sigma v(a_n = v)\urcorner$ are ficture and ψ^n is a relational predicate in the active voice, and the object denoted by 'a', bears the ψ^n-relation to the objects denoted by 'a_2', ..., 'a_n' in that order.

For the difficult question of the quantifiers, we might have something like

(6) If ϕ does not occur in a work of fiction and ϕ is $\ulcorner\Sigma v(\psi v)\urcorner$ then ϕ is true in fiction if χ is a substitution instance of ϕ and χ is a truth-of-fiction. If ϕ is $\ulcorner\Sigma v(a = v)\urcorner$ then ϕ is true in fiction if $\ulcorner\exists v(a = v)\urcorner$ is possibly not true, yet ψ is a substitution instance of ϕ and ψ is a truth-of-fiction.

We may note, in passing, that the quantifiers of clause (6) seem to call for a substitutional construal (of which more in §13), and that clause (5) seems in its antecedent to provide for a blend of the substitutional idiom and the referential (see also §13). In particular, the quantified sentence there first mentioned displays the standard existential quantifier, which is assumed to be referentially construed. The question, in any case, remains: how can real objects involve themselves with objects that do not exist, yet are not merely intentional objects? How can we possibly give sense to "the object denoted by 'a_1' bears the ψ^n-relation to the objects denoted by 'a_2', and ..., and 'a_n'"? And what, pray, *is* that relation?

§13. *The fill-question.* – We have been supposing that part and parcel of what it is to understand a work of fiction involves the reader's ability to fill the story in, in various places, with sentences that do not occur in the story or logically follow from those that do, but which somehow need to be true for the story to make full and proper sense. Thus, clause (3) of the previous section. Perhaps the most compelling reason for thinking this to be so, is that much of the action of a story is not wholly explained – sometimes not explained at all – by the explicitly declared sentences of the story together with their logical consequences. The story, just as it stands, presents only enthymematic explanation-sketches, the missing 'premises' of which it is the reader's job to furnish. Thus, if fictional character A strikes fictional character B on the head with the butt of a musket, and B falls instantly to the ground, it seems entirely unproblematic – provided the story affords nothing to the contrary – to propose the causal sentence "It was because of the blow to the head that B fell down", even though the author nowhere explicitly so declares or asserts anything that logically implies as much.

Another assumption of normal literate practice is that an author speaks up to his maximum, in the sense that he will declare all departures from the normal for his creations or at least will weaken normalcy assumptions appropriately. Otherwise his creations are assumed to be normal cases of their kinds; and by these lights, Holmes will be allowed to have had an alimentary canal. The fill-problem, then, is to ascertain whether there are general recipies by which to determine when an unauthored and logically unimplied fictional sentence should be deemed true. Roughly speaking, we seem entitled to make those fill-assumptions about fictional objects of kinds K_i that we make about real objects of kinds K_i, unless deviations are explicitly declared by the author. Even when we are ignorant of its details, we assume the truth of the various sciences for the objects of our everyday encounters; and it seems, that we should do the same for the creations of fiction. I assume, for the objects in my room, for the persons of my acquaintance, for the starry heavens above me, the truths of mechanics, psychology, and astronomy, some of which I may know, but the very great majority of which I do not. Shall I do the same for Sherlock? Shall I do the same for Don Quixote? The fill-problem for Don Quixote includes the problem of whose physics to assume for him – ours? his? Copernicus'? or Cervantes'?

Don Quixote was published in two parts, the first in 1605, the second in 1615. Kepler's first two laws of planetary motion were published in 1609; the third appeared in 1619. Shall we therefore say that the heavenly bodies on or under which Don Quixote – of the first part – slept, described circular orbits, yet those of the second part described elliptical orbits? And shall we say that nowhere in the world of this great novel – part one and part two – is it the case that the square of the period of revolution of a planet is propositional to the cube of its average distance from the sun – for, this the third law, did not appear until after the publication of the novel was completed, and was not proved in Kepler's time?

And how shall we fill *Ulysses*? Not certainly, *in general*, in quite the way that we might fill *The Case of the Speckled Band* or *Remembrances of Things Past*. Great literature creates the need for literary commentary, for cultural historians, whose very demanding task it is to advise interested readers how to fill. It is problematic how such truths are discovered, and it is, for the most part, beside the point of our enquiry. Our purpose, we have said, is to expose the logical structure of fictional truths. We can say, with some confidence, that fictional truths exemplify at least three types. They are the actual sentences of the novel (and their past tensifications), the mixed, parasitic fictional sentences such as, "Freud psychoanalyzed Gradiva", and the logical consequences of fictional sentences. Our task is to discern the logical structure of sentences of at least these sorts. It is not especially likely that their rational reconstruction would be vitiated simply by expanding the set $\mathscr{E}$ by inclusion of an assortment of fill-sentences according to some adequate theory of Literature. In consequence, we may ignore the fill-question; and do.

§14. *The quantificational problem. The modal problem.* – The problems of the naive account create problems for any serious theory of the language of fiction. They roughly classify themselves into two categories, the logical and the semantical. Chief among the semantic problems is (1), whether to allow for the truth of fictional sentences; and if not, how to evaluate them. True, the naivist may have landed himself in a semantic mess with his sayso semantics for fictional sentences, but a competitor would still (2), need to state truth conditions for fictional sentences, assuming them to be true, or he needs to provide an alternative account with as little violence as possible to such facts as a bet is won by him who says that Holmes lived in Baker Street, and it is lost by him who places him elsewhere. In a word, he must be able to account for the bet sensitivity of fictional sentences, true or not.

The logical problems are not of course entirely isolable from the semantical ones. But the job (3) of making sense of a fictional sentence's contradicting the facts, (4) the problem of author-endorsed self-contradictions, and (5) the problem of a fictional being's deviation from Excluded Middle, are incomparably more severe when harnessed to a semantic theory by which fictional sentences can be true. Even so, they remain problems when unharnessed, for they all pertain to the general puzzle (6) of the logical structure of fictional sentences.

To speak of the logical structure of fictional sentences is to speak of the formal sentences of a language L of a base logic by which they are to be represented. I assume that a satisfactory specification of the logical structure of fictional sentences will carry us to acceptable decisions concerning the following matters: whether the general sentences of fiction are to be represented by formulas of L in which only the standard quantifiers occur; whether the negative existential sentences concerning fictional beings are to be represented by formulas of L in which there occurs a predicate constant representing the predicate 'exists' of E; whether, if the latter question is answered affirmatively, the quantificational structure of L shall be that of a free logic; whether the base logic will represent the singular terms by means of individual constants, and if so, whether these constants shall be supposed to be contextually eliminable; and, whether the sentences of fiction shall be represented only by those formulas of L prefixed by a special sentence-operator. All these questions but the last can corporately be displayed as the problem of the quantificational structure of fictional sentences, or, more shortly, the QUANTIFICATION PROBLEM. The last question concerns the problem of the modality of fictional sentences, or, more shortly, the MODALITY PROBLEMS.

We turn now to the quantification problem.

III

FREE LOGIC AND FACTS

§1. *Free logics.* – A FREE LOGIC IN THE WIDE SENSE is a logic admitting non-denoting terms without paraphrase, or whose terms may denote non-actual individuals. Some of the logical bases proposed in the previous chapter are free in this sense. In particular, a logic whose terms may denote fictional beings as well as actual individuals, and whose bound variables may have these as values is a widely free logic. One similar such logic is that of Lejewski.[1] A significant difference, however, is that Lejewski's system does not tolerate empty singular terms (e.g. 'the present king of France') and does not have either a distinguished predicate for existence or a quantifier whose range is restricted to actual individuals.

By a FREE LOGIC IN THE NARROW SENSE, or a NARROWLY FREE LOGIC, we shall mean any quantificational system whose domain of interpretation can be empty; whose terms (free variables or individual constants) need not denote (however, if they do denote they are presumed to denote some actually existing individual); whose predicates denote properties and relations defined over existing individuals; and whose quantifiers range over existing individuals, all of which are in the domain of the theory's interpretation. Logics free in the narrow sense may or may not recognize a special existence predicate. In the former case we may speak of a NARROWLY FREE e-LOGIC; in the latter case sentences containing non-denoting terms may be evaluated as classically truth-valueless, and so may be called narrowly free non-bivalent logics. In the

[1] Casmir Lejewski, "Logic and Existence", *British Journal for the Philosophy of Science*, 5, 104-119.

latter case, too, existence may be expressed through identity and the standard quantifiers. These, for simplicity, can also be referred to as e-logics.

Several classical treatments of non-denoting singular terms are not free logics in the senses mentioned here.

Frege's early theory,[2] in which it is proposed that non-denoting terms be given a denotation, namely a null-entity outside the domain of the theory, is not a narrowly free logic since the null-entity is not in the domain of interpretation. It can, however, be thought of as widely free.

Russell's theory of descriptions[3] is not free in any sense, since empty definite descriptions are paraphrased away. Quine's extension[4] of Russell's treatment to all singular terms is open to the same remark.

In one of Leonard's systems[5] we have a treatment that is free except that it has theorems that fail to hold in the empty domain. The system of Hailperin and Leblanc[6] is a narrowly free e-logic. Hintikka's[7] theory, on the other hand, although it shares some of the insights of the Hailperin and Leblanc treatment (and which was developed independently of it) is not narrowly free; some of its theorems fail in the empty domain.

The theory of Smiley[8] comes close to being a narrowly free non-bivalent logic; however certain sentences with non-denoting terms fail in the empty domain, and so Smiley's theory is not narrowly free.

---

[2] Gottlob Frege, *The Basic Laws of Arithmetic*, ed. and transl. by Montgomery Furth (Berkeley and Los Angeles: University of California Press, 1967).
[3] Bertrand Russell, "On Denoting", *Mind*, N S., 14, 479-493.
[4] W. V. Quine, "Designation and Existence", *The Journal of Philosophy*, 36, 701-709.
[5] Henry Leonard, "The Logic of Existence", *Philosophical Studies*, 7, 49-64.
[6] T. Hailperin and Hughes Leblanc, "Nondesignating Singular Terms", *The Philosophical Review*, 68, 239-243.
[7] Jaakko Hintikka, "Existential Presuppositions and Existential Commitments", *The Journal of Philosophy*, 56, 125-137.
[8] Timothy Smiley, "Sense without Denotation", *Analysis*, 20, 125-135.

Schock's system,[9] which reports an earlier paper,[10] is a narrowly free e-logic.

Lambert[11] has proposed (different) systems of narrowly free e-logics, both of which are incomplete. His later systems,[12] also narrowly free e-logics, avoid these troubles.

Van Fraassen[13] has produced an axiom set for systems with empty domains, and proved it semantically complete. It is the first such proof for a narrowly free e-logic.[14]

In Chapter Two certain base logics for the logical reconstruction of a theory of fictionality were hinted at. Aside from a **BL** in which there are the standard quantifiers, the neutral quantifiers and a special predicate for existence (which systems are widely free), we also mentioned extensions of such systems in which classical Non-Contradiction and Excluded Middle fail. Such then purport to be both free e-logics and free non-bivalent logics; but it is not safely supposed that they are narrowly free, since they were not set up with a view to handling problems of the empty domain.

One hard question for the logical reconstruction of a theory of fictionality is: shall it be a significant part of the quantification problem for a theory of fiction that it proclaim a policy regarding preservation of a distinction between non-entities and nonesuches (between, that is to say, the terms 'Sherlock Holmes' and 'The present king of France')?[7] I shall, for the time being, suppose an affirmative answer; I also suppose the policy to be one of maintaining such a distinction. That done, another question comes

---

[9] Rolf Schock, "Contributions to Syntax, Semantics and the Philosophy of Science", *Notre Dame Journal of Formal Logic*, 5, 241-289.

[10] Rolf Schock, "A Natural Logic without Existence Assumptions" (Address, 1961).

[11] Karel Lambert, "Notes on E! III: a Theory of Descriptions", *Philosophical Studies*, 13, 51-59 and Karel Lambert, "Existential Import Revisited", *Notre Dame Journal of Formal Logic*, 4, 288-292.

[12] For example, Karel Lambert, "Notes on E! IV: a Reduction in Free Quantification Theory with Identity and Descriptions", *Philosophical Studies*, 15, 85-88.

[13] Bas C. van Fraassen, "The Completeness of Free Logic", *Zeitschrift für Mathematische Logik und Grundlagen der Mathematik*, 12, 219-234.

[14] This very brief historical sketch does not pretend to be complete. It merely samples the recent history of free logic.

hard on the heels of the first: do we satisfactorily handle the quantification problem for a theory of fictionality by incorporating in **BL** a widely or narrowly free logic?

§2. *Neutral Logics.* – The decision of Chapter I, §1, to equip the naivist with the existence-neutral quantifiers 'Σ' and and 'Π', and therewith to allow him the satisfiability of "Some things don't exist", suggests as part of the solution to the quantification problem some or other NEUTRAL LOGIC in the sense of Routley.[15] A neutral logic is here understood to contrast with a narrowly free logic, it is a system whose quantifiers bind variables whose values need not be existent individuals, and whose individual constants can name things that do not exist. In such logics, Routley's **R₁***, for example, it is a theorem that some things do not exist – +$\Sigma v \neg (Ev)$. We read 'E' as the non-descriptive, categorical or natural-kind[16] predicate 'exists'. Routley's systems, therefore, are free e-logics in the wide sense.

Routley's neutral logic **R*** has a normal-enough looking first order language whose logical symbols include a (truth-functional) implication sign, '$\rightarrow$', a (truth-functional) negation-sign '$\neg$', parentheses, the comma, and the existence-neutral quantifier 'Π' read 'for all (possible) objects'. The language contains variables 'x', 'y', 'z', etc., individual constants 'a', 'b', 'c', etc., and the primitive predicate constant, 'E', read 'exist(s)'. The axioms and rules of inference for **R*** are:

(1) If ϕ is truth-functionally deducible, then ϕ is **R*** deducible.

(2) $\Pi v(\phi \rightarrow \psi) \rightarrow (\phi \rightarrow \Pi v\, \psi)$, provided that v is an individual variable not occurring free in ϕ.

(3) $\Pi v \phi \rightarrow S_{v_0}^{v_1}\phi|$, where v_1 is an individual variable or an individual constant that possibly has a referent.[17]

---

[15] Richard Routley, "Some Things Do Not Exist", *Notre Dame Journal of Formal Logic*, 7, 251-276.

[16] Natural kinds are scrutinized in Woods, "Semantic Kinds".

[17] The substitution notation is that of Church. See Alonzo Church, *Introduction to Mathematical Logic* (Princeton: The Princeton University Press, 1956), 192.

(4) Detachment: *From* ϕ, $\ulcorner \phi \rightarrow \psi \urcorner$ to *infer* ψ.

(5) Generalization: *From* ϕ to *infer* $\Pi v \phi$.

Thus, **R*** provides that names of fictional objects may interpret its individual constants and that the quantifier 'Π' may bind variables referring to fictional objects.

The remaining quantifiers of **R*** 'Σv' ("for some possible v"), '$\exists v$' ('for some actual v'), and '$\forall v$' (for all actual v') are introduced by definitions.

(6) $\Sigma v \, \phi = \mathrm{df} \, \neg \Pi v \neg \phi$
(7) $\exists v \, \phi = \mathrm{df} \, \Sigma v (\phi v \, \& \, Ev)$
(8) $\forall v \, \phi = \mathrm{df} \, \neg \exists v \neg \phi$.

It is provable in **R*** that

(9) $\forall v \, \phi v \leftrightarrow \Pi v (Ev \rightarrow \phi v)$.

$\ulcorner \Pi v \, Ev \urcorner$ is not a theorem and is not a valid sentence. Neither $\ulcorner \Sigma v \, vE \urcorner$ nor $\ulcorner \Sigma v \, \neg Ev \urcorner$ is a theorem of **R***, even though $\ulcorner \Sigma v \, Ev \urcorner$ is a self-sustaining sentence; i.e. to utter it is to guarantee that *it* at least exists. A stronger system, **R*$_1$**, can be got from **R*** by addition of the axioms

(10) $\neg \Pi v \, Ev$.
(11) $\neg \Pi v \, \neg Ev$.

That is, by the lights of **R*$_1$** some things do and some things do not exist. **R*** and **R*$_1$** further provide that

(12) $\Pi v (\phi v \, \& \, \neg \phi v) \rightarrow \neg Ev$,

whence that

(13) $\neg \exists v (\phi v \, \& \, \neg \phi v)$.

But they do not solve the contradiction problem; they do not, that is to say, permit any theorem of the form $\ulcorner \phi \, \& \, \neg \phi \urcorner$. It is just as well, since **R*** and **R*$_1$** have no provision for staunching the flow from contradictions. Without what Routley describes as a radical amendment of quantification theory,[18] the presence in

[18] Routley, "Some Things Do Not Exist", 259.

R* or **R*₁** of any theorem ⌜φ & ¬φ⌝ results in absolute inconsistency.

Neither can **R*₁** accommodate mixed modes of being. If it is true at *t* that Holmes had tea with Gladstone, and also (really) true that Gladstone at *t* was fasting in Abyssinia, then if we represent these English sentences in **R*₁**, we shall have a sentence of the form ⌜φ & ¬φ⌝; and **R*₁**, and hence our theory would be inconsistent.

Of course something like that 'radical amendment' of first order logic was, in effect, the job of the rule for the special predicate '$\mathscr{F}$'. But it must not be supposed that the (implied) base logic of the naive approach is an **R***-logic. Whereas **R*₁** is a logic that is bivalent (because two-valued), quantifier non-classical (because it has four quantifiers, not two), non-narrowly free (because its variables are not restricted to existing objects), the implied logic of the naivist seems to be quatravalent, quantifier non-classical, existence-neutral, and subject to the inference-inhibitions of the predicate '$\mathscr{F}$'. Its four sentential values are truth, falsehood, history-constitutiveness with respect to ... and fictionalizationhood with respect to ....

The 'radical departure', represented by the rule for '$\mathscr{F}$' in self-contradictory contexts, we are already familiar (not to say, happy) with. Whatever the explicit structure of such a theory of inference, it ventures the possibility of the theoremhood of *some* sentences of the form ⌜φ & ¬φ⌝, without falling into absolute inconsistency and so may be called a 'Meinong-logic'. True, the inference-abating predicate-constant '$\mathscr{F}$' appears to discharge some of the functions of the predicate 'E' of **R***. For example, it is a theorem of **R*** that if something behaves self-contradictorily then it does not exist. That is,

(14) $\vdash \Pi v((\phi v \,\&\, \neg \phi v) \to \neg Ev)$.

And in a Meinong-logic it would surely be desirable to have it as a theorem that something behaves inconsistently only if it satisfies the predicate '$\mathscr{F}$'. That is,

(15) $\vdash \Pi v((\phi v \,\&\, \neg \phi v) \to \mathscr{F} v)$.

Given these, and numerous other such parallels, it would be natural to think of the extension of '$\mathscr{F}$' as comprising such things as fictional and mythological beings, and the extension of 'E' as comprising neither; perhaps to the point of the interdefinability of these predicates: $\mathrm{E}v = \mathrm{df} \neg \mathscr{F}v$.

Even so, a Meinong-logic is not a narrowly free-logic, since the latter's quantifiers bind variables that range over existent entities only; and a Meinong-logic, though it is a neutral logic, is not an R^*- or R^*_1-system, in which latter, as in narrowly free logic too, self-contradictions have no place.

§3. *Impossibilia logics.* – Some philosophers[19] have attempted to expose the structure of what may be called IMPOSSIBLIA-LOGICS, that is, logics that endorse some contradictions. They differ from Meinong-logics chiefly by the absence of an inference-arresting device such as '$\mathscr{F}$'. Their efforts, I fear, have not met with very much success. In particular, attempts to re-vitalize a distinction of ancient purport, between sentence-and predicate-negation, so as to describe the impossible goings-on of *Meinonge* in an idiom that does not beget the theoremhood of every sentence, seem to us to fail. For, this is conceived to be an enterprise that requires us to characterize, and to accomodate among our theorems, the impossibility of such goings-on in a way that does not overturn the Law of Non-Contradiction. Predicate negation is so characterized as to differ from sentence negation chiefly on the question of bivalence. For any sentence, ϕ, either it or its sentential negation $\ulcorner \neg \phi \urcorner$ is true, and the other false. Yet for some ϕ neither it nor its predication $\ulcorner \text{un-} \phi \urcorner$ needs be true; both might be false, as when ϕ represents "The present king of France is bald" and $\ulcorner \text{un-} \phi \urcorner$ "The present king of France is non-bald". It may be true, as Routley says, that neither the Law of Non-Contradiction nor the Law of Excluded Middle is universally valid in cases of *predicate* negation, but this is a circumstance that serves only the cause of impossibilia, e.g. Meinong's round square, which is both round and not-round. For all that, predicate-negation will not be able to

[19] E.g. Routley, "Some Things Do Not Exist", 259ff.

handle any *truth-functional* contradictions that an author may choose to visit upon such putative possibilia as Sherlock Holmes or Watson.

There is also the point that predicate negation is difficult to interpret save as reflecting a notion of contrariety. So regarded, any pair of mutual predicate negations is true of a given object x only because some pair of logical contraries is true of x. (For example, the round square is both round and not-round only because it is both round and square.) But it is immediate that if ϕ is a contrary of ψ and ψ is true of x then it is not the case that ϕ is true of x, *i.e.* the sentence negation of ϕ, $\ulcorner \neg \phi \urcorner$, is true. And if we were to have it, by hypothesis, that ϕ is true of x as well, that would be a pity, for now we have an inconsistency that *is* a departure from the Law of Non-contradiction.

§4. *Possibilia.* – The semantics of neutral logics postulate domains of POSSIBLE INDIVIDUALS. It is not transparent what might be intended by the appellation "possible" applied to individuals. Routley characterizes an individual as a possible individual when and only when it is the referent of a consistent singular term. By a consistent singular term, I think he means a term whose sense (assuming such to have sense) can be likened to a function, from term to a bearer, that takes the term to the bearer in such a way that does not logically imply that the bearer satisfies contradictory predicates. Thus, as inconsistent singular terms, we would have the likes of 'the round square' and 'the second least even prime'; and as consistent terms we would have (just about) all the other well-formed singular terms of our language – 'Sherlock Holmes', 'Mrs. Sherlock Holmes', 'The chubbiest girl-friend of Sherlock Holmes not known to Mrs. Sherlock Holmes' mother's Confessor', 'the most happy fella', 'the Creator' 'the present king of France', 'the fourteen trillionth Premier of Italy', 'the phlogiston in Tommy Tweed's beard' and so on.

Not the least of the objectives of neutral logics is the accommodation of discourse about all manner of objects whose non-existence is known or at least in doubt – point masses, ideal gases, Lycurgus of Sparta, God, and fictional beings. Fictional beings, in fact, are taken as paradigms of possible non-actual individuals, as, on Routley's test, they should be in view of the self-consistency of their names.

However, I think it may justly be argued that a possible object semantics does not accommodate the prime purport of a theory of fictionality. For, it is entirely possible that the most singular of all the properties of fictional objects is that, in at least one very important sense, they are *not* a species of possible individual. Fictional individuals seem, on the contrary, very much to be impossibilia. For suppose that we agree that

1. An object x is a possible individual exactly when x belongs to a possible world.[20]

2. W is a possible world if and only if it is either the actual world or is some totality of unactualized states of affairs under some suitably complete, self-consistent description.

3. If x is not a member of the actual world but $x \in W$, then if W were to be ACTUALIZED then x would be REALIZED (i.e. the existence of individuals coincides precisely with their membership in an actualized possible world).

Given this understanding, fictional individuals are not possible individuals. They are impossibilia, not in Routley's sense that they inhabit worlds whose every "accurate" or "faithful" description or whose "definition" involves a contradiction (though sometimes they are impossibilia in this sense too), but rather in the sense that they cannot be members of any world that can be actualized. A possible individual is one whose existence is possible; but it is in the very nature or essence of fictional beings not to exist – of fictional objects *esse est esse fictive*.[21]

[20] The concept of possible worldhood is reviewed below, §4.4. And a conception of possible individuals, different from Routley's, may be found in Woods' "The Formal Ontology of Death".

[21] The Latin, but not the interpretation, is Ockam's. The expression "termini ficti" appears in the *Summa Logicae* II, ch. 12 and ch. 14. Ockam there explicitly rejects the view that termini ficti denote *figmenta* (i.e. non-existent things).

Consider a world in which one of either of the following circumstances obtain.

(1) Holmes, the character who was *in fact* created by Doyle's literary efforts, proceeded from an entirely nonliterary paternity.
(2) The selfsame Holmes, created in our world by Doyle, *becomes* in that possible world *real*. (That is to say, in the new world there is some individual x from the actual world, with whom Holmes interacts in such a fashion as to guarantee his reality in that new world – for example, he actually kills him.)

To view a fictional being as *essentially* fictional involves finding these conditions incoherent; "incoherent" in the sense in which it is incoherent to suppose Gladstone becoming a transcendental number (and surviving the change). But it is also true that to regard fictionality as an essential characteristic, or property, of him who has it is to countenance a philosophical doctrine of essentialism, as we have had occasion earlier to remark.

Holmes' 'residency' in possible worlds, W_i, alternative to the one he currently 'inhabits' (*viz.* our own or anyhow a temporal predecessor of ours), cannot (I am saying) depend upon his meeting the condition: if x is in W_i then x exists iff W_i is actualized. Nor can Holmes' residency in our world involve satisfaction of the condition that membership in its population coincides exactly with existing. Whatever its precise details, the correct story of Holmes' 'residency' must preserve the truth that he, being fictional, is an unrealizable member of the host world, this or any other. Holmes, being fictional, is an impossibile. And so we are speaking, really, of two varieties of world-habitation, the one such that to belong is to be a possibile, the other such that to belong cannot be to be a possibile. In this second sense of 'habitation', fictional beings 'inhabit' the real world, for Holmes inhabited

---

'Figmenta' is often used to refer to impossibilia, but Ockam is careful to point out that every terminus fictus is complex and that its simple parts refer to real things. So 'fictus' is an adjective of second intention, conveying a property of terms, not of things. However, in his youth (*Commentary on the Sentences*, first rescension), Ockam used "fictum" to mean *idea*. That use accords rather more with our own.

London and London is as faithful a sample of reality as one could wish for. It is clear, then, that in the second sense, "inhabit" is used as a metaphor whereby Holmes' habitation of our world amounts to no more than that "Holmes lived in London" is a fictional sentence that we are quite right to assent to, and London is a location in the real world.

It can now be appreciated that fictional objects do not satisfy *strong* versions of Meinong's principle of the independence of *Sosein* from *Sein*. For if *Sein* is taken narrowly, as existence, and if Holmes' *Sosein* includes his fictionality, then Holmes' *Sosein* implies his incapacity for *Sein*, and Meinong's principle is breached.

We should be clear that Holmes may not even meet what I presume to be Routley's test of possibility (i.e. having a self-consistent name) and that he might not be admissible into the range of the variables bound by 'Π' and 'Σ'. But Holmes, not to harp upon it, could logically misbehave, say by squaring the circle, and cause $\mathbf{R}^*$ and $\mathbf{R}^*_1$ to be absolutely inconsistent. Of course, amendments of Routley's criterion quickly spring to mind. For example a is a possible individual iff 'a' is co-referential with no self-inconsistent singular term. So, if Holmes ever did square the circle, we should have some singular term co-referential with 'Holmes', say, 'the only detective to have squared the circle prior to the invention of the A-bomb', by the evident inconsistency of which Holmes would be an impossible.

It is not obvious that every fictional being is obligated to *behave* so as to violate the Law of Non-Contradiction. But if one were to accept the appropriate reduction postulates for the iterated alethic modalities, the essential kind-predicate 'is fictional' indeed implies a contradiction; for, 'x is fictional' entails, for some ϕ, the modal predicate $\ulcorner possibly\ \phi x$ and $\neg \phi x \urcorner$. A fictional object, x, satisfies the modal predicate by virtue of the circumstance that had the author so chosen, x would have behaved differently, and the author could have so chosen. Now, to satisfy this predicate is to depart the modalized Law of Non-Contradiction, and since there are reduction laws according to which $\ulcorner$Possibly $\phi\urcorner$ entails $\ulcorner$Necessarily (Possibly ϕ)$\urcorner$, then, by such laws, a fictional object has an essence incompatible with the Law. Whence the Routley-inconsistency of any such singular term as 'the fictional person who ...'. That is to say, if our language L were distinctively to represent the essential predicate 'is fictional', and if it represented, as well, a modal expression 'possibly', and if, moreover, the semantics for L provided, via appropriate reduction laws, that anything satisfying the representation of that predicate was necessarily capable of self-contradictory behaviour, then L would represent such an object as an impossibile.

The languages of **R*** and **R*$_1$** are not languages of this kind. And neither **R*** nor **R*$_1$**, contains such a reduction law. It is nonetheless the intent of **R*** and **R*$_1$**, that both the present king of France and Sherlock Holmes be possible objects falling in the range of their quantifiers 'Π' and 'Σ'. It is also the case in **R*** and **R*$_1$** that, short of being distinct possible objects, no semantic distinction is marked between the present king of France and Sherlock Holmes. Whence, Routley's systems are logics for nonentities and nonsuches alike, and so, by the decision of §1, not adequate (enough) for the logical reconstruction of a theory of fictionality. More generally, no logic of possibilia seems rightly tooled for singular terms that denote fictional beings. They are better for theories of empty singular terms, terms that do not denote at all. Names for fictional beings, unlike, for example, improper definite descriptions, do not fail to denote. They denote impossibilia. A semantics is therefore suspect if it does not reflect the purport between terms that denote essentially non-existent objects and terms that do not denote at all, but which might denote in worlds alternative to the one in which they do not.

How might a semantics honour this distinction between individuals and nonsuches? The language L could subclassify its names into those that denote and those that do not. Nonsuches could be characterized as values only of free variables. Individuals could be taken to be the values of bound variables. Names of individuals would instantiate quantification contexts; nonsuch terms would be substitutable only for free variables. In such a set-up, I believe, the theorist would elect to place 'Holmes' in the former class of names and modify the quantificational base of the language in such a way as to preserve "there are things that do not exist".

§5. *Narrowly free* e-*logics.* – By these, and similar, lights widely free e-logics, such as those of Routley, do not work for fiction. Neither likewise do narrowly free e-logics, such as those of Lambert. Basic narrowly free e-logics are bivalent, quantifier-standard quantificational structures, to the languages of which is added a predicate constant 'E!', the special axioms for which might be, for example,

1. $\exists v\, \phi v \rightarrow \exists v (E!v\, \&\, \phi v)$

2. $\phi v_0 \rightarrow (E!v_0 \rightarrow \exists v_1\, \phi v_1)$.

'E!' is a primitive predicate constant borrowed from Whitehead and Russell, and is read '... exists'. The individual variables range, classically, over actual objects, and the quantifiers '$\exists$' and '$\forall$' are construed accordingly. The axioms for '$\forall$' are standard:

3. $\forall v(\phi v \rightarrow \psi v) \rightarrow (\forall v\, \phi v \rightarrow \forall v\, \psi v)$

and

4. $\forall v_0\, \phi v_0 \rightarrow \phi v_1$.

The Law of Universal Generalization is a version of the Hilbert-Ackermann

5. *From* ⌜$\phi \rightarrow \psi$⌝, *if v is not free in* ϕ, *to infer* ⌜$\phi \rightarrow \forall v\, \psi$⌝.

Important theorems include

(T1) $\forall v(E!v \rightarrow \phi v) \rightarrow \forall v\, \phi v$
(T2) $\forall v(E!v \leftrightarrow \forall v(E!v \rightarrow E!v)$
(T3) $\forall v_0\, \phi v_0 \rightarrow (E!v_1 \rightarrow \phi v_1)$
(T4) $\forall v\, E!v$

Now in the two special axioms, there is no need to restrict the range of singular terms; 'Pegasus', 'Sherlock', 'the present king of France' all may be represented here. The correctness of singular inferences is, in this system, expressly divorced from such semantic considerations as whether a singular term denotes or whether a predicate is true of any actual object. So, in such a system there is no need, and perhaps no advantage, to ascribe to these singular terms any semantic property other than that of *failing to denote*. To that extent, narrowly free logics ignore the intuitive distinction between non-entities and nonesuches.[22] For our current interests, the chief difference between free logic and neutral logics is their respective stands on

(1) $\forall v \, E!v$.

In our narrowly free logic, it is a theorem that everything exists (so, there, neither the present king of France nor Holmes is a somebody), whereas in our widely free neutral logic the negation of (1) is a theorem (and, there, both Holmes and the present king of France are somebodies).[23] In the former instance we are too hard on Holmes; in the latter, too easy 'on' the present king of France.

§6. *Facts.* – No apologia for it can be guaranteed to root out all of a considerable cumulative scepticism regarding the naive theory of fictionality. Doubtless it will still be protested that the naive concept of fictionality exacts excessive concessions. For the not entirely essential fact of our daily lives, that, concerning people who get into disagreements and make bets with one another about where Holmes lived, there is a clear winner and a clear loser, we must pay an astonishing price. We must either amend the Law of Non-contradiction, say by inventing a new predicate '$\mathscr{F}$' where-

---

[22] However, Lambert has said, in conversation, that he is not even the slightest inclined toward that intuition. For him, "Sherlock Holmes" and "Mrs. Sherlock Holmes" are up for precisely the same semantic treatment. That, as always, is the trouble with intuitions.

[23] The differences between such neutral logics as R* and narrowly free logic do not prevent free logic's being a subsystem of R*. Let FR* be the restriction of R* such that the language of FR* is the language of R* minus the quantifiers 'Π' and 'Σ' and all constants. As Routley points out ("Some Things Do Not Exist", 256), FR* is a free logic in the sense of Lambert ("Notes on E! III"). It is provable (though Routley's proof is defective) that every theorem of R* that is a sentence of FR* is a theorem of FR*. That is, FR* is a *conservative restriction* of R*.

with to stem inferential floods, or we must make a distinction between truth values and history constitution-values with whose motivation and meaning there is reason to be dissatisfied.

It is of some importance that every one of these unorthodoxies arises from insisting that fictional sentences are *true* and that fictional goings-on are *knowable*. And that surely argues (I don't say, conclusively) that they are *not* true and therefore *not* known. Yet if no sentence about Holmes is true *de re* it must be faced that he loses his place in our objectificatory scheme of things, and sentences 'about' him take on the non-subject-predicate structure of such minor classics as "The present King of France is bald". Unless we can give an alternative account in which fictional sentences are *not* true, but which is strong enough not only to make possible settlement of arguments about the fictional by appeal to works of fiction, yet also to reveal why that method is sufficient (indeed necessary), we shall find ourselves in the paradoxical position of knowing full well who it is that there is nonesuch as, who it is that cannot be identified, and who it is of whom it is true that there are no truths about him. It would be well to be clear that not the only cause for skepticism concerning truths about fictional objects is their capacity for departing from laws. Nomological misbehaviour is troublesome enough, but it does not exhaust the difficulties of the naive approach. Far the more implausible circumstance is that self-consistent fictional goings on contradict the facts. And so, if fictional truths are to be counted true, there is need for some such manoeuvre as that by which fictional truths are regarded not as history-constitutive of fictional beings but as mere fictionalizations of reality.

No doubt this gambit has its attractions, but not quite so many as to quell the following kind of uneasiness. If fictional truths are (true) fictionalizations of the world, there is no reason not to bestow the same, generous, construal, upon mythology and legend. So, a person who 'knows' that Zeus lived atop Olympus and not in the Cascades is one who embraces some true 'mythologization' about the world. And he who 'knows' that Nero fiddled while Rome burned, and did not, then or ever, play hockey, is one who assents to some true 'legendization' concerning the world. But we know it to be non-history-constitutive not only of the world, but also of Nero, that he fiddled, for there were at the time no fiddles. How then can such a statement, being non-history-constitutive of everyone and everything, compel a verdict of 'true'? If our answer is that such a verdict is unwarranted, even though you win your argument with me if you take the position that Nero fiddled rather than played hockey, while Rome was incinerated, then it looks as though we have lost our strongest argument for the truth of fictional statement. For, it ought to be possible to account for the phenomenon of bets, properly won and lost, without having to enlarge the extensions of 'true' so as to guarantee a place for the winning fictional sentence.

The chief part of our problem, no doubt, is that fictional goings-on did not really happen, and that entirely accurate descriptions of fictional goings-on are not really true, are not, as we might say, *factual*. Here is the possibility, at least, of a needed and useful distinction between sentences that are (really) true because they describe and are made true by the facts, and sentences that, even though, they describe no facts, are allowably utterable; true in a sense, but not, as we might say, 'factually true'. Philosophers are familiar enough with a use of the word 'fact', by which the world, or reality, is the totality of facts. This accords well with our disinclination to place fictional beings in the real world, and to look upon their deeds and passions as elements in reality's chronicle. If only facts were well understood.

Facts have recently enjoyed a revival from their lonely retirement to the prehistory of semantics. Their resurrection is due to van Fraassen.[24] Let us say that PRIMITIVE STATES OF AFFAIRS are those in virtue of which the atomic sentences of a language are true. Thus, primitive states of affairs are what Russell and Whitehead called complexes, and they are, for the sentences 'Fa' and 'G(a,b)', THAT-A-HAS F and THAT-A-BEARS G-TO-B. It is also supposed that some primitive states of affairs OBTAIN and that others do not.

[24] Bas C. van Fraassen, "Facts and Tautological Entailment", *The Journal of Philosophy*, 66, 477-486.

Thus *that-Pierre-Trudeau-is married* is a primitive state of affairs that since only rather recently obtains; previously, to the giddy optimism of countless Canadian women, it did not obtain.

The question whether primitive states of affairs are all that is needed to account for the truth of every true sentence, whether compound facts or states of affairs are needed, has a long and rather untidy history. It shall be our policy to admit into the discussion as few kinds of fact as we can get away with. What we can get away with varies with what we take our various needs to be. If our concern is simply to find truth conditions for sentences of a standard language we would need no appeal to facts. Facts can help in the specification of such truth conditions, but they are not demanded by them. Of course some of the sentences whose logical structure we wish to represent are the sentences of fiction, are sentences whose semantics seems nonstandard. Hence *their* truth conditions may turn out to require a concept of facts; but we will want to develop that latter notion without any such antecedent assumption.

What is a primitive state of affairs? What sort of entity is it? Let us say that the primitive state of affairs (psa) *that-a-G-b* consists of the ordered triple $\langle G, a, b \rangle$ the first member of which is the relation in extension, G and the second and third members, respectively, are in the domain and converse domain of that relation. In general,

(1) A psa is an $n+1$-tuple whose first element is a relation of degree n.

Facts can now be represented as sets arising from operations on psas. Atomic facts are singletons of psas. The conjunctive fact *that-ϕ & ψ* is the union of the fact *that-ϕ* and the fact *that-ψ*.

Facts are presumed to make sentences true; they are also presumed to make for other facts. If a given fact obtains it is natural to think that certain other facts likewise must obtain, and certain others not. That is to say, we ought to look for relations, over the domain of facts, analogous to the logical relations among sentences, such as compatibility and entailment. If the fact

$\{\langle F, x \rangle\}$ is incompatible with the fact that $\{\langle F', x \rangle\}$, then these two facts clearly cannot co-obtain: $\{\langle F, x \rangle\} \cup \{\langle F', x \rangle\} = 0$.

Similarly, if a fact cannot obtain without another's obtaining, we may say that the first *compels* the second. Thus $\{\langle G, x_1, ..., x_n \rangle\}$ compels $\{\langle G', y_1, ..., y_n \rangle\}$ if and only if the former is a subset of the latter. This also allows for a distinction between a sentence's *being made true* and its *diffusely being made true*; a sentence is diffusely made true by any fact that compels a fact that makes it true.[25]

Facts are construable in the metatheory of standard logic. In ordinary interpretations of first order languages, valuations are defined for sentences relative to a model and under an assignment of values to the sentence's variables. It is supposed that a model $\mathcal{M}$ is a sequence of a domain D of objects and n-ary relations G_k^i over the domain. There is a function f from variables to objects in the domain; and the atomic sentence $\ulcorner \phi(v_0, ..., v_n) \urcorner$ is true in $\mathcal{M}$ under f if $\langle f(v_0), ..., f(v_n) \urcorner$ is a member of G_i^n, where G_i^n is the extension of the ith atomic n-place predicate of our language.

A psa in $\mathcal{M}$ is any $n+1$-tuple whose first term is an n-ary relation over D and whose remaining members are members of D. A fact in $\mathcal{M}$ is a nonempty set of psas in $\mathcal{M}$. A conjunctive fact in $\mathcal{M}$ is the set $F_1 \cup ... \cup F_n$, where the F_i are facts in $\mathcal{M}$. A fact F_1 compels in $\mathcal{M}$ a fact F_2 if F_1 and F_2 are facts in $\mathcal{M}$ such that $F_1 \subseteq F_2$. A psa $\langle G, a_1, ..., a_n \rangle$ obtains in $\mathcal{M}$ iff $\langle a_1, ..., a_n \rangle \in G$. A fact F obtains in $\mathcal{M}$ iff every object $x \in F$ obtains in $\mathcal{M}$.

It is now possible to define a notion of *factual truth*, a notion, that is, such that for every sentence ϕ of our language there is a set, $T(\phi)$, of facts which *make ϕ true* in $\mathcal{M}$, and a set, $\bot(\phi)$, of facts that *make ϕ false* in $\mathcal{M}$. For the atomic sentences, let ϕ be the atom $\ulcorner \psi(v_0, ..., v_n) \urcorner$. There is but one fact that makes ϕ true in $\mathcal{M}$ under f; it is $\{\langle R, f(v_0), ..., f(v_n) \rangle\}$, where R is the extension of the predicate ψ. Likewise, one fact only makes for ϕ's falsity in $\mathcal{M}$, the fact $\{\langle \check{R}, f(v_0), ..., f(v_n) \rangle\}$, where $\check{R}$ is the set

---

[25] van Fraassen credits such a notion to McKinsey and to Schock; see "Facts and Tautological Entailment", 483.

theoretic complement in $\mathcal{M}$ of R. For the molecular sentences we have:

$T(\neg \phi) = \bot(\phi); \bot(\neg \phi) = T(\phi)$
$T(\phi \& \psi) = T(\phi) \cap T(\psi)$, the intersection of $T(\phi)$ and $T(\psi)$.
$T_f((\forall v)\phi) = \cap T_{f*}(\phi)$, where $f*$ is like f save perhaps at v.
$\bot_f((\forall v)\phi) = \cup T_{f*}(\phi)$, where again $f*$ is like f save perhaps at v.

The relation of *making* in $\mathcal{M}$, between sentences and the sets $T(\phi)$ and $\bot(\phi)$, is defined as follows.

(i) ϕ is made true (is factually true) in $\mathcal{M}$ iff $\exists F(F \in T(\phi))$
(ii) ϕ is made false (is factually false) in $\mathcal{M}$ if $\exists F(F \in \bot(\phi))$.

Let us now characterize the sets $T^e(\phi)$ and $\bot^e(\phi)$, respectively, as the set of facts that compel some fact $F_i \in T(\phi)$, and the set of facts that compel some fact $F_k \in \bot(\phi)$. $T^e(\phi)$ is the set of facts that diffusely make ϕ true; and $\bot^e(\phi)$ the set of facts that diffusely make ϕ false. Clauses (i) and (ii) still hold true if we were to replace '$T(\phi)$' with '$T^e(\phi)$' and '$\bot(\phi)$' with '$\bot^e(\phi)$'.

As has already been remarked, facts are not needed to define truth in $\mathcal{M}$. If facts are to be interesting they must be expected to provide for definitions of new, nonstandard semantic relations. To take a particular example, the standard semantic relation of entailment such that ϕ entails ψ if whenever ϕ is true in $\mathcal{M}$, ψ is also true in $\mathcal{M}$ can be defined without bothering with factual truth. But what of the more intimate-sounding fact-dependent relation that holds from ϕ to ψ exactly when anything that *makes* ϕ true also *makes* ψ true? If we denote that relation by the expression '$\Rightarrow$', we can write the definition:

$\ulcorner \phi \Rightarrow \psi \urcorner$ is true if $T^e(\phi) \subset T^e(\psi)$, in any model $\mathcal{M}$.

van Fraassen has noticed that this new relation is that of tautological entailment, of Anderson and Belnap, and it is to van Fraassen's credit to have provided an interpretation of it within ordinary model theory. The proof[26] that the $\Rightarrow$-relation is tautological entailment are one and the same is straightforward and we shall not reproduce it here.

[26] See van Fraassen, "Facts and Tautological Entailment", 486.

Short of a passion for tautological entailment, it is hard to think of an urgent need of the apparatus of facts and of notions such as *making true*. Why, then, should one be inclined towards countenancy of facts?

Facts can be used to explicate something like a concept of *history-constitution values*. We might imagine such sentences as describe what actually happens, as describing and being made true by facts; and such sentences as describe the goings-on of fiction as counter-describing the facts. So conceived, fictional truths are truths that are not *made* true; in fact they are *made* false. Thus, "Holmes lived in London" is true, but no fact makes it true. And "Holmes lived in Gutherie" is false, and is made false by the facts. So, as things stand, there is no semantic difference between fictional falsehoods and factual falsehoods, but we could recover such a distinction by putting it that fictional falsehoods have at least one fictionally true presupposition.

We are nevertheless left with the contradiction problem. Fictional sentences are true and factual falsehoods are false. So fictional sentences can be both true and false. To have the theory we again would have to restrict the Law of non-Contradictions, somewhat as follows: for every ϕ it is not the case that both ϕ and $\ulcorner \neg \phi \urcorner$ are *factually* true or *factually* false.

But what of those other aspects of the contradiction problem – when ϕ and ψ are fictional sentences that are one another's contraries, true, let us say, by the sayso of different authors? And what, again, if ϕ is a fictional truth in the form $\ulcorner \psi \ \& \ \neg \psi \urcorner$? A theory of facts is here of no use to us. We might, of course, adopt an earlier suggestion of not representing such inconsistencies in L. That removes, after a fashion, the inconsistency-problem, but it replaces it with another – the problem, namely, of saying what such "orthographic inconsistencies" really mean, given that they do not mean what they appear to mean.

It is also worth noting, if only for the irony of it, that in the system of tautological entailment self-contradictions do not entail every sentence, and the Lewis-proof is invalid. But the system in which this is so is one in which there are no true self-contradictions; the system for which this is not so is the system which, on the face of it, is distinguished by the need to reckon with contradictions that are true. The system of tautological entailment has the resources for stemming the spread from contradictions but it does not apply to those parts of $\mathscr{E}$ where self-contradictions threaten to be true.

Facts are of no conspicuous help to us so long as we allow fictional sentences to be true. And once that is disallowed facts are unneeded, for we have all the contrast we need in a distinction between truth and falsehood, provided we also hit upon a way of representing a *truth-like* semantic property for fiction. Pending a full development, let us allow that what it is that is distinctive about "Holmes lived in Baker Street" by which that sentence wins a bet, is that it is TRUE-BY-CONVENTION. Truths-by-convention are understood to have two significant properties: (1) they are not true and (2) they warrant a class of false assertions.

§7. *The substitution interpretation of quantification.* – Truth-by-convention is not a truth value. It is a property of false sentences; yet sentences having it are properly assertable. The class of a theory's assertable sentences is not, therefore, exhausted by its theorems, or by its truths. How shall we represent such a property? Should we trifle with it at all? Will not its recognition hopelessly complicate the semantics of $\mathscr{E}$? These questions, and sundry others, argue the wisdom of a pause. Let us make another try at locating ourselves closer to a standard base logic.

In elementary logic texts, the approach taken to the quantifiers tends to be a substitutional rather than a referential approach. By "A REFERENTIAL APPROACH TO THE QUANTIFIERS" is intended a model theoretic semantics postulating (usually) a countably infinite domain of interpretation for the sentences of L, over denumerably long sequences of which are defined such notions as satisfaction, truth, and validity. If, in particular, ϕ is some quantified sentence '$(\exists x_k)(F(x_k))$' then ϕ is satisfied by a sequence, s, from the domain for L if it is not the case that no such sequence differing from s in at most its k-th place satisfies '$F(x_k)$'. And if φ is the closed formula '$G(a)$' s satisfies φ provided the individual constant 'a' names something in the domain that is in the extension of the predicate 'G'. Thus it is a basic insight of such a semantics that names name only existent individuals and that existential formulas *impute* existence to elements from the domain. But one pays a price for that insight, since the sentence that represents "Someone solved the Case of the Speckled Band" is satisfied by no sequence, and so neither is the sentence implying it, "Holmes solved the Case of the Speckled Band".

On the other hand, the substitutional account of the quantifiers originates in such a different insight. It is that a sentence $\ulcorner(\exists v_k)(\phi)\urcorner$ is satisfied if there is some singular term, a, of its language such that the result of substituting occurrences of a for appropriate occurrences of v_k in φ is a sentence ψ for which there is a valuation, V, such that $V(\psi) = T$ ('T' for the truth value, truth). ψ is called a "substitution instance" of $\ulcorner(\exists v_k)(\phi)\urcorner$.

It is clear that, for the substitutionist, the existential quantifier does not impute existence; it imputes the truth of a substitution instance. Thus, the sentence φ representing "Someone solved the Case of the Speckled Band" will be satisfied, on this account, for there will be in L a singular term representing the name 'Holmes', and a predicate representing the predicate 'solved the Case of the Speckled Band', whose concatenation is a true substitution instance of φ that represents the truth of English, "Holmes solved the Case of the Speckled Band".

According to the referential account, the inference representing

(1) Holmes solved the Case of the Speckled Band
(2) Therefore, someone did

is vacuously valid, owing to the unsatisfiability of (1); whereas according to the substitutionist, the inference is properly valid, not valid on a technicality. Although these two semantics can be shown to be formally isomorphic[27] with respect to validity, it may be supposed that the one that represents our inference as non-

---

[27] Not to say equally adequate to all useful purposes. See John Wallace, "Convention T and Substitutional Quantification", *Noûs*, 5, 199-211.

vacuously valid answers better to our primal logical intuitions. It might be supposed, too, that the semantics that represents (2) as true squares better with what we think we know to be so.

Our two semantics differ from one another with respect to sentences that are not logical truths. The question of how to represent sentences of English that are not logical truths is not, therefore, a narrowly logical question. It is a question of which of the two approaches preserves more truths of English without occasioning differences in what they agree on as logical truths and in what inferences they mark as valid.

That being so, the substitutionist cannot but offer his approach as the base logic for our logical reconstruction of the sentences of fiction. It is a sober and reasonable proposal. It invites us to represent the world of fiction in a standard first order logic.

If, to return to the recurring contradiction problem, it is complained that some fictional truths are self-contradictory, the substitutionist need only suggest that their inconsistency is orthographic, not logical, and counsel their representation in L by atomic sentences.

He who would argue that the truth of a singular truth comes to much the same as an imputation of existence to its subject does not take substitutionists' semantics seriously; and anyway he must deal with the fictionalist for whom the situation is conspicuously otherwise. But we suppose $\mathscr{E}$ to contain not only sentences of fiction but also those that chronicle the unfolding of history. There still remains, therefore, a contradiction problem – the problem of the conflicting deviation of fiction from what actually occurs. One method of its treatment is to refuse fictional sentences the truth value truth; but that not only ignores the desires of the fictionality theorist, it also withdraws a claim by which the substitutionist can argue the intuitive superiority of his approach to the quantifiers. The alternative would seem to involve allowing such sentences as (2) to be true, but to add to the semantic component of **BL** additional equipment by way of history constitution values, or some such. The upshot here is that although the quantificational structure of fictional discourse may be represented classically, its semantics cannot be. And so it does not seem that one can avoid the reconstruction of $\mathscr{E}$ in some or other deviant logic.

We shall, after all, therefore, consider truth-by-convention.

IV

TRUTH-BY-CONVENTION

§1. *The value* **c**. – Essential to sentences true-by-convention ('**c**', for short) is that though not true, we are perfectly right to affirm them. That is to say, some of our most sober pronouncements, correct, accurate, entirely right, that win bets for us, are nonetheless not true. So either the classical epistemology is sound and the class of known statements is but a proper subclass of the class of what is rightly affirmable; or the classical epistemology is incorrect, and the class of truths is but a proper subclass of what is known. This might suggest a non-classical analysis of knowledge, by which a person x knows that ϕ, only if ϕ is true or true-by-convention. For the present we do not debate the worthiness of such a reform.

Formally the advantages of the present proposal are considerable. (I) The abnormalities resulting from the ascription of truth to fictional sentences disappear in one fell swoop. The Law of Non-Contradiction is restored unrestricted; no sentence, $\ulcorner \phi \mathbin{\&} \neg \phi \urcorner$, will be true, though it may be true-by-convention. The theory of inference of our base logic no longer requires the rule for '$\mathscr{F}$', for though it may be true-by-convention that Holmes violated such and such law, it will not be true. In general, putting '**c**' for 'true-by-convention' and '**t**' for 'true' it need not be invariable that if $\ulcorner \mathbf{c}(\phi) \urcorner$ and $\ulcorner \mathbf{t}(\phi \to \psi) \urcorner$ are theorems of our metalanguage then $\ulcorner \mathbf{c}(\psi) \urcorner$ is a theorem as well.

The logical consequences of truths-by-convention need not themselves be true-by-convention, i.e. truth-by-convention is not closed under consequence. Intuitively, this is as it should be, since, although the disjunction "Holmes lived in London v Podunk Center, Iowa has been offered for sale" is a logical consequence[1] of "Holmes lived in London", the latter is **c** whereas what it implies might be, to the very palpable bemusement of local dignitaries, **t** and therefore not **c**. And in case we should have ⌜c(ϕ)⌝ and ⌜c($\neg\phi$)⌝, even if ⌜c(ϕ & $\neg\phi$)⌝ is a consequence, it certainly need not follow that **t**(ψ), for arbitrary, ψ, the truth of ⌜(ϕ & $\neg\phi$)→ψ⌝ granted.

(II) The proposal also provides for the incompleteness of fictional individuals, for saying that fictional objects really are *Meinonge*, and to that extent intentional objects. Though this is not something I am tempted to say, it must be admitted that the earlier rejection of *Meinonge* on grounds of ω-inconsistency loses any bite it may have had. For it simply need not be the case that the set $\{$⌜c$\Sigma v\phi$⌝, ⌜$\neg$c(ϕa_1)⌝, ⌜$\neg$c(ϕa_2)⌝, ..., ⌜$\neg$c(ϕa_n)⌝, ...$\}$ is ω-inconsistent. Neither will it be obvious that ⌜t(ϕ ∨ $\neg\phi$) → c(ϕ ∨ $\neg\phi$)⌝ is a valid conditional.

(III) Though untrue, such claims as place Holmes and his kind so comfortably within the framework of objectifactory discourse – *e.g.* that there is such as Holmes, that it is known who he is; more generally, that fictional individuals enter the identity relation, are countable, are individuated, and have properties and histories – all emerge as true-by-convention, and hence as perfectly open to affirmation, in contradistinction to such sentences as "The present King of France is wise" which is not true, not true-by-convention and not rightly affirmable.

(IV) Freud will have been spared whatever embarrassment attends the preparation of psychiatric study not only about a non-entity (fair enough) but also about a nonesuch. He will have been provided or not with the needed object of his endeavours just according as "$\Sigma x(x =$ Gradiva)" is either true or true-by-convention. It will also be clear that "$\Sigma x((x =$ Gradiva) & (x does not exist))", by the consistency of which the naivist pleaded the need of a non-existential particular quantifier, probably is *not*

---

[1] Provided that 'v' is defined for sentences that are **c**.

consistent,[2] although it could be true-by-convention. In that event, to insist on replacement of '∃' by 'Σ', without new arguments, might have little to recommend it other than doggedness (if that).

Though there is much that favours the present proposal, it would lose nearly all its attraction if two fundamental questions remained unsettled. First, we must know how to interpret the predicate 'true-by-convention'. Second, we must understand what justifies our saying of an untruth that if it is true-by-convention it is properly open to affirmation.

§2. *Truth-by-convention.* – Regarding the question of what is meant by "is-true-by-convention", we propose this definition:

Def. The sentence ϕ is true-(false-) by convention iff (i) ϕ is non-bivalent and (ii) if ϕ were bivalent it would be true (false)

Intuitively, ours is an account of truth-by-convention such that every singular atomic sentence about a fictional being is either true-by-convention or false-by-convention, and such that the other atomic non-truth valued sentences are neither true-, nor false-by-convention. It hardly seems likely that if "The present king of France is bald" were truth valued it would stand any better a chance of being true than false. It is fortunate that this should be so, for it allows for the preservation of the nonentity-nonesuch distinction. Two concrete examples satisfying **Def** are these. First: if the sentences comprising Sir Arthur Conan Doyle's *The Case of the Speckled Band* were truth-valued then, in particular, the sentence "Holmes lived in London" would be true. Second: if the (faulty) recounting that Tommy Tweed gave of the *Case of the Speckled Band* were truth valued then it would be false, in particular, that Holmes solved that case while in Luxembourg. In the first example we have truth-, in the last falsehood-, by-convention. We might remark that a like treatment awaits insolubilia involving the fictional. However, the important point to notice is that *all* atomic sentences 'about' the present king of France are, in a sense, insolubilia, whereas this is so only of some sentences concerning the

[2] "Not consistent" in the sense that it is satisfied by no interpretation.

fictional. So there would still be a significant difference between Holmes and 'his' wife: Holmes, the non-entity, is the subject of some c-truths, whereas 'she', the nonesuch, is subject of none.

§3. *Conditionals.* – Here we have position – we might call it the CONVENTIONALIST THEORY OF FICTIONALITY – whose logical reconstruction may be presumed to proceed as follows. Those sentences of $\mathscr{E}$ that are about fictional beings are represented in L in the usual way. A fictional sentence is understood to be any sentence about a fictional being, and so includes, in addition to an author's contributions, those sentences recording our concourse with fictional beings ("Freud psychoanalyzed Gradiva"). The semantics for L is a non-bivalent one. In particular, if ϕ is a sentence of L representing a fictional sentence of $\mathscr{E}$, then by the semantic component for L, there is a valuation, V, from sentences into the truth-values, such that $V(\phi) \neq T$ and $V(\phi) \neq F$. Such a semantics might propose a third truth-value for ϕ, or it might simply leave V undefined for ϕ. Depending on one's choice on that point, the base logic for E might be non-bivalent narrowly free, a presuppositional logic (say) in the sense of van Fraassen,[3] which admits of truth-value gaps, or it might be a three-valued system in the manner of Woodruff,[4] in which there is a third 'truth'-value, **u**, that closes truth-value gaps.

What is truly distinctive, however, about the conventionalist's proposal is not his toleration of non-bivalent logics. On that score, fictional sentences such as "Holmes was wise" are treated indistinguishably from such nonesuch sentences as "The present king of France is wise". The conventionalist wants to recognize the non-bivalence of both kinds of sentence; yet for fictional sentences, and only for these, he wishes to summon a fourth and fifth semantic property, truth-by-convention and falsehood-by-convention. I say fourth and fifth "semantic property" so as to discourage one

---

[3] Bas C. van Fraassen, "Singular Terms, Truth-value Gaps, and Free Logic", *The Journal of Philosophy*, 63, 481-494.
[4] Peter Woodruff, "Logic Truth Value Gaps", *Philosophical Problems in Logic*, ed. by Karel Lambert (Dordrecht: Reidel, 1970), 121-142.

from supposing these to be additional 'truth'-values and **BL** to be, really, a five-valued logic. In a very important sense our **BL** is not a five-valued logic, since it allows different sentential values to converge. In particular, it allows fictional sentences, and only these, to be assigned the non-bivalent truth value, **u**, and also either of the semantic objects truth-, falsehood-by-convention.

If susceptibility to be assigned one or other of these new semantic properties, is to represent what is distinctive about fictional sentences, the job of explicating truth-, and falsehood-by-convention is the distinctive feature of the conventionalist's proposal. The definition, **Def**, of truth-by-convention, places very considerable weight upon conditions rendered subjunctively. But subjunctive conditionals are notoriously problematic in their own right, and it would be incautious, to say the least, to allow the conventionalist to rest his case on so dark a saying as **Def**.

What is needed is an account of subjunctive conditionals, wherewith to illuminate **Def**.[5] We require, that is to say, a theory of (relevant portions of) our semantic meta-language SML for L, for the likes of such expressions as ⌜Were ϕ, non-truth-valued it would be that ϕ is true (false)⌝.

By "a subjunctive conditional" I mean a conditional sentence intermediate in strength as between a material conditional and a

---

[5] The account of conditionals here presented is essentially an account developed in John Woods', "Subjunctive Conditionals and Middling Modalities", Mimeo (University of Toronto, 1967); slightly revised version in *Manitoba Modern Languages Bulletin*, 8, 25-31. It is very similar to Robert C. Stalnaker's theory, "A Theory of Conditionals", *American Philosophical Quarterly Monograph Series*, 2, 98-112, which was developed independently. My earlier proposals were not exactly those of Stalnaker, however. In particular, my theory did not accept that:
(1) Either ⌜ψ, given that ϕ⌝ or ⌜$\neg\psi$, given that ϕ⌝ is a theorem
for, although these conditionals cannot both be true, they can both be false. Another important difference is that Stalnaker's theory was presented in an axiomatic form that is provably complete (see Robert C. Stalnaker and Richmond H. Thomason, "A Semantical Analysis of Conditional Logic", *Theoria*) whereas my theory was not presented axiomatically. Because Stalnaker's axioms are complete I have decided to resolve these differences his way. I am not sure whether this makes for a theory that captures precisely the right intuitions, but I believe it does so nearly enough to be safely employed for our current purposes.

strict conditional. I do not assume, moreover, that a subjunctive conditional needs to be counterfactual or even that it demands expression in the grammatically subjunctive mood.

We assume a semantic meta-meta-language whose resources may be supposed to include a Kripke-semantics for systems of modal logic. We have need to speak of what Kripke calls a "model-structure". A MODEL-STRUCTURE is a formal set theoretic object, a triple $\mathscr{W}$ where $\mathscr{W}$ is $\langle W, A, \mathscr{T} \rangle$. W is understood to represent the set of all possible worlds; A to represent a relation of world-alternativeness (it is read 'is an alternative possible world with respect to possible world ...'); and $\mathscr{T}$ to represent the world in which everything is the case.

We put it that A is reflexive. Thus $\mathscr{W}$ is equivalent to the von Wright modal system M. If one's intuitions concerning being possible with respect to warranted it, A might also be characterized as transitive. In that event $\mathscr{W}$ would be equivalent to Lewis' modal system S4. Similarly, if A were characterized as symmetrical as well, $\mathscr{W}$ would be the equivalent of Lewis' S5. However, it suffices for present purposes to have A a reflexive relation only.

'$\mathscr{T}$' represents the world in which everything is the case. A complete description of such a world would, of course, be inconsistent, for every sentence is the case only if $\ulcorner \neg \phi \urcorner$ is the case. $\mathscr{T}$ is the world in which self-contradictions hold. One is therefore tempted to call $\mathscr{T}$ "Meinong's world". Perhaps it is rather more apposite to call it "Tertullian's world", and we shall do so here. $\mathscr{T}$ is not customarily a member of a Kripke-structure. It is a bizarre abstraction; Formally, however, $\mathscr{T}$ is as metaphysically solid as an entity as any model-structure.

$\mathscr{T}$ is understood to be that member of W that bears A to no

---

It is necessary to add the very agreeable discovery of two further independent developments of conditional-theory. The one, by J. Howard Sobel, "Utilitarianisms: Simple and General", *Inquiry*, also does not endorse (1). The other, by David Lewis, I have seen in (photocopied) typescript only (David Lewis, "Completeness of Three Logics of Counterfactual Conditionals", Photocopy of typescript (Oxford, 1970)). Both papers incorporate the basic intuitions of Woods' and Stalnaker's accounts, and both are very much more finished systems than the one presented here.

other member of W and to which no other member of W bears A.

It will be necessary to introduce a notion of FIXED WORLDS. Fixed worlds are worlds, the conditions of the truth in which it is our theory's job to state for middling conditionals. It is, of course, not in general the case that the worlds in which a subjunctive conditional is true is a world in which its antecedent or consequent is true; nor, likewise, that worlds in which its antecedent and consequent are true are worlds in which the conditional is true.

C is some set of formal sentences that represent some of the sentences of $\mathscr{E}$, of (some of) ordinary English. The sentences of C represent conditional sentences in $\mathscr{E}$. We suppose now a function f, from the set of ordered pairs $\langle x, y \rangle$, such that x is a sentence of C and y is a world of W, into the set W of worlds.

For each sentence of C, ⌜ψ, given that ϕ⌝, the function f chooses a world in which the antecedent ϕ is true. Intuitively, a conditional ⌜ψ, given ϕ⌝ is *true domestically* (*i.e.* true with respect to the real world) if its 'consequent' ψ is true in the chosen world. Thus, more generally, ⌜ψ, given ϕ⌝ is true in a world w if ψ is true in $f(\langle \phi, w \rangle)$; and ⌜$\psi$, given that ϕ⌝ is false in a world w if ψ is false in $f(\langle \phi, w \rangle)$.

Our function chooses worlds according to the following conventions. Since it is advisable to preserve the truth of "Tommy Tweed is bearded, given that Tommy Tweed is bearded", we require the condition,

(C1) For all ϕ and for all p, if ϕ is an antecedent and p is a fixed world, ϕ is true in the chosen world $f(\langle \phi, p \rangle)$.

We must also devise a strategy for conditionals whose antecedents are inconsistent. Thus,

(C2) For all such ϕ and p, $f(\langle \phi, p \rangle) = \mathscr{T}$ only if there is no possible world w such that w A p where ϕ holds true.

(C2) motivates Tertullian's world. It is the world that f chooses for conditionals whose antecedents are formally inconsistent. It is, plainly, a formal contrivance without which f would be undefined for such sentences.

Conditions (C1) and (C2) do not yet capture our function. It is not enough that f choose a world under just those governances.

For suppose that we have some sentence, "Canadians would renounce the monarchy, given that a set theory is developed, and generally accepted, in which the Continuum Hypothesis is false". Then, unless we constrain f further, this sentence will be a domestic truth if f but chooses an appropriate possible alternative to the real world. What is worse, we also would have it that our republican-toned sentence is false, since f might also choose a possible world in which the Continuum Hypothesis is confuted though the monarchy there flourishes. This suggests the need to make f a one-one function, that is, a function for whose every distinct argument there is a distinct unique image. I confess that my intuitions on this point are not as clear as they might be, but I shall nevertheless suppose that f always chooses a unique world from W. This restriction will cancel the second of our objections, but it does nothing to annul the first. To that end, we imagine that f always choose a world that differs *as little as possible* from the fixed world under review. If $\langle \phi, p \rangle$ is an argument to the function, then f takes us to a world, w, in which both ϕ and ψ are true and in which other things are as equal as can be. $f(\langle \phi, p \rangle)$ is, then, a maximally similar alternative to p; only those differences are tolerated between p and $f(\langle \phi, p \rangle)$ as are occasioned by the truth of ϕ in $f(\langle \phi, p \rangle)$, adjusting, of course, for consistency, and by the truth there of ψ, as well, if ψ there is true. So we shall need the condition

(C3) For all ϕ and p, if ϕ is true in p, then $f(\langle \phi, p \rangle) = p$. (If ϕ is true in the fixed world p, then the alternative world maximally similar to p is p itself.)

We also observe that

(C4) For all fixed worlds p and antecedents ϕ and ϕ^*, if ϕ holds in $f(\langle \phi^*, p \rangle)$ and ϕ^* holds in $f(\langle \phi, p \rangle)$, then $f(\langle \phi^*, p \rangle) = f(\langle \phi, p \rangle)$.

(C3) and (C4) jointly provide that f linearly orders the set of all the choosen possible worlds with respect to each possible world, with the fixed world as least element under that ordering. The unique fixed world represents the real world, which is the world the statement of the conditions of truth in which for conditionals is the first task of any theory of conditionals.

The sentence $\ulcorner \psi$, given that $\phi \urcorner$ can be written with the help of the (subjunctive) conditional connective '$\leadsto$' thus: ⌜$\phi \leadsto \psi$⌝, an alternative reading of which is ⌜Were it to be the case that ϕ, it would (also) be the case that ψ⌝.

The Stalnaker-Thomason axiom schemata for the $\leadsto$-sign are as follows ('$\to$' is for material implication):

(AC1) If ϕ is a logically valid formula of **BL** then ϕ is an axiom

(AC2) $(\neg(\phi \to \psi) \leadsto (\phi \to \psi)) \to ((\neg\phi \leadsto \phi) \to (\neg\psi \leadsto \psi))$
(AC3) $(\neg(\phi \to \psi) \leadsto (\phi \to \psi)) \to (\phi \leadsto \psi)$
(AC4) $(\neg(\phi \leadsto \neg\phi)) \to ((\phi \leadsto \psi) \to \neg(\phi \leadsto \neg\psi))$
(AC5) $(\phi \leadsto (\psi \lor \chi)) \to ((\phi \leadsto \psi) \lor (\phi \leadsto \chi))$
(AC6) $(\phi \leadsto \psi) \to (\phi \to \psi)$
(AC7) $(\phi \leftrightsquigarrow \psi) \to ((\phi \leadsto \chi) \to (\psi \leadsto \chi))$

(AC2) reflects the familiar intuition that if a material conditional is necessary, then the necessity operator distributes over the material conditional. (AC3) establishes that a logically necessary material conditional materially implies the corresponding strong conditional of its antecedent and consequent. (AC4) represents the circumstance that a possible sentence is one that does not subjunctive imply both a formula and its negation.

There are two rules of inference in this system:

(RC1) MODUS PONENS: *From* $\vdash\phi$ *and* $\vdash\phi \to \psi$ *to infer* $\vdash\psi$.
(RC2) NECESSITATION: *From* $\vdash\phi$ *to infer* $\vdash(\neg\phi \leadsto \phi)$.

The deductive system Δ resulting from these axioma-schemata exhibits two properties of particular note. In Δ '$\leadsto$' obeys neither transitivity nor contraposition.[6]

I now assume that the language of C, the set of sentences representing the subjunctive conditionals of $\mathscr{E}$, includes enough of its own metalanguage to enable it to represent such sentences of $\mathscr{E}$ as ⌜$\mathscr{S}$ is truth-valued⌝ and ⌜$\mathscr{S}$ is true⌝ and ⌜$\mathscr{S}$ is false⌝. The formal language of C is thus a sublanguage of the language L of

---

[6] Cf. J. L. Austin, *Philosophical Papers*, ed. by J. O. Urmson and J. G. Warnock (Oxford: The Clarendon Press, 1961), 157. Austin may be credited with the discovery that, in some uses, 'if' does not contrapose. But it must also be said that he was mistaken in thinking those uses to be very special uses.

our **BL** for $\mathscr{E}$. **BL** is now assumed to include the system Δ and to represent the sentences of $\mathscr{E}$, some of which will be subjunctive conditionals involving semantic predicates. One such is

(1) If "Holmes lived in London" were truth-valued, it would be true.

Another is a fictional sentence, ϕ, in the form $\ulcorner \psi(a) \ \& \ \neg \psi(a) \urcorner$, in which the singular term 'a' denotes a fictional being. ϕ then can justly be said to be neither true nor false. Yet if ϕ enjoys the explicit backing of the author's sayso the inclinations of very many conventionalistic members of the $\mathscr{E}$-linguistic community would be to accord ϕ the semantic property truth-by-convenion. By the definition, **Def**, of truth-by-convention, such an ascription involves the recognition of ϕ's non-bivalence together with the claim that were ϕ bivalent it would be true. And by our theory of the middling conditional, this latter commits us to saying that there is a chosen world w^* in which ϕ is bivalent and in which it is also the case that ϕ is true. But w^* can only be Tertullian's world $\mathscr{T}$; whence the unwelcome consequence that the only world in which ϕ is true-by-convention is the world in which everything is the case, hence is a world in which, among other things, it is the case that ϕ is *not* true-by-convention.

Just as things stand, the conventionalist theory of fictionality cannot solve the contradiction problem. But, that it cannot may be a matter of some importance. For, it is plausibly argued that if, under an intuitively good definition of truth-by-convention, and under at least a very promising theory of conditionals, it turns out that fictional sentences in the form $\ulcorner \psi \ \& \ \neg \psi \urcorner$ cannot, even on their author's sayso, be true-by-convention – to say nothing of their being true – then a perfectly legitimate restriction to place on the author's sayso condition is that it not be allowed to licence sentences in that form. Perhaps that is as good a solution to the contradiction problem as one could reasonably hope for.

§4. *Possible worlds.* – True, both the intuitive and the conventionalist theories remain problematic in other ways. On the naive approach, it was necessary *somehow* to populate the actual world with non-actual individuals, whereas on the conventionalist approach we were at liberty to populate possible worlds with individuals *tout court*, undifferentiated as between actuality and non-actuality. And too, on the second approach, it was necessary to make some sense out of TERTULLIAN'S WORLD. Though it is more likely than not that if the general notion of a possible world could be made clear, our cavils concerning Tertullian's world could come to seem to us no more justified than complaints about the empty set or the integer zero.

Certainly the general notion of a possible world lies at the centre of a burgeoning amount of current logical and philosophical analysis. It is hard to imagine theories for the modalities, for conditionals, for formal pragmatics, for some conceptions of essential kinds, and much else besides, in which there do not occur formal analogues of possible worlds. And even apart from the apparent philosophic need for possible worlds, it has been suggested that here is a concept no less clear, no less intuitive and no less worthy than the concept of an abstract set.[7] And at least one philosopher has taken the position that even in the absence of a needed explanation "the notion [of a possible world] has enough intuitive content to make it fruitful in semantics". Apparently clarity enough would be achieved with respect to the identity of a possible world by specifying "a domain of individuals said to exist in that world".[8] It is not necessary to belittle a concept just because, intuitive, picturesque, and innocent, it has attended certain of our philosophical or pre-philosophical meanderings. But there are grounds for worry if, for example, such a concept is invited to bear a theoretical burden for which it is unprepared; especially if, on the grounds of intuitiveness alone, it is pretended that burdens are capably accommodated. At the very least, it ought to be established with respect to any such notion what are to be the adequacy conditions that will place the concept suitably half-

[7] David Lewis, *Convention* (Cambridge, Mass.: The Harvard University Press, 1969), 208.
Robert C. Stalnaker, "Pragmatics", *Synthese*, 22, 272-289.

way between its formal analogues ('concepts without intuitions') and its natural, over-picturesque representatives ('intuitions without concepts ...'), halfway, for example, between Kripke-structures and Leibniz's possible worlds. What, then, are the philosophical adequacy conditions that an account of possible worlds must meet? It seems reasonable to ponder at least these four:

(1) The (actual) world is a possible world.

(2) There exists an alternativeness relation A, suggestive of the idea of compossibility, from possible worlds to possible worlds. A is reflexive.

(3) Since the world contains all there is for it to contain, any possible world must be a complete totality in the sense that it not fail to contain any containable item.

(4) Although on the face of it, it does not seem necessary or reasonable to require that every possible world entirely differ in membership from every other possible world, there ought in any case to be some policy regarding the results of addition and subtraction of members from a given possible world.

No doubt, other conditions could be suggested, and some of those listed could be disputed. But if all or most of these were to go, so would our intuitive grasp on that notion of possible worldhood.

The idea of a possible world originates expressly with Leibniz,[9] and has been adumbrated by Mates and others.[10] There is something initially very attractive about the Mates-Leibniz reconstruction of a possible world as *something answering to a maximal consistent set of sentences*. A set Γ of sentences of a language L is maximal consistent iff the extension of Γ to Γ^+ by addition of any sentence of L that is not a member of results in the absolute inconsistency of Γ^+. Now, for every sentence ϕ of L either it or its

---

[9] Though anticipated, certainly, by Buridan.
[10] Benson Mates, "Leibniz on Possible Worlds", *Logic, Methodology, and the Philosophy of Science III*, ed. by B. van Rootselaar and J. F. Staal (Amsterdam: North-Holland, 1968), 507-529; Alvin Plantinga, "World and Essence", *The Philosophical Review*, 79, 461-492.

negation occurs in every maximal consistent set of sentences of L; and every consistent sentence of L or consistent set of sentences of L can (with the axiom of choice) be extended to a maximal consistent set Γ of sentences of L in which that original sentence (or set of sentences) is a member (or is included). Thus, maximal consistent sets are satisfiable (they describe possible states of affairs); and they are genuine totalities, for they could not take on new members without becoming inconsistent. So they are POSSIBLE TOTALITIES. Mates' general idea is to have possible worlds be the images of some suitable function or functions from maximal consistent sets of sentences.

It is not obvious how to specify these functions. If we had only a function from the Γ_i to {T, F}, then possible worlds would be the truth-values. Clearly a more promising strategy would be one that maps the Γ_i onto sets of not-necessarily realized *states of affairs*, or sets of not-necessarily obtaining *facts*, or, in the manner of Plantinga, sets of *propositions*.

It is here that ancient arguments threaten to rage. Whether facts, states of affairs or propositions are themselves any the less in need of a theory than possible worlds is a moot question, and a hard one. But I mean to leave such a question to one side, and to turn briefly to other matters. It will suffice to suppose that possible worlds are images of maximal consistent sets of sentences under a suitable choice of a function. We shall sometimes say, appropriating Jeffrey's metaphor,[11] that possible worlds are images of complete novels, or for short, of NOVELS.

Possible worlds are images of maximal consistent sets of sentences. Our question is: do possible worlds, so conceived, abide by our four conditions? As for condition 1, viz. that the actual world is a possible world, there is a difficulty. We are used to thinking of our natural world as one historically continuous changing world, not as a sequence of different, though similar, worlds one each for each newly truth-value-changed sentence, i.e. for each successive new Novel. However, perhaps we could be persuaded to abandon

---

[11] Richard C. Jeffrey, *The Logic of Decision* (New York: McGraw-Hill, 1965), 196.

the continuous conception of the world for the discretist perspectives of our present analysis. Pending a decision on that matter, let us agree that condition (1) is well-enough met. What, then, of condition (2), viz. that there exists an alternativeness relation defined over possible worlds? It is clearly met, if only in the trivial sense that every maximal consistent set is accessible to itself. And that is all that (2) absolutely requires of alternativeness. At condition (3), however, we encounter more serious difficulties. For, let w and w' be distinct possible worlds. Then, unless we are prepared to say that only those worlds are alternatives to a given world that are identical to one another, either we need an appropriately expanded view of worldhood or a carefully relaxed notion of alternativeness. Let it be clear why this is so. Since w and w' are distinct possible worlds, they are images of distinct Novels N and N'. And since Novels are maximal consistent sets, their union is inconsistent, and so is not a Novel and does not describe a possible world. Clearly the problem is that the requirement of complete totality-hood and the requirement of the compossibility of distinct possible words are not jointly satisfiable. So one of conditions (2) and (3) requires amendment. Otherwise, we would have it that for all w and w', where w and w' are not necessarily distinct, w A w' iff w = w'. In that event, too, the alternativeness relation, A, could consistently be supposed to have the properties, respectively, of transitivity and symmetry wherewith to interpret, respectively, the Lewis systems S4 and S5, only if every world standing in that relation, A, were just the same world. But that would argue the philosophical need, at any given time, only for the actual world, and a possible worlds semantics would cease discharging any interesting and distinctive responsibilities. The point rests upon the technicality that possible worlds semantics for the systems S4 and S5 require the alternativeness relation to be transitive and symmetrical,[12] and also that there exist more than one possible alternative to any given world. Since there is but one Mates-world, Mates' account does not semantically suffice for two of the most interesting

---

[12] A good account of Lewis' systems may be found in C. E. Hughes and M. J. Cresswell, *An Introduction to Modal Logic* (London: Methuen, 1968), 213-254.

and intuitive systems of modal logic. This is unfortunate, not only because possible worlds seem semantically so natural for S4 and S5, but also because one's hopes are dashed for a unified account of possible worlds – an account semantically adequate not only for von Wright's system for M, for S4 and S5, and for much more besides.[13]

It could be argued, of course, that the notion of possible world alternativeness is not, in the first place, properly served by the set theoretic concept of union. Union was introduced with an eye on the idea of compossibility, but perhaps that is an idea that alternativeness should not be asked to convey. It might be better to amend condition (3) and to think of alternativeness along the lines of set theoretic intersection, and to think of two worlds as alternatives, one to the other, when they share at least one element. Thus, if N and N' are distinct novels, they are alternatives if there exists at least one sentence ϕ such that $\phi \in N$ and $\phi \in N'$. Read this way, alternativeness cannot represent compossibility, which might more usefully be defined over proper subworlds of non-compossible possible worlds.

Such a relation, A, is reflexive, since every maximal consistent set trivially intersects with itself. And A would also seem to be symmetric. But it is not transitive. It is not, therefore, a relation that will do justice to the semantic interpretation (in the manner of Kripke) of any system of modal logic as strong as S4. This is not so much a complaint as an observation. It is an instructive observation, for it teaches us that the apparatus of a maximal consistent set may well enough reflect the notion of a possible world *tout court*, yet not every useful notion of *relatively* possible worldhood.

Normally a formal language is not so constructed as to contain

---

[13] However, it should be pointed out that Kripke-structures, though formally adequate to S4 and S5, do not faithfully represent S2 and S3, and will not do at all for S1 except in a conspicuously complicated version. See A. Shukla, "Decision Procedures for Lewis' System S1 and Related Modal Systems", *Notre Dame Journal of Formal Logic*, 11, 141-180, and M. J. Cresswell, "The Completeness of S1 and Some Related Systems" (unpublished typescript, Victoria University of Wellington).

its own theory, and so does not have the wherewithal to refer its own elements. But $\mathscr{E}$ is a fragment of English, and English consistently contains some of its own theory. If N, then, were to represent some maximal consistent set of sentences of $\mathscr{E}$, and if $\mathscr{E}$ contained resources enough to say, whenever S is (represented) in N, that this is so, then N would seem to contain that second sentence as well. Under that assumption, it is instructive to examine the following argument.

Let N be a Novel and let $\phi \in N$. Then, because N is a maximal consistent set, we have it that $\ulcorner \neg \phi \urcorner \notin N$. Yet since $\ulcorner \neg \phi \notin N \urcorner$ is itself true and consistent with N (since, after all, it tells the truth about N), and because N is maximal, we need to say that $\ulcorner \neg \phi \notin N \urcorner \in N$. But it would seem that N cannot contain this sentence unless it also contains the sentence $\ulcorner \neg \phi \urcorner$ to which it refers. So, N is not maximal consistent. Clearly something has gone amiss, and unless we can isolate a definite fallacy we can hardly persist with the model of a maximal consistent set.

The argument of the previous paragraph relies upon the (sound) principle (a): If $\phi \in \Gamma$ and ϕ refers to ψ, then Γ refers to ψ. But this principle, (a), must not be confused with either of the two further principles,

(b) ϕ is referred to by sentences of Γ only if ϕ is a member of Γ, where ϕ is a sentence and Γ a set of sentences;

(c) ϕ occurs in a sentence that is a member of Γ only if ϕ likewise is a member of Γ.

It is easy to see that (b) and (c) are false, and therefore that the foregoing argument collapses. For let ϕ be "What Zachary said about Sally was libelous" in which non-identifying reference is made to a sentence that need not occur in Γ even if ϕ does. And to see that (c) fails to hold – technically, saying it does not hold amounts to saying that maximal consistent sets are not closed under the subformula property – it suffices to suppose that Γ is a maximal consistent set of sentences and both ϕ and $\ulcorner \neg \phi \to \psi \urcorner$ are members of Γ. It is immediate that Γ cannot also contain $\ulcorner \neg \phi \urcorner$ as an element even though $\ulcorner \neg \phi \urcorner$ occurs in an element of Γ.

In the light of principle (b) it is necessary explicitly to acknowledge a distinction between

    (i) sentences in a Novel, N.

and

    (ii) sentences in the image of a Novel, N.

Clearly, (i) and (ii) do not in general coincide. Corresponding to the contrast between (i) and (ii) is a distinction, noted by Buridan, in the *Sophismata* chapter eight, between sentences true *of* a given possible and sentences true *in* a given possible world. Buridan noticed that truth of a world does not in general coincide with truth in a world. If a sentence ϕ is true *of* a world, w, then ϕ must be an element of N, where w is the image of N, yet need not be an element of w. If ϕ is true *in* w, then ϕ must be an element not only of N but also of w, the image of N. Buridan's classic illustration is the sentence "There are no negative sentences", which is false of any world containing that sentence, hence true *of* worlds *in* which it would not be true.

It seems reasonable to propose yet another condition on an adequate theory of possible worlds. It is that

(5) Buridan's distinction be preserved and clarified.

The conventionalist of current persuasion may assume a solution to the quantificational problem in a near standard first order logic. Provided the system allows for a sentence-value of the likes of **c** and indicates how it may behave over standard truth-tables, even the semantics of L need not be terribly non-standard. However, since c is interpreted, in the metalanguage, as truth-by-convention, and since we have provided a meta-metalinguistic account of that notion in terms of subjunctive conditionals, the semantics of our meta-metalanguage is nonstandard. The question is, do we need to countenance possible world in order to produce an adequate theory of fictionality? In the light of Buridan's problem, we might better look elsewhere.

V

MANY-VALUED AND MODAL LOGICS

§1. *The system $\mathscr{L}^3$*. – Our purpose, as we have said, is twofold. It is, on the one hand, to sketch a logical reconstruction of sets of fictional sentences of English. It is, second, and secondarily, to scrutinize an array of nonstandard logics in an effort to discern what might be their value for certain philosophical problems. This last task is pursued, in part, by attempting to mobilize various nonstandard systems as segments of a base logic adequate to the purposes of a logical reconstruction of fictionality.

It is apparent that both the naive and the conventionalist approaches to the logical reconstruction of fictional sentences are approaches that suggest a many-valued base logic. For, what is the base logic of the naive account if not the quatravalent system of truth, falsehood, history-constitutiveness with respect to ... and fictionalization with respect to ...? And what is the conventionalist approach if not the (at least) quatravalent system of truth, falsehood, truth-by-convention and falsehood-by-convention? True, as we have already remarked, neither could be thought of as a very ordinary sort of four-valued logic, in view of the capability of different values to characterize certain selfsame formulas; but the idea of a many-valued system persists and we would do well to examine it.

In considering many-valued systems of logic, it is nearly automatic to begin with Łukasiewicz's three-valued system $\mathscr{L}^3$.[1] Though

---

[1] Jan Łukasiewcz, "On Three-valued Logic", *Ruch Filozoficzny*, 5, 169-171, translated in *Polish Logic:* 1920-1939, ed. by Storrs McCall (Oxford: Oxford University Press), 15-18.

our first two passes at a theory of fiction suggest a four-valued system, it is helpful to understand precisely why a three-valued system will not do.

The semantics for $\mathscr{L}^3$ include three values, T, for truth, F, for falsehood I, for some suitably interpreted third alternative. (It is in Łukasiewicz possibility; in Bočvar's system[2] it is interpreted as meaninglessness, and it is undefinedness in Kleene's system.)[3] Both T and I shall be designated values in our version of $\mathscr{L}^3$.

In $\mathscr{L}^3$ it is not the case that all valuations V_i are such as that $V_i(\ulcorner \neg(\phi\ \&\ \neg\phi)\urcorner) = T$ or $V_i(\ulcorner(\phi \vee \neg\phi)\urcorner) = T$. That is, the classical laws of Non-Contradiction and Bivalence fail to hold. This alone is encouraging, for by the failure of the one Law, fictional beings are given needed room for nomological misdeeds, and, by the failure of the other, fictional beings can straightforwardly be construed as ontologically incomplete.

We have in $\mathscr{L}^3$ the following valuation-equations:

$\mathscr{L}^3$ ($\neg$): $\neg(T) = F$; $\neg(F) = T$; $\neg(I) = I$
$\mathscr{L}^3$ (&):   &(T, T) = T;   &(T, I) = I;   &(T, F) = F;
              &(I, T) = I;   &(I, I) = I;   &(I, F) = F;
              &(F, T) = F;   &(F, I) = F;   &(F, F) = F
$\mathscr{L}^3$ (v):   v(T, T) = T;   v(T, I) = T;   v(T, F) = T;
              v(I, T) = T;   v(I, I) = I;   v(I, F) = I;
              v(F, T) = T;   v(F, I) = I;   v(F, F) = F
$\mathscr{L}^3$ ($\rightarrow$): $\rightarrow$(T, T) = T; $\rightarrow$(T, I) = I; $\rightarrow$(T, F) = F;
              $\rightarrow$(I, T) = T; $\rightarrow$(I, I) = T; $\rightarrow$(I, F) = I;
              $\rightarrow$(F, T) = T; $\rightarrow$(F, I) = T; $\rightarrow$(F, F) = T.

The rules $\mathscr{L}^3$ ($\neg$), ..., $\mathscr{L}^3$ ($\rightarrow$) establish that, *if I is taken to be intermediate in 'truthfulness' between truth and falsehood*, then the negation $\ulcorner\neg\phi\urcorner$ of a statement ϕ will always take as value the exact opposite of the value of ϕ, except where ϕ is I (in that event $\ulcorner\neg\phi\urcorner$ takes the same value as ϕ); that a conjunction ψ has the least-

---

[2] D. A. Bočvar, "On a Three-valued Logical Calculus and its Application to the Analysis of Contradictions", *Matématičésky Sbornik*, 4, 287-308.

[3] S. C. Kleene, *Introduction to Metamathematics* (Amsterdam: North Holland, 1952), 332ff.

true value of its constituents; and that an implication $\ulcorner(\phi)\to(\phi')\urcorner$ is evaluated exactly as in classical systems (i.e. $V(\ulcorner\phi\to\phi'\urcorner) =$ $= V(\ulcorner\neg\phi \vee \phi')\urcorner)$ save that where $V(\phi) = V(\phi') = I$, $V(\ulcorner\phi\to\phi'\urcorner)$ is adjusted to come out T so as to preserve the validity of $\ulcorner\psi\to\psi\urcorner$. (We also remark that $V(\ulcorner\phi\leftrightarrow\phi'\urcorner) = V(\ulcorner(\phi\to\phi') \& (\phi'\to\phi)\urcorner)$, as in the usual two-valued case.)

Now a three- or n-valued logic is interesting only insofar as it differs structurally from its two-valued counterpart.[4] For example, if σ is a sentence-connective of a many valued system S and σ' is its two valued counterpart, then the semantics of S for σ are STANDARD if S contains at least one designated value (e.g. T) and one contra-designated value (e.g. F), and S provides that $V(\sigma(\phi)) = V(\ulcorner\sigma'(\phi)\urcorner)$ if $V(\ulcorner\sigma(\phi)\urcorner) = T$ or $V(\ulcorner\sigma(\phi)\urcorner) = F$, for all σ and σ'. That is, σ and σ' have identical matrices for T and F. $\mathscr{L}^3$ is in this sense standard.[5]

A semantics S for an n-valued negation-connective is KLEENE-REGULAR iff $V(\ulcorner\neg(\phi)\urcorner) = T$ (or F) just in case $V(\phi) = F$ (or T).

The negation modality is STABLE iff nowhere do the semantics for '$\neg$' permit a valuation V such that $V(\phi) = V(\ulcorner\neg\phi\urcorner)$.

$\mathscr{L}^3$ is Kleene-regular but unstable with respect to negation.

Might $\mathscr{L}^3$ serve as base sentence logic of the sentences of fictional discourse? Could one not suppose, in particular, our representation function to take all atomic singular sentences of $\mathscr{E}$, in which there occurs an empty singular term, into the atomic sentences ϕ of $\mathscr{L}^3$ for which the semantics of $\mathscr{L}^3$ provide a valuation, V, such that $V(\phi) = I$? Certainly, if it *is* to serve, it would be useful if it were to turn out either (1) that for no sentence ϕ and for no valuation V_i is it the case that $V_i(\ulcorner\phi \& \neg\phi\urcorner) = T$; or (2) that for no sentences ϕ and ψ is it the case that $V_i(\ulcorner(\phi \& \neg\phi)\to\psi\urcorner) = T$ for all valuations V_i; or that for no ϕ and ψ is it the case that $V_i(\ulcorner((\phi \vee \psi) \& \neg\psi)\to\phi\urcorner = T$, for all valuations V_i (i.e. Disjunctive

---

[4] For a good survey of many-valued systems see Nicholas Rescher, *Topics in Philosophical Logic* (Dordrecht: Reidel, 1968), 54-116. Cf. A. A. Zino'vev, *Philosophical Problems of Many Valued Logic* (Dordrecht: Reidel, 1963).

[5] However, the systems of Post are not standard. See E. L. Post, "Introduction to the General Theory of Elementary Propositions", *American Journal of Mathematics*, 43, 163-185.

Syllogism does not obtain). It is easily verified that all three conditions are met in $\mathscr{L}^3$. That this is so constitutes an argument of sorts for $\mathscr{L}^3$ as part of the **BL** for $\mathscr{E}$. Chief among the advantages of $\mathscr{L}^3$ are these:

(1) In $\mathscr{L}^3$ there can occur author-authenticated contradictions, for these do not entail the truth of every $\mathscr{L}^3$-sentence. There is no need, therefore, for an inference-inhibiting rule such as the semantic rule for '$\mathscr{F}$'. Neither is it necessary to exclude or ignore fictional self-contradictions by representing them by means, say, of atomic formulas of L of **BL**. However it also emerges that $I \neq c$, i.e. that the third value of $\mathscr{L}^3$ cannot be given the interpretation 'true-by-convention', according to the theory of truth-by-convention developed for the conventionalist approach to a theory of fictionality. On the conventionalist approach, there is no V_i such that $V_i(\ulcorner \phi\ \&\ \neg\phi \urcorner) = c$, whereas in $\mathscr{L}^3$ there is a valuation V_j such that $V_j(\ulcorner \phi\ \&\ \neg\phi \urcorner) = I$.

(2) Another advantage, of a sort, of $\mathscr{L}^3$ is that there disjunctive syllogism does not hold universally. So any Lewis-style proof of the claim that a sentence of the form $\ulcorner \phi\ \&\ \neg\phi \urcorner$ entails every sentence is aborted.

(3) $\mathscr{L}^3$ can be supposed extended by addition of a quantification profile, that is, of axioms for the quantifiers and for identity and perhaps, too, for definite descriptions. In that extension, $\mathscr{QL}^3$, there would be natural means of reflecting the Meinongean incompleteness of fictional beings, safe from inconsistency, ω- and absolute-.

(4) In $\mathscr{L}^3$ and $\mathscr{QL}^3$ all representations of fictional sentences are non-bivalent, are classically truth-value gappy. This could be understood to reflect the point that no fictional sentence ϕ, or its negation, 'refers to reality'. Non-congress with the world is made explicit.

However, there is, in $\mathscr{L}^3$, a deep disadvantage for the concept of fictionality. As we have seen, negation in $\mathscr{L}^3$ is not stable. It is Kleene-regular, of course, since in $\mathscr{L}^3 \neg(T) = F$ and $\neg(F) = T$.

But it is not stable because it allows for *self-annulment*: $I = \neg(I)$. Negation in $\mathscr{L}^3$ is far better suited to represent talk of nonesuches than talk of non-entities, to talk 'of' the present king of France than to talk of Sherlock Holmes. For as between the canonical representations in $\mathscr{L}^3$ of

(i) The present king of France is bald

and

(ii) The present king of France is not-bald,

there is rightly nothing to choose. Certainly there is no rational bet to make on the outcome of the 'conflict' between (i) and (ii); and since in $\mathscr{L}^3$ they are both represented by sentences that are assigned the third value, I, then '$\neg$' is unstable in nonesuch-contexts, and $\mathscr{L}^3$ is a natural logic for nonesuches.

But concerning Holmes there is clearly something to choose as between

(iii) Sherlock Holmes lived in Baker Street

and

(iv) Sherlock Holmes did not live in Baker Street,

and, certainly, the rational bet to make is on (iii). Since $\mathscr{L}^3$ cannot distinguish a winner from a loser, and provides no grounds for affirming (iii) that are not grounds for affirming (iv), it will not do.

§2. *The system $\mathscr{L}^4$.* – It is plain that a logical reconstruction of fictional discourse requires a concept of negation that is both Kleene-regular and stable. That, in turn, is pretty strongly to suggest the need of a non-3-valued logic. Suppose, then, that we explore a 4-valued sentence logic, $\mathscr{L}^4$, with a value, T, for truth, F, for falsehood, I_1 for fictruth and I_2 for ficfalsity. We designate T and I_1, and, for the present, contra-designate F. We might also presume to be associated with $\mathscr{L}^4$ a non-classical epistemology:

P knows that ϕ iff ϕ has a designated value.

The connectives '$\neg$', '&' and '$\rightarrow$' are defined as follows:

Negation	
ϕ	$\ulcorner\neg\phi\urcorner$
T	F
I_1	I_2
I_2	I_1
F	T

Conjunction		
ϕ	ψ	$\ulcorner\phi\,\&\,\psi\urcorner$
T	T	T
I_1	T	I_1
I_2	T	I_2
F	T	F
T	F	F
I_1	F	F
I_2	F	F
F	F	F
T	I_1	I_1
I_1	I_1	I_1
I_2	I_1	I_2
F	I_1	F
T	I_2	I_2
I_1	I_2	I_2
I_2	I_2	I_2
F	I_2	F

Implication[6]
$\ulcorner\phi\to\psi\urcorner$
T
T
T
T
F
I_1
I_1
T
I_1
I_1
I_1
T
I_2
I_2
I_1
T

Now the negation-function of $\mathscr{L}^4$ is both Kleene-regular and stable, and so is non-self-annulling. In $\mathscr{L}^4$ there exist the means of distinguishing those fictional sentences that we may assent to, that we non-classically know, from those that we may not assent to, that we do not, even non-classically, know. As such, $\mathscr{L}^4$ is adequate to talk of non-entities (such as Holmes) but not of nonesuches (such as the present king of France).

As in $\mathscr{L}^3$, neither the Law of Non-Contradiction nor the Law of Excluded Middle is classically valid in $\mathscr{L}^4$. And here too, as in $\mathscr{L}^3$, neither $\ulcorner(\phi\,\&\,\neg\phi)\to\psi\urcorner$ nor $\ulcorner((\phi\vee\psi)\,\&\,\neg\phi)\to\psi\urcorner$ is classically valid. The aforementioned advantages, of these same properties of $\mathscr{L}^3$, for the concept of fictionality are therefore preserved by $\mathscr{L}^4$.

However these selfsame conditionals so behave in $\mathscr{L}^4$ that for all valuations, V_i, $V_i(\ulcorner(\phi\,\&\,\neg\phi)\to\psi\urcorner) = T$ (or I_1), and

[6] The connectives in $\mathscr{L}^4$ do not all interdefine. For example, $\ulcorner\phi\to\psi\urcorner$ and $\ulcorner\neg(\phi\,\&\,\neg\psi)\urcorner$ do not exactly agree in truth-value; the implication takes I, in the sixth row, whereas the negated conjunction takes I_2. True, it seems slightly counterintuitive to evaluate $\ulcorner\phi\to\psi\urcorner$ as I_1, when its antecedent is 'truer' than its consequent. But, if we altered the defining matrix of '$\to$' so as to change the value of $\ulcorner\phi\to\psi\urcorner$ at row six to I_2, $\mathscr{L}^4$ would be strictly isomorphic to classical sentence logic, provided T and I_1 were designated and F and I_2 were counter-designated. So we shall, for the present, tolerate row six in the matrix for '$\to$', as is.

$V_i(\ulcorner((\phi \vee \psi) \mathbin{\&} \neg\phi) \to \psi\urcorner) = T$ (or I_1); that is, these conditionals are *non*-classically valid in the sense that under every valuation they are given one or other *designated* value.

So, it is just as well that no sentence $\ulcorner\phi \mathbin{\&} \neg\phi\urcorner$ receives in $\mathscr{L}^4$ a designated value. In fact, provided that we contra-designate both F and I_2 (more of this shortly), $\ulcorner\phi \mathbin{\&} \neg\phi\urcorner$ is a non-classical inconsistency, receiving only contra-designated values and therefore not reasonably open to assent and not an object even of non-classical knowledge. This means that, as with the conventionalist theory of fictionality, $\mathscr{L}^4$ may not tolerate any description of a fictional being's nomological misbehaviour expressly in the form $\ulcorner\phi \mathbin{\&} \neg\phi\urcorner$. Hence to represent fictional sentences in $\mathscr{L}^4$ is to permit no contradictions, and avoids the need for an inference-restrictor like '$\mathscr{F}$'.

The need to contra-designate both F and I_2 is fairly well determined by the problem of mixed modes of being. In order properly to state the problem, let us imagine $\mathscr{L}^4$ to be extended by addition of a quantificational profile. The problem posed by Holmes' having had tea with Gladstone can now be construed as the problem of how in $\mathscr{2L}^4$ to evaluate such sentences as:

(1) $(\exists x)$ (x = Holmes & Gladstone had tea with x).

(2) $(\exists x)$ (x = James Bond & Kingsley Amis admires x).

Suppose that $\mathscr{L}^4$ has been extended, as indicated, to $\mathscr{2L}^4$. Suppose, in particular, that the language of $\mathscr{2L}^4$ is that of $\mathscr{L}^4$ augmented by the classical quantifier '$\exists$', by the identity-sign '$=$', and that '$\exists$' and '$=$' are governed by standard axioms.[7] Then, given that Kingsley Amis does indeed admire James Bond, and that James Bond does not *really* exist, we can put it that each component of (2) receives the value I_1, so that (2) itself has the designated value I_1. This is an agreeable result, for it preserves that part of the naivist's

---

[7] $\mathscr{2L}^4$ might be extended to a neutral logic, $\mathscr{2}$N, as follows: for every formula $\ulcorner E\upsilon\,\phi\urcorner$ of $\mathscr{2L}^4$ there is a formula $\ulcorner \Sigma\upsilon\,\phi\urcorner$ of $\mathscr{2}$N such that if $\ulcorner E\upsilon\,\phi\urcorner$ is either T or I_1 then $\ulcorner\Sigma\upsilon\,\phi\urcorner$ is T, and if $\ulcorner E\upsilon\,\phi\urcorner$ is either F or I_2 then $\ulcorner\Sigma\upsilon\,\phi\urcorner$ is F. It would probably emerge that $\mathscr{2}$N is a bivalent neutral logic in the manner of R^*_1, retaining the inadequacies of R^*_1 concerning, *e.g.* mixed modes of being.

insight by which any assent-worthy sentence that implies or presupposes a fictruth is itself a fictruth.

With I_2 contra-designated, we also have a representation of perfectly familiar phenomenon: sentence (2) is not 'exactly' false, but then not 'exactly' true either, yet is 'closer to the truth' than its negation.

But there is also the Cook Wilson intuition that sentence (1) records a tea-party that is vastly more a 'fact' about Holmes than it is about Gladstone. By the present policy, (1) is given the value I_1, as is its $2\mathscr{L}^4$-equivalent:

(1′) $(\exists x)(x =$ Gladstone & Holmes had tea with x)

Even so, whereas both conjuncts of (1) are assigned the value I_1 (suggestive of a fact about Holmes), in (1′) only one conjunct is assigned I_1; the other, affirming the existence of Gladstone, is assigned T (suggesting that (1′) is not 'really' a fact about Gladstone). So the something like Cook Wilson's intuition is honoured by $2\mathscr{L}^4$.

Representing $\mathscr{E}$ in the language, L, of $\mathscr{L}^4$ involves the blindness of the representation relation to authored self-contradictions. The semantic metalanguage for L will define a truth-predicate in much the usual way, and an I_1-predicate along the general lines of a sayso semantics. We may also imagine that the representation theory maps bet-winning-capable fictional sentences of $\mathscr{E}$ into the I_1-sentences of $\mathscr{L}^4$ and the bet-winning-incapable fictional sentences to I_2. But what of those other sentences of $\mathscr{E}$ that contain occurrences of empty singular terms, terms purporting reference to nonesuches? It is no good to represent them as we represented fictional sentences, for presumably, *every* such sentence should be contradesignated. Yet if ϕ is a nonesuch-sentence and is contradesignated in $\mathscr{L}^4$, its negation $\ulcorner \neg \phi \urcorner$ is designated in $\mathscr{L}^4$. On the other hand, if we were systematically to represent nonesuch-sentences by means of logically distinct contradesignated formulas of $\mathscr{L}^4$, it would no longer be possible there to preserve the circumstance that "The present king of France is bald" and "the present king of France is not bald" are, in $\mathscr{E}$, each other's predicate-negations.

§3. *Dimensions.* – Much of the time philosophers and linguists who labour to bring some light to bear upon the logical structure of fictional discourse attempt to persuade one another of the theoretical utility of a concept of LINGUISTIC DIMENSIONS. Such a notion is invoked when it is pointed out, for example, that "Holmes solved the Case of the Speckled Band" is true in one linguistic dimension (in the 'language of fiction') but false in another dimension (the 'language of reality'). Similar inventions are sometimes thought to dissolve apparent problems of mixed modes of being. That Holmes lived in London is acknowledged to be true in the one dimension yet not the other.

These are dark sayings. Pending an explication of 'true in a dimension' there is little to choose between the explanations of the preceding paragraph and explanations of the form: "'That Holmes lived in London' is true but it is also false. There is no contradiction here, for, you know *perfectly well* what I mean."

Pending the explication, there is a problem lately discussed in Chapter Two, to which we must recur. If we were to represent fictional sentences in $\mathscr{L}^4$, we would have it that if ϕ and ψ take the value I_1, then so too does their conjunction. Yet if we have ϕ represent the Doyle-authenticated sentence

(1) Holmes was the first Honorary Mayor of Tunbridge Wells.

and ψ the Disraeli-authored

(2) Sibyl was the first Honorary Mayor of Tunbridge Wells.

then since ⌜(1) & (2)⌝ is inconsistent, so too should ⌜ϕ & ψ⌝ be. But $\mathscr{L}^4$ accords to ⌜ϕ & ψ⌝ a designated value, and our representation of ⌜(1) & (2)⌝ in $\mathscr{L}^4$ fails to preserve inconsistency. Such a problem was anticipated in §2.6, where a conception of inconsistency was sketched, by which (1) is inconsistent with (2) only if they are both same-author fictionalizations about Tunbridge Wells. A similar disposition might be expected from a multi-dimensionalist; fictional sentences authenticated by one author are true in one dimension and those authenticated by another author are true in a different dimension. And where ϕ and ψ are true in different dimensions, it does not follow that their conjunction is true in either dimension or any.

Pending, I have twice said, an explication of 'true in a dimension' we may or may not have something in such a proposal. It would, in any event, be prudent to scrutinize our intuitions about the kind of dissolution presently imagined. Whatever an explication of 'true in a dimension' might come to, it is clear that we are considering *something* like the relativization of the totality of assent-worthy fictional sentences to the literary corpuses in which they originated. That is, we are proposing that the set of fictional 'truths' is partitioned by the equivalence relation, *is a member of the same literary corpus as* ....Very roughly speaking, literary corpuses are construed as equivalence classes under that relation, and so are pairwise disjoint subclasses of the class of fictional 'truths'. Our problem is solved by forbidding truth-functional compounds of ϕ and ψ if ϕ and ψ are from different such equivalence classes.

Evidently the proposal's chief drawback is the weight it places on the still unexplicated notion of a LITERARY CORPUS. In particular, it is not clear that we are left any room for sentences in which to conduct literary criticism, even modest ones with which we seek to record only the more harmless platitudes, thus: "Hamlet was a strategist and Holmes was a strategist, but they were two very different kinds of strategist."

It is not really surprising that a good deal more would need to be said of corpuses, for, they are proffered in the same explanatory role as that for dimensions.

A slightly less energetic strategem, perhaps, is to take very seriously our actual practice with respect to the likes of (1) and (2). It is, as we have previously surmised, to admit their conjunction and to ignore its look of inconsistency. There is no deep mystery as to why we do this and as to why we think ourselves justified in doing it – (1) is Doyle's sentence and (2) is Disraeli's, and that is why they do not really conflict. The problem is how best to represent the logical structure of such a conjunction. One way, of course, is to add structure in moving from the English sentence to its canonical representation, as when, in representing (1) "Holmes was the first Honorary Mayor of Tunbridge" by ⌜d(ϕ)⌝, where ϕ is some quantificationally adequate representation of (1) and 'd' is an operator suggestive of (1) 's origins in a work of fiction by Doyle.

(2) would likewise be represented by ⌜d'(ψ)⌝ (suggestive of Disraeli, if the pun be forgiven). And the representing language, L, could be set up as governed by a set of rules that do not provide that from ⌜d(ϕ)⌝ and ⌜d'(ψ)⌝ to infer either ⌜d(ϕ & ψ)⌝ or ⌜d'(ϕ & ψ)⌝ although in which it is perfectly permissible to form their conjunction, ⌜d(ϕ) & d'(ψ)⌝. We note in passing that the operators 'd' and 'd'' are tantamount to modal operators (suggestive of the olim-operator **O**), and our **BL**, if it would avail itself of them for $\mathscr{E}$, would be tantamount to a modal logic.

Another method of representation for ⌜(1) & (2)⌝ exists, which avoids the need to make **BL** a modal logic. It is, to return to still another point already met, simply to ignore the apparent inconsistency of (1) with (2), to regard it as an orthographic and phonetic accident. Such a representation-function might take ⌜(1) & (2)⌝ into a sentence of L, ⌜ϕ & ψ⌝, where, in L, ϕ and ψ are logically distinct. That, it will be recalled, was one way, previously considered, of representing self-contradictory yet designated fictional sentences of $\mathscr{E}$. As before, however, (1) and (2) cannot mean what they seem to mean. What, then, do they mean?

§4. *The composition system $\mathscr{L}^8$.* – Can anything be made of a multi-dimensions approach to the logical reconstruction of $\mathscr{E}$? In particular, can we come up with a suitably well-behaved formal analogue of a dimension – short of adopting a special modal logic? One proposal, at least, recommends itself. It involves the basic idea of a many-valued COMPOSITION SEMANTICS for the language L of **BL** in which the sentences of $\mathscr{E}$ are canonically represented. For simplicity we shall assume that the sentences of $\mathscr{E}$ are initially mapped into one or other of three proper subsets of L – L_1, L_2, and L_3. Intuitively, we suppose L_1 to represent those sentences of fiction, such as "Holmes lived in London", originated by the creator of the character involved, or that follow from such. L_2 we reserve for the purpose of representing those fictional sentences recording guest appearances of characters not of the borrowing author's own creation, and for their logical consequences as well. L_3 is the language in which the sentences of science are represented, where science is conceived, broadly, and picturesquely, as the chronicle of reality.

It is not ruled out that a given sentence of $\mathscr{E}$ be represented in more than one, or in all, of our three formal languages. That is, we do not take the expression "is a member of a same L_i" to express a relation that partitions L into the disjoint sublanguages, L_i. In the event that some sentences ϕ might be members of all the L_i, we postulate a vocabulary sufficiently common to all the L_i to make this possible.

It is necessary to suppose a simplification (or regimentation). In order to remove such problems as the apparent inconsistency of (1) and (2), these sentences will be taken into logically independent sentences of L.

We now suppose a satisfactory **BL** for each of the languages $L_i (1 \leqslant 1i \leqslant 3)$, $\mathscr{F}_1$ for L_1, $\mathscr{F}_2$ for L_2 and $\mathscr{R}$ for L_3. Details of those logics are not here developed, but we may suppose that they are as nearly as possible classically two-valued. In particular, although this too is a simplification, such logics might in the L_i uniformally represent sentences in $\mathscr{E}$ about nonesuches and their apparent predicate negations by logically independent (false) sentences, thus closing truth-value gaps by the expedient of refusing recognition of "The present king of France is not bald" as a predicate-negation of "The present king of France is bald". Of course, if ϕ represented such a sentence, then its sentence-negation $\ulcorner \neg \phi \urcorner$ would be assigned the value truth. Needless to say, the logics for the L_i might be free logics in the wide or narrow senses lately distinguished in §3.1.

The distinctive feature of the currently proposed treatment of fictional sentences is that they, along with the other sentences of $\mathscr{E}$, be represented in L, via the vocabulary common to all the L_i, and that there be defined for L the following many-valued composition semantics $\mathscr{L}^8$.

$\mathscr{L}^8$ is an 8-valued composition of the sublogics $\mathscr{F}_1$, $\mathscr{F}_2$, and $\mathscr{R}$. That is to say, $\mathscr{L}^8$ is understood to be the Cartesian product, $\mathscr{F}_1 \times \mathscr{F}_2 \times \mathscr{R}$, in the precise sense that every one of the eight truth values of $\mathscr{L}^8$ is a member of the Cartesian product of one or other of the truth-values of $\mathscr{F}_1$, $\mathscr{F}_2$, $\mathscr{R}$. Since $\mathscr{F}_1$, $\mathscr{F}_2$, and $\mathscr{R}$ are presumed to be classically truth-valued, and putting 'T' for truth and 'F' for falsehood, the values of $\mathscr{L}^8$ are ordered triples of Ts and Fs. In particular, if ϕ is a sentence of $\mathscr{L}^8$ and $j(1 \leq j \leq 8)$ is its truth-value then $j = \langle \pm T, \pm T, \pm T \rangle$ where ϕ receives the classical truth-value $\pm T$ in $\mathscr{F}_1$, $\pm T$ in $\mathscr{F}_2$, and $\pm T$ in $\mathscr{R}$, and $+T = T$ and $-T = F$.

The *truth-values* of $\mathscr{L}^8$ are

$$1 = \langle TTT \rangle$$
$$2 = \langle TTF \rangle$$
$$3 = \langle TFT \rangle$$
$$4 = \langle TFF \rangle$$
$$5 = \langle FTT \rangle$$
$$6 = \langle FTF \rangle$$
$$7 = \langle FFT \rangle$$
$$8 = \langle FFF \rangle$$

Negation is given by the matrix:

ϕ	$\ulcorner \neg \phi \urcorner$
1	8
2	7
3	6
4	5
5	4
6	3
7	2
8	1

Conjunction is defined by the following abbreviating equations.

(1) 1&1=1; 1&2=2; 1&3=3; 1&4=4; 1&5=5; 1&6=6; 1&7=7; 1&8=8
(2) 2&1=2; 2&2=2; 2&3=4; 2&4=4; 2&5=6; 2&6=8; 2&7=8; 2&8=8
(3) 3&1=3; 3&2=4; 3&3=3; 3&4=4; 3&5=7; 3&6=8; 3&7=7; 3&8=8
(4) 4&1=4; 4&2=4; 4&3=4; 4&4=4; 4&5=8; 4&6=8; 4&7=8; 4&8=8
(5) 5&1=5; 5&2=6; 5&3=7; 5&4=8; 5&5=5; 5&6=6; 5&7=6; 5&8=8
(6) 6&1=6; 6&2=8; 6&3=8; 6&4=8; 6&5=6; 6&6=6; 6&7=8; 6&8=8
(7) 7&1=7; 7&2=8; 7&3=7; 7&4=8; 7&5=6; 7&6=8; 7&7=7; 7&8=8
(8) 8&1=8; 8&2=8; 8&3=8; 8&4=8; 8&5=8; 8&6=8; 8&7=8; 8&8=8

Note, in particular, that "1 & 1 = 1" is short for "if $V(\phi) = 1$ and $V(\psi) = 1$, then $V(\ulcorner \phi \& \psi \urcorner) = 1$".

The values for '&' are computed as follows:

i & h = $\langle \pm T, \pm T, \pm T \rangle$ & $\langle \pm T, \pm T, \pm T \rangle$ = $\langle \pm T \& \pm T, \pm T \& \pm T, \pm T \& \pm T \rangle$ = $\langle \pm T, \pm T, \pm T \rangle$,

according as $\pm T$ is T or F, and the following conditions are met: T & T = T, T & F = F, F & T = F, F & F = F.

As an example, suppose we have the formula $\ulcorner \phi \& \psi \urcorner$, and that ϕ receives the value 4 and ψ the value 3. To compute the value of $\ulcorner \phi \& \psi \urcorner$ we write,

4 & 3.

Then replacing 4 and 3 with the triple of classical values with which they have been identified, we have,

$\langle TFF \rangle$ & $\langle TFT \rangle$

But since in general $\langle \pm T, \pm T, ..., \pm T \rangle$ & $\langle \pm T, \pm T, ..., \pm T \rangle$ = = $\langle \pm T \& \pm T, \pm T \& \pm T, ..., \pm T \& \pm T \rangle$, we write $\langle T \& T, F \& F, F \& T \rangle$,
which reduces to

$\langle T, F, F \rangle$.

And, since this triple is identified with the value 4, we conclude that, 4 is the truth value of $\ulcorner \phi \& \psi \urcorner$ if 4 is the truth-value of ϕ and 3 of ψ. And this is just what the third entry from the left of row (4) says.

In $\mathscr{L}^8$, the values 1, 2, 3 and 4 are designated, and the values 5, 6, 7 and 8 are contradesignated. The principle by which it is determined whether an $\mathscr{L}^8$-value is designated is by whether or not its first element is classically designated.

It is easy to see that negation in $\mathscr{L}^8$ is stable; nowhere do we have $V(\phi) = V(\ulcorner \neg \neg \phi \urcorner)$. And if we were to identify the $\mathscr{L}^8$-value $1 = \langle TTT \rangle$ with the classical value T, and $8 = \langle FFF \rangle$ with F, negation in $\mathscr{L}^8$ would be Kleene-regular, as well. In fact, since negation in $\mathscr{L}^8$ is mirror-imagistic, it is an orthodox notion of negation;

for it always sends a designated value into a contradesignated value, and vice versa.

An $\mathscr{L}^8$-sentence ϕ is $\mathscr{L}^8$-valid iff it receives a designated value for all $\mathscr{L}^8$-assignments to its components. An $\mathscr{L}^8$-formula is $\mathscr{L}^8$-inconsistent if it receives none but contra-designated values. ϕ is $\mathscr{L}^8$-valid iff ⌜¬ϕ⌝ is $\mathscr{L}^8$-inconsistent.

Some valid $\mathscr{L}^8$-sentences are classically valid, putting $1 = T$ and $8 = F$. Examples include Modus Ponens, Non-Contradiction, Double Negation and Excluded Middle. Bivalence, of course, does not hold; however, $\mathscr{L}^8$ has a 'bivalent climate' about it, in the sense that its every sentence is either designated or not.

Composition logics have been investigated, for example by Prior,[8] with a view to providing a formal semantics for chronological languages, and by Rose,[9] in an attempt to find a common semantics for different systems of geometry.[10] One of their principle advantages is that these are semantics that need involve objects no more arcane than the ordinary truth values and n-tuples of these.[11]

The language L_1, we said, represents author-originated sentences, their negations and other truthfunctional and quantificational compounds, and sentences presupposing such. L_2 represents authored sentences that are original-author-parasitical, their negations, and other truthfunctional compounds, etc. $\mathscr{R}$ represents sentences reporting what actually happens, their negations, etc. We suppose that $\mathscr{F}_1$ will provide a sayso semantics for L_1, that $\mathscr{F}_2$ will provide a suitably modified parasitic-sayso semantics for L_2, and that $\mathscr{R}$ will provide a standard model theoretic semantics for L_3.

We can postulate a semantics for all of L, i.e. for $L_1 \cup L_2 \cup L_3$, by which there is a valuation function V that is the *composition* of the valuation functions V_1, V_2, and V_3, for L_1, L_2, and L_3 respectively. V provides that every ϕ from L is either 1, 2, 3, 4, 5, 6, 7, 8 depend-

[8] A. N. Prior, *Time and Modality* (Oxford: Oxford University Press, 1952).
[9] Alan Rose, "Eight Valued Geometry", *Proceedings of the London Mathematical Society*, Series 3, No. 2, 30-44.
[10] See also Rescher, *Topics in Philosophical Logic*, 89-90.
[11] This, the leading idea of many-valued composition logics, must be credited to Post in "Introduction to the General Theory of Elementary Propositions".

ing on the order of $V_1(\phi)$, $V_2(\phi)$, and $V_3(\phi)$. Thus, if ϕ represents the fictional sentence of $\mathscr{E}$, "Holmes solved the Case of the Speckled Band", $V(\phi)$ would be 3, since $V_1(\phi) = T$, $V_2(\phi) = F$ and $V_3(\phi) = F$; that is, the sentences representing "Holmes solved the Case of the Speckled Band" is true in Doyle's stories, false (not true) in Disraeli's and Kafka's, and false in the Chronicle of reality. And so homely a domestic truth as "John is father of Cathy, Kelly, and Michael" will be represented by a sentence ϕ such that $V(\phi) = 7$; so sentences that are this world's truths *only* are contra-designated in $\mathscr{L}^8$. Thus $\mathscr{L}^8$ provides a partial reconstruction of 'true in the dimension of fiction'. It also affords a graphic means of conveying that such a sentence is *somehow* both 'true' and 'false'; for it displays the circumstance that our sentence is 'true in reality' but 'false (everywhere) in fiction'. Yet since '$V(\phi) = \neg$' and '$V_3(\phi) = T$' do not contradict each other, we also have the means of representing apparent clashes between fiction and reality as only apparent. In $\mathscr{L}^8$ are the beginnings, too, of a distinction between the two style's of world-habitation noted in §3.4. Holmes, we said, somehow inhabits the real world, without there being actual, whereas the present king of France is not a member of the real world, yet is a member of some or other non-natural possible worlds. That distinction can be caught in $\mathscr{L}^8$ as follows: "The present king of France is bald" is represented by a sentence ϕ of $\mathscr{L}^8$ whose truth-value is 8; its predicate-negation is also assigned the value 8. Sentences about nonesuches are therefore classified as counter theorems of $\mathscr{L}^8$; they are untrue (false) both in fiction and in reality. Their sentential negations, therefore, are theorems.

The canonical representatives of fictional sentences fare quite differently. If ϕ $\mathscr{L}^8$-represents "Holmes lived in London" then $V(\phi) = 4$; the value of its predicate negation is 8; yet the value of its sentence-negation is 5.

The classical tautologies are, as one would want them to be, 1 in $\mathscr{L}^8$, and the classical inconsistencies 8.

$\mathscr{L}^8$ allows for an acceptable solution to problems of mixed modes of being. If ϕ were to $\mathscr{L}^8$-represent "Holmes had tea with Gladstone", then $V(\phi) = 4$, which is a designated value, yet one which shows that ϕ is not designated either in $\mathscr{F}_2$ or in $\mathscr{R}$.

As before, fictional 'truths' whose orthography suggests a self-contradiction might be represented by a consistent sentence of $\mathscr{L}^8$; or, as before, the sayso criterion of 'truth' for fictional sentences might be amended so as to preclude our classifying fictional self-contradictions as 'true'.

In either case, $\mathscr{L}^8$ must deal with self-contradictory 'truths' of fiction by ignoring them. And that, it may be protested, is a weakness of the many-valued treatment. Another is that $\mathscr{L}^8$ contains a somewhat counterintuitive notion of countervalidity. For, ϕ is $\mathscr{L}^8$-invalid if for every valuation V_i to ϕ's sentential parts, $V_i(\phi)$ is a triple whose common first member reflects that the sentence from $\mathscr{E}$ canonically represented by ϕ is 'false in non-parasitical fiction'. But, as we earlier chanced to remark, that is hardly really a fault of $\mathscr{L}^8$. In fact, if we are really going to take the logics of the sentences of fictional seriously, then we must be prepared for the prospect of an appropriately relaxed concept of invalidity. This we have in $\mathscr{L}^8$; there a sentence is countervalid if for no valuation is it true *even in* (non-parasitical) *fiction*.

"Yes, yes, I can hear the objections being shouted from all corners." – so, again, Scott, "Advice on Modal Logic", 153. "If one is going to use undefined terms why not undefined truth values? Is not that more natural? Maybe so, but I have yet to see a really workable [many-] valued logic. I know it can be defined, and at least four times a year someone comes up with the idea anew, but it has *not* really been developed to the point where one could say it is pleasant to work with."[12]

It is not to my purpose to plead a vindication of any system of 8-valued logic. I meant only to raise possibilities. It is doubtless true, as Quine has said, that

Primarily the motivation of [many-valued] studies has been abstractedly mathematical: the pursuit of analogy and generalization. Studied in

---

[12] Scott's complaint specifies *three*-valued systems, as it might be expected to do. I do not attribute to Scott the amended sentiments here quoted; I only borrow his pungent idiom.

this spirit, many-valued logic is logic only analogically speaking; it is uninterpreted theory, abstract algebra. (*The Philosophy of Logic*, 84)

Yet, think (commands Quine) of "the handicap of having to think within a deviant logic. The price is perhaps not quite prohibitive, but the returns had better be good" (*The Philosophy of Logic*, 86).

I of course did not mean to propose that we consciously set out to conduct the business of reason in $\mathscr{L}^8$; I only suggested that whether $\mathscr{L}^8$ suitably represents some of how we think is something to think about. Much depends on how good the returns are; and that in turn depends finally on what inferences and sentences of English we find that we assent to and with what degree of vigour.

In the particular case of $\mathscr{L}^8$, however, it is necessary to remark that, formally speaking, it is not really a non-standard system. $\mathscr{L}^8$ has exactly the same number of designated values as it has contradesignated ones, and negation in $\mathscr{L}^8$ is stable and Kleene-regular. So it is easy to see that $\mathscr{L}^8$ is isomorphic to classical sentence logic; for let us introduce a truth value, t, that applies to an $\mathscr{L}^8$-sentence ϕ exactly if ϕ receives a designated value of $\mathscr{L}^8$; and let us introduce a truth value, f, that applies to an $\mathscr{L}^8$-sentence ϕ exactly when ϕ takes a contradesignated value of $\mathscr{L}^8$. Clearly t and f are, formally speaking, just the classical truth values; and every sentence ϕ that is $\mathscr{L}^8$-valid will be assigned nothing but ts and every sentence ψ that is $\mathscr{L}^8$-inconsistent will everywhere be f. Small wonder, then, that $\mathscr{L}^8$ can tolerate no sentence in the form $\ulcorner \phi \mathbin{\&} \neg \phi \urcorner$, that in $\mathscr{L}^8$ the only accommodation of the contradiction problem is either to ignore the contradictoriness of self-contradictory fictruths or to constrain the author's sayso condition in such a way as to withhold fictruth from such. As it happens, then, $\mathscr{L}^8$ *is* a logic in which to conduct our quotidian ratiocinations, for it is ordinary textbook logic.

Many-valued logics, unless they have an unstable notion of negation, do not solve the contradiction problem. They force us to ignore it, to accept that fictional contradictions do not mean what they seem to mean. But they do not make it easy to see what such really mean. If only on that account, a theory of fictionality would do well to seek its base logic elsewhere. But there is also the point that if truths and fictruths as well are to be designated, and if falsehoods and ficfalsehoods are to be contradesignated, then an accommodating many-valued system will need to have a stable conception of negation. If such a system has as many designated values as contradesignated values, and if its connectives are interdefinable, it is isomorphic to classical logic. Yet from the beginning it has never been doubted that classical logic is not an adequate sentence logic for the reconstruction of fictionality. And many-valued systems begin to look very much ill-suited to our particular needs, quite apart from questions of how they fare elsewhere.

§5. *Ambiguity.* – We said, many sections ago,[13] that a sayso semantics has limited scope. The class of sentences for which a sayso semantics is appropriate needs, therefore, to be, in some or other common way, distinctive. It is not enough that they are different from the other sentences; they must differ distinctively. A sayso semantics is an extraordinary semantics; it undertakes to characterize a truth-predicate in terms of a condition of material adequacy,

(M): x is true iff y

wherein 'x' is a structural descriptive name (or a Gödel number-name) of some sentence distinct from a sentence 'y' and distinct from any translation, in our SML or elsewhere, of 'y'. Roughly, then, what is distinctive about a sayso semantics is that, in (M), y and what x names do not t-mean the same.[14]

How shall a formal semantical theory for $\mathscr{E}$ know where to apply (M) and where to defer to the more usual (to say the least) Tarski-condition (T)?[15] Shall the sentences, for which (M) is the appropriate choice, contain some structural feature that the semantic component of our theory of $\mathscr{E}$ might be presumed to be able to recognize, 'mechanically' as it were?

[13] In §2.4.
[14] In the sense of 't-mean' of §2.4.
[15] (T) is exactly like (M) save that x is a name of y or a translation of y.

The fictional truths of English do not always phonetically or orthographically proclaim themselves fictional, but it is nonetheless because they *are* fictional that they seem to call for a semantics of the (M)-sort rather than of the (T)-sort. The adverbial clause 'in fiction' naturally enough attaches to verbs descriptive of fictional deeds and suffering, as do their cognates 'only in fiction', 'in fiction and in real life too'. But in most of their occurrences, the fictional sentences of English do not display such modification; it is understood. It is just as well, since versimilitude is no friend of "Holmes lived in London only in fiction".

'Only in fiction', even where it is available to us, is not a standard verb phrase adverbial modifier. It is not strictly an adverb of a verb phrase at all, since it conveys neither the manner, place, duration, nor other circumstance in which Holmes resided in London – provided we discount the limiting case of adverbial verb-modification, negation.

'Only in fiction' has the effect of averting certain improper semantic consequences of fictional chat, for example, that Holmes did, in fact, live in London. Its effect, that is to say, is primarily semantic and functions as much like an annexed bit of meta-language as it does like contained syntax. 'Only in fiction' is therefore kin to a sentence operator. The modality problem for the logical reconstruction of fictional discourse is whether to represent what is semantically distinctive about fictional sentences by means of a certain kind of sentence operator. An affirmative answer no doubt would place heavy emphasis upon the fact that we *know* that there is something semantically distinctive about the sentences of fiction and, knowing this, it is reasonable to seek to capture that feature (whatever it is) by representing fictional sentences in L by means of modalized olim-sentences $\ulcorner O(\phi) \urcorner$. But that, we said, means that the sentences of fiction do not mean just what they appear to mean. And we asked, half-despairingly – and rightly despairingly, in the light of the conclusion of the previous section – "What, then, do they mean?"

We need not, as it happens, have been buffaloed by that question. Resources enough are at hand to deal with it. What is more, in so doing we can also answer the question of what is semantically distinctive about (the structure of) fictional sentences. Our first task is done once it is remarked that, in one good sense of the word 'meaning', to give the meaning of the sentences of a language is to explicitly define or to recursively characterize a truth-predicate for those sentences. That is, we accept the position that "to give truth conditions is a way of giving the meaning of a sentence".[16] And we also accept that

To know the semantic concept of truth for a language is to know what it is for a sentence – any sentence, to be true, and this amounts, in one good sense we can give the phrase, to understanding the language.[17]

Fictional sentences are distinctive in that, on their face, they admit of two truth definitions, one under the governance of (M), the other under the governance of (T). But it is not just that they are sentences for whose truth-predicate there are a pair of definitions; it is rather that, so defined, the truth predicate collects different and incompatible sets of truths. 'True', constrained by (T), collects

(1) Holmes never lived in London;

constrained by (M) it collects

(2) Holmes lived in London.

Up to a point we may say what we like. It is, however on the far side of that point that there is an ambiguity, somewhere, pertaining either to the sentences of fiction or to the predicate 'true'. That (1) is correctly said to be true and to be false pretty well secures this verdict of ambiguity, since postulation of multivocality is one's best method of resolving inconsistencies without prejudice to the theories or contexts in which they may appear to occur. Our task, then, is to locate and represent the ambiguity attaching to

(3) "Holmes lived in London" is true and is false.

[16] Donald Davidson, "Truth and Meaning", *Synthese*, 3, 304-322.
[17] "Truth and Meaning", 310.

One method of treatment is to fix on 'true', to proclaim it n-ways ambiguous, and to recommend its replacement by n different truth-predicates. Such an approach is tantamount to proposing that (3) be represented in a language whose underlying logic is many-valued. But we have not found much comfort in many-valued systems.

Another approach is to soften the focus on 'true', to lighten the emphasis on its apparent susceptibility to multiple characterization, one via condition (T), another via condition (M), and to put it that the real source of the ambiguity is not an ambiguous semantic metalanguage, but rather an ambiguous quantificational component in the object language. Such a view, lately met in §3.6, would stress the point that the quantifiers, under a substitutional interpretation, just do not mean what they mean under a referential interpretation. In any language, therefore, into which both interpretations of the quantifiers are admitted, the locus of our ambiguity would be 'exists' rather than 'true', and (3) could be explained in terms presuppositious of the two different senses of 'exists' – one for which the contained sentence is true, the other for which it is not true, yet for the same sense of 'true'.

For what it may be worth, a language admitting two such interpretations of the quantifiers has an underlying logic that is in all essentials a multi-sorted quantificational system. Unless the language in question, L, is one in which its quantificational ambiguity cannot be disclosed or proclaimed, it will have syntactic resources whereby to mark the relevant differences. It might contain but one undefined quantifier yet at least two sorts of variable; or it might have but one sort of variable yet two undefined quantifiers. Either way there would be a false sentence in L representing "Holmes lived in London" and a different true sentence in L representing "Holmes lived in London", depending on what its quantificational ancestry is judged to have been. That is tantamount to saying that the ambiguity in "Holmes lived in London" is with the name 'Holmes'. It is not easy to imagine a semantically relevant structural feature of a name by which the ambiguity of "Holmes lived in London" is explained. Of course, we could always propose that, from the logical point of view, names have one or other signature according to the quantificational ancestry of the sentences in which it occurs – and hence that names have a bit of structure not disclosed in their ordinary orthographic presentations. One drawback to such a proposal is that it just does not seem that 'Holmes' is ambiguous.

§6. *The olim modality.* – One could say: "By virtue of no *structural* feature are these ambiguities accounted for; it is, rather, a matter of what a sentence is used for, of the special context in which it is uttered." No doubt that may be so. But notice that use-features and context-features are trades-off for our postulated structural ones. In a semantic theory, as contrasted with a pragmatic theory, semantically relevant structure tries to go proxy for semantically relevant context and use. To demand that considerations of structure give way to the pragmatic ones of context and use is tantamount to abandoning a semantics for fictionality.

Short of that, yet another procedure recommends itself. It is to broaden the scope of the proposal of late in §5. Rather than supposing names to have appropriate signature, let us attach the ambiguity to the entire sentence. Our proposal is to make the English sentences of fiction ambiguous, without ascribing the origins of that ambiguity to any of its displayed subsentential components, and to postulate a representation procedure for $\mathscr{E}$ that associates with (1) and (2), for example, a *pair-set* of formal L-sentences, $\langle \phi, \ulcorner O(\phi) \urcorner \rangle$. In this way the ambiguity of (1) and (2) is preserved in L; and in this way, too, it is indicated how that ambiguity is to be understood. L is a clearer language than $\mathscr{E}$.

The rationale for our present course is that the English sentences of fiction, granted that they are ambiguous, do not contain *any* subsentential components that are obviously ambiguous in ways that would account for the truth of (3). That being so, it is natural to assume that their orthography under-represents their logical form, that they have a subsentential component, undisclosed orthographically, whose presence in such sentences accounts for the ambiguity of their English formulations. The advantages of this hypothesis are threefold. It is an hypothesis that saves us from the need to invent ambiguities for the *parts* of such straightforward utterances as "Holmes had tea with Watson"; and it is an hypothesis that can explain the orthographic non-recognition of the presence in English fictional sentences of this semantically relevant bit of structure, by appeal to the demands of verisimilitude. But, perhaps, most important of all, the hypothesis begins to make it clear why, and in what sense, a sentence of the English language might ever be thought of as taking truth-predicate some of whose satisfaction-conditions explicitly honour the authors-sayso.

We may, then, presume L to contain a Formation Rule and a Vocabulary such that if ϕ is a sentence of L so too is $\ulcorner O(\phi) \urcorner$. A set of axioms can be imagined for 'O', and the semantics for L can be thought of as follows:

(1) Since a proper part, L', of L just is a first order formal language, the semantics for L' is a usual model theoretic semantics in something like the manner of Tarski.[18] That is, we define a SATISFACTION RELATION over countably infinite sequences of the elements of a D (of objects) of an interpretation for L. Truth is then defined, in the normal way, as satisfaction by every sequence.

(2) Because L contains the operator 'O' it is necessary to extend the satisfaction-concept so as to take account of $\ulcorner O(\phi) \urcorner$. Thus, we might say that if ϕ is the L-sentence $\ulcorner O(\psi) \urcorner$, and ψ is atomic then any sequence s satisfies ϕ if $\ulcorner O(\psi) \urcorner$ is (the canonical representation of a) sentence (of $\mathscr{E}$) for which the sayso condition holds. Here then, something like the non-standard condition (M) would be a schema of one of many conditions on SATISFIABILITY; it need no longer be thought of as a condition of the material adequacy of a truth-definition for L. It is not even an entirely normal-looking condition on satisfaction, for it does not always appeal to a notion of denotation and it does not always invoke the truth values. It is easy to see that satisfaction, under this and similar conditions, sometimes answers to a substitutional idiom: it appeals (as we shall see) to sentences and their substitution instances,

---

[18] Alfred Tarski, *Logic, Semantics, and Metamathematics*, ed. by J. H. Woodger (Oxford: Oxford University Press, 1956), 189-264.

not to truth values; to names not their denotations, to variables, not their values.

Before hazarding a fuller specification of the satisfaction-conditions for olim-sentences, it is necessary briefly to return to the sayso semantics. The specification of satisfaction conditions will proceed in two stages. At the first stage, a stock of sentences is introduced as meeting a basis condition on satisfaction. At the second stage, the remaining conditions are recursively specified from that basis. The sayso condition is needed for stage one, for specification of the basis.

Let us say that a sentence $\ulcorner O(\phi) \urcorner$ meets the ELEMENTARY SAYSO CONDITION iff the following condition is met:

(S1) $\ulcorner O(\phi) \urcorner$ represents a sentence that occurs in a work of fiction.

And let us say that a sentence $\ulcorner O(\phi) \urcorner$ meets the author's SAYSO CONDITION iff

(S2) $\ulcorner O(\phi) \urcorner$ meets the elementary sayso condition

or

(S3) ϕ is a logical consequence of ψ, ψ is consistent, and $\ulcorner O(\psi) \urcorner$ meets the author's sayso condition.

The basis of the definition of SATISFACTION OF A SENTENCE, ϕ BY A SEQUENCE, s, can now be given, as follows.

1. If ϕ is $\ulcorner O(\psi) \urcorner$ and $\ulcorner O(\psi) \urcorner$ meets the sayso condition, s satisfies ϕ.

The recursion clauses are:

Provided that ϕ does not meet 1., then:

2. *Negation.* If ϕ is $\ulcorner O(\neg \psi) \urcorner$ then s satisfies ϕ iff there is a sentence $\ulcorner O(\chi) \urcorner$ that is satisfied by S and no sequence satisfying χ^* fails to satisfy $\ulcorner \neg \psi^* \urcorner$, where any sentence Γ^* is just like the sentence Γ save for showing a free variable wherever Γ^* displays a fictional name.

3. *Negation.* If ϕ is $\ulcorner \neg O(\psi) \urcorner$, then ϕ is satisfied by s iff $\ulcorner O(\psi) \urcorner$ is not satisfied by s.

4. *Conjunction.* If ϕ is $\ulcorner O(\chi_1)\urcorner$ and ψ is $\ulcorner O(\chi_2)\urcorner$ then s satisfies $\ulcorner \phi \ \& \ \psi \urcorner$ iff s satisfies both ϕ and ψ.
5. *Conjunction.* If ϕ is $\ulcorner O(\psi \ \& \ \chi)\urcorner$ then s satisfies ϕ if and only if s satisfies $\ulcorner O(\psi)\urcorner$ and $\ulcorner O(\chi)\urcorner$.
6. *Implication.* If ϕ is $\ulcorner O(\chi_1)\urcorner$ and ψ is $\ulcorner O(\chi_2)\urcorner$ then $\ulcorner \phi \rightarrow \psi \urcorner$ is satisfied by s iff s satisfies ψ or does not satisfy ϕ.
7. *Implication.* If ϕ is $\ulcorner O(\phi' \rightarrow \psi)\urcorner$ then s satisfies ϕ iff s satisfies some sentence $\ulcorner O(\chi)\urcorner$ and no sequence that satisfies χ fails to satisfy $\ulcorner \phi' \rightarrow \psi \urcorner$.
8. *Quantification.* If ϕ is $\ulcorner \exists v_i O(\psi)\urcorner$ then ϕ is satisfied by s iff at least one of these conditions is met.
    (i) $\ulcorner O(\psi)\urcorner$ contains free occurrences of the variable v_i and v_i denotes the i-th element of some sequence s' differing from s in at most the i-th place, a is the name of that element and χ is a substitution instance of $\ulcorner O(\psi)\urcorner$ with respect to a, and χ meets the sayso condition.
    (ii) If $\ulcorner O(\psi)\urcorner$ is $\ulcorner O(\chi(v_i, a))\urcorner$, then v_i denotes the i-th element of some sequence s' differing from s in at most its i-th place; that element knows $\ulcorner O \exists v_k (v_k = a)\urcorner$ to be true; the predicate χ is such that in general $\ulcorner \chi(v_j, v_h)\urcorner$ is semantically equivalent to $\ulcorner v_j$ believes that $\chi(v_j, v_h)\urcorner$; and the element denoted by v_i believes that $\ulcorner \chi(v_i, a)\urcorner$.

§7. *Quantification.* – If ϕ is $\ulcorner O(\exists v(\psi))\urcorner$ then ϕ is satisfied by s iff for some name or singular term a of L, free for a free variable in ψ, $\ulcorner O(S^v_x(\psi))\urcorner$ is satisfied by s.

A truth-definition now easily drops out. Truth is satisfaction by every sequence. And truth, it should be noted, is governed by a single condition of material adequacy:

(T) *x* is true iff *y*

where *x* is the name of a sentence of L and *y* is the sentence named or a translation of it in SML. In particular,

"O(Holmes lived in London)" is true iff O(Holmes lived in London).

These satisfaction conditions on olim-sentences may need some explanation. By condition 8., no quantified olim sentence ⌜$\mathcal{Q}M\phi$⌝, where $\mathcal{Q}$ is a quantifier M the olim operator, and a ϕ a sentence, is ever satisfied, except in the two rather special circumstances described by clauses 8(i) and 8(ii), about which a word anon. Condition 9. provides that a sentence of the form ⌜$M\mathcal{Q}\phi$⌝ is satisfiable, and some may be satisfiable by every sequence. Thus to return to an annoyance of §2.9, "Moriarty discovered that Holmes really existed" is represented as unsatisfiable (as it should be), whereas "**O**(Moriarty discovered that Holmes really existed" is not. In like fashion the nasty problems of §2.12. concerning mixed modes of being, are here contained. "Holmes had tea with Gladstone" is represented as the harmless ⌜**O**(T(h, g))⌝; the truths "Someone [i.e. Amis] admires James Bond", "Someone [i.e. Freud] psychoanalyzed Gradiva", "Someone [i.e. an eminent European philosopher, here unnamed] loves Molly Jeavons" are rendered in the form ⌜$\exists v$ **O**$(\psi(v, a))$⌝. At this point it is worth noticing that condition 8. provides (at (ii)) that a real object may enter into something like intentional relations with the fictional. For, suppose that our European philosopher claims to love Molly Jeavons. It is hard to imagine how he does this. Taking loving the best way, conservatively model theoretically, he does no such thing. But it would be arch to charge him with insincerity. For, imagine that he *says* he loves her, and that, of course he knows it is a love logically outside the usual patterns of amatory pursuit, that his is, as we might say, a *contemplative* love. Sub-clause 8(ii) rules that, although he does not love Lady Molly, he may be said to **O**-love her, as it were. It is fitting that our friend's word here be given such weight, verbs of contemplative loving being intentional verbs. It is also fitting that his word does not compel more than a verdict of **O**-loving, for a contemplated embrace is not an embrace.

It will be objected that it is improper[19] to intrude into the canonical representative of "Someone loves Lady Molly" an occurrence of the olim-operator. For it well may seem that, in the sense appropriate to our example, "to be in love with" is just an

---

[19] For one thing, one chances the confusion that '**O**' is *synonymous* with the English expression 'fictionally', a confusion we have been at pains to discourage.

intentional verb requiring no more specialized a treatment than any intentional verb in its occurrence as the principal verb of any declarative sentence. The issue, however, is not whether the intentionality of that particular verb, just as it stands, requires or will tolerate the afixing of an occurrence of 'O'. It is a question, rather, regardless of whether 'to be in love with' is in fact an intentional verb, as to whether one can be in love with a being that one knows to be merely fictional. Nothing of paramount importance for our discussion hinges on our choice of the verb 'to be in love with'. Our philosopher friend could merely admire Lady Molly or could be obsessed by her strangely tranquil yet disorderly domesticity, or could regret the impossibility of meeting her, and so on. It does not much matter whether the verbs that express such states are intentional verbs or not. It does matter that the sentences that record such states of affairs are, or have the feel of, truths *de re*, of truths concerning Molly. And it is not by any means typical of intentional verbs, V, that truths in the form 'xVy' even *seem* to admit of the *de re* construal '$\exists x \exists y (xVy)$'. Something then is altogether missed by any theory that requires "Zachary is in love with Lady Molly" to be represented in a staunchly anti-*de re* fashion.

On the other hand, it should be clear from the kind of case under review that not every verb will tolerate the sort of treatment that seems so right for "Zachary loves Molly". 'To punch' won't work this way; neither will 'to shake hands with', 'to kiss', 'to minuet with', and so on and on. That this *suggests* that intentional verbs alone enter into sentences that can be treated as we are treating "Zachary loves Molly" may be the case; certainly it does not demonstrate that it is the case. It is of no less importance that for those verbs that *do* enter sentences to be understood the "Zachary loves Molly"-way, there is little doubt that they do not enter except with certain restrictions understood. Zachary cannot have a consummatable love for Molly, and Freud's psychoanalysis of Gradiva was required to be technologically circumspect; as we have said, there could be no question of house-calls.

Jointly we seem to have it that it is entirely possible for there to be states of affairs that seem most naturally construed *de re*, but that also seem to involve one's recognition that the object of the *de re* involvement does not exist, it being merely fictional. Now, since the principal verb, V, of such constructions is such that for x to bear V to y it is necessary and sufficient that x believe that x bears V to y, there is a self-consistent way of preserving the truth that some sentences, "x bears V to y" admit of *de re* construal. It is that such sentences, though true, reveal their subjects to have inconsistent beliefs, reveal their subjects to be slightly irrational. If I know that Lady Molly is only fictional yet I love her for all that, then I believe that I cannot love *her* yet that I do. So I am irrational. Were I not, literature could not engage me as it does. This is an irrationality that is not to be disparaged; in fact it requires to be recognized by any adequate recount of the logical structure of fiction. And it is to that end that the olim-operator is, by clause 8(i), introduced into the *de re*-making position, between the quantifier and the predicate.

Subclause 8(i) defines satisfaction for what were earlier called fictionalizations. That some (real) person, e.g. Gladstone, had tea with Holmes, is satisfied when for at least some appropriate sequence the sentence formed by placing the name of an appropriate element into the free occurrence-places of the variables in "x had tea with Holmes" is a sentence, "**O** Gladstone had tea with Holmes" that is an assertable fictionalization, true by the sayso condition.

Needless to say, a language whose sentences were subject to such conditions as ours would need a stock of constant singular terms wherewith to represent names. But this is not to say that everything in the domain of such a language need be named. The real numbers might be in our domain and they cannot all be named. Even if our story provides that there is some unnameable real number, $\ulcorner \mathbf{O} \exists v_k (v_k$ is real & v_k is unnameable$)\urcorner$, that may, by condition 1. be accepted as true even though the contained quantified sentence has no true substitution instance.

Of course, the provision for L of a stock of names, some of which do not name any element of the domain of interpretation of our theory, is non-standard from the point of view of ordinary model theory. Model theory does not recognize names that do not name. Of course, we could decide simply to over-rule model theory on this point, augmenting L with a special stock of symbols – they needn't be *called* 'names' – that represent what we in English call names of fictional beings. Or, we could decide to keep these new symbols compliably in the category of name, but select some unique special designatum for them all to name in a sense recognized by model theory – say the domain, D, of interpretation itself and nothing else, and then to distinguish them further by the condition that they represent only those expressions of $\mathscr{E}$ that are supposed to denote fictional beings. So there should not be too much trouble with the notion of a fictional name.

Neither is there likely to be much of a problem concerning the learnability of fictional names, for these are provided by fiction, in finitey manageable assortments. Likewise, for the totality of sentences collected by the sayso condition. Apart from the logical truths, these are modestly finite. And the logical truths, though infinite, present no known challenge to intelligibility.

The logical problems, especially those of self-contradiction, are mitigated by our satisfaction rules. Condition 3., on negation, covers three kinds of case concerning $\ulcorner \neg \mathbf{O}(\phi) \urcorner$:

(i) when ϕ represents the unmodalized "Holmes lived in Bombay"[20]
(ii) when ϕ represents the unmodalized "Doyle lived in Bombay"
(iii) when ϕ represents the unmodalized "Doyle lived in England"

For case (i), there is the purported truth "$\neg$ (**O**(Holmes lived in Bombay)". Now it is true that case (i) holds, since the sentence $\ulcorner \mathbf{O}(\text{Holmes lived in Bombay}) \urcorner$ is not satisfied. It is also true that Holmes' non-residency in Bombay may also be handled as an instance of $\ulcorner \mathbf{O}(\neg \phi) \urcorner$, and, under condition 2 is seen to hold. For, there is the true sentence "**O**(Holmes lived in London)", and no sequence satisfying "x lived in London" ever fails to satisfy "x did

---

[20] "Lived" here means 'permanently resided'; and permanent residence is understood to attach only to one place of habitation at a time.

not live in Bombay". However, cases (ii) and (iii) are seen to hold for quite different reasons; not because, to put it loosely, they contradict truths of fiction, but because, as with (ii), we have an unauthored falsehood, and, as with (iii), a truth, but an unauthored one. The point of greatest importance, however, is that ⌜¬O(ϕ)⌝ does not imply ⌜O(¬ϕ)⌝. For let us consider the case (ii). Plainly, "¬O(Doyle lived in Bombay)" is true, since no sequence satisfies "O(Doyle lived in Bombay)". But neither is it the case that any sequence satisfies "O¬(Doyle lived in Bombay)". So the implication is seen to fail and therewith a problem is solved in favour of the proponent of the indeterminacy of fictional beings. For let ⌜O(ϕ)⌝ rpresente "Holmes had a mole on his back"; clearly neither ⌜O(ϕ)⌝ nor ⌜O(¬ϕ)⌝ is true; yet we do no violence to Excluded Middle.

Thus we have it that the semantics for the olim-operator defeat the equivalence of ⌜O(¬ϕ)⌝ and ⌜¬O(ϕ)⌝. It is established, moreover, that ⌜O(ϕ)⌝ and ⌜O(¬ϕ)⌝ are not one another's contradictories, for, at least they can both be false.

Are they, perhaps, one another's contraries? No, they are not even that. For, let ⌜O(ϕ)⌝ represent some story-constituent truth S; every sequence satisfies (that representative of) S; and let ⌜O(¬ϕ)⌝ represent some story-constituent sentence ⌜¬S⌝, true, whether by the same author, as before, or not; then every sequence satisfies (that representative of) ⌜¬S⌝. Although ⌜S & ¬S⌝ is a self-contradiction, greatly to be disesteemed, our rules provide that ⌜O(ϕ) & O(¬ϕ)⌝ is true and self-consistent. Similarly, if ⌜¬S⌝ is deducible from the unmodalized part of some true olim-sentence, we can have it jointly that ⌜O(ϕ)⌝ and ⌜O(¬ϕ)⌝ are true and compatibly so.

A problem is herewith dissolved. It is that, logically speaking, different authors do not contradict one another. Nor does an author contradict himself.[21]

So too, by these lights, is another logical problem dispatched: ⌜O(ψ & ¬ψ)⌝ is satisfiable; it implies ⌜O(ψ) & O(¬ψ)⌝ which is

---

[21] This is a logical, not a stylistic point. No storied sequence of sentences, ⟨O(ϕ_1), O(¬ϕ_1), O(ϕ_2), O(¬ϕ_2),..., O(ϕ_n), O(¬ϕ_n)⟩ is likely to claim the *Prix Goncourt* or the Governor-General's Medal for Fiction.

also satisfiable. Neither permit a Lewis-reductio, since ⌜$O(\psi)$⌝ does not contradict ⌜$O(\neg\psi)$⌝. Such may represent what *appear* to be authored self-contradictions, what lazy orthography misleadingly displays as self-contradictory. In our semantics such have satisfiable representations. Fictional contradictions do not mean what they seem to mean; their meaning indeed is given by the semantics for 'O'.

The semantics for a theory of fictionality of the olim-kind are turgid to state. I am not at all confident that they are here correctly stated, even as far as they go. Nonetheless it is worth noting that our conditions essay a blend of two distinctive idioms, the referential and the substitutional, and it elects to have them converge over a hybrid notion of satisfaction, especially at condition 8. It is no part of our programme to settle the logical question of which idiom is best for ordinary first order languages; but it *is* suggested that a good theory of fictionality, anyhow a theory of fictionality admitting the olim-operator, cannot get by in an exclusively referential metatheoretical idiom. It is also suggested, though not proved, that a language countenancing mixed modes of being is best not thought about in an exclusively substitutional idiom either. Roughly speaking, quantified fictional discourse is reckoned the substitutional way; the rest the referential way. Even so, we do not need to be committed to multivocalism with respect to 'exists'. Quantified fictional discourse is olimized; and English sentences, quantificational or otherwise, are supposed to be ambiguous as between ϕ and ⌜$O(\phi)$⌝.

If the concept of existence is spared, by these means, a proliferation of senses, so too, by these means is the concept of truth spared a like proliferation. It is a commonplace that a sentence is satisfied by a sequence – or any object – or not according as that sentence exhibits or does not certain structural features. The conditions on satisfiability accordingly vary over differences of structure. And since our theory is consistent, in the sense that for no sequence and no sentence ϕ is it the case that any sequence satisfies both ϕ and $\neg\phi$, there is no need to recognize different senses of 'satisfaction'. True, some sentences have very different satisfaction conditions from others, but that does not make for the multivocality of 'satisfaction'. Even in the semantics of a first ordinary theory, the satisfaction conditions on sentential atoms differ strikingly from those on quantifier-closed formulas. But these differences reflect semantic differences, differences of meaning if you like, not at the level of the semantic predicate 'satisfies', but rather at the level of sentences of the object language. What is disclosed by these differences in satisfaction conditions is that, from the perspective of the theory of truth, a sentential atom differs in meaning from a quantified formula; or, to return to our own preoccupations, that a sentence ϕ differs in meaning from a sentence $\ulcorner O(\phi) \urcorner$.

§8. *Quantified modal logic.* – It is natural to think of '**O**' as a modal operator, an operator of what Quine calls a third grade of modal involvement[22] in view of satisfaction-condition 8, which permits '**O**' to cross over quantifiers. An axiom set for '**O**' might be expected to include some of the following (putting '$\Diamond$' for possibility)

(A1) $\Diamond \phi \leftrightarrow \Diamond(\mathbf{O}(\phi)\ \&\ \phi)$
(A2) $\Diamond(\mathbf{O}(\phi)\ \&\ \neg \phi)$
(A3) $(\neg \Diamond \neg \phi) \rightarrow \mathbf{O}(\phi)$
(A4) $\mathbf{O}(\phi\ \&\ \psi) \leftrightarrow (\mathbf{O}(\phi)\ \&\ \mathbf{O}(\psi)\urcorner$
(A5) $\mathbf{O}(\mathbf{O}(\phi)) \rightarrow \mathbf{O}(\phi)$
(A5) $\Diamond(\neg \Diamond(\phi\ \&\ \psi)\ \&\ \Diamond(\mathbf{O}(\phi)\ \&\ \mathbf{O}(\psi))$

Axiom (A1) conveys that a fictional truth can be a real-world truth; (A2) that a fictional truth can be a real-world falsehood; (A3) conveys the notion that logical truths are fictional truths; (A4) allows the olim-operator to pull out of conjunctive contexts and to return; (A5) acknowledges the 'play-within-a play' phenomenon; (A6) allows for the possibility that the olim-nation of sentences that are jointly inconsistent need not themselves be jointly inconsistent. We may note that it is not intended that the converses of (A3) and (A5) hold in our theory. That converse (A3) fails is obvious. (A5) is a reduction axiom; it does not hold

[22] W. V. Quine, *The Ways of Paradox* (New York: Random House, 1966), 156.

conversely since not every fictional truth is a truth of a fictional work of fiction. An axiomatization of the language L of a modal theory of fictionality might be supposed to contain such Rules of Inference as,

(R1) *Generalization.* From ⌜$\phi(a)$⌝ to infer ⌜$\exists v(\phi v)$⌝ provided that ϕ is not ⌜$\mathbf{O}(\psi)$⌝.

(R2) *Instantiation.* From ⌜$\forall v(\phi v)$⌝ to infer ⌜ϕa⌝, provided a nowhere occurs in ψ, where ψ is an atomic formula ⌜$\mathbf{O}(\chi)$⌝.

(R3) From ⌜$\mathbf{O}(\phi(a))$⌝ to infer ⌜$\mathbf{O}(\exists v(\phi v))$⌝.

(R4) From ⌜$\mathbf{O}(\alpha = \beta)$⌝ and ⌜$\mathbf{O}(\phi(\alpha))$⌝ to infer ⌜$\mathbf{O}(\phi(\beta))$⌝.

(R5) *Detachment.* From ⌜$\mathbf{O}(\phi \to \psi)$⌝ and ⌜$\mathbf{O}(\phi)$⌝ to infer ⌜$\mathbf{O}(\psi)$⌝.

Yet we would not expect to have

(R3′) From ⌜$\mathbf{O}(\exists v(\phi v))$⌝ to infer ⌜$\mathbf{O}(\phi(a))$⌝, (since our hypothesis might represent the sentence of fiction "There is an unnameable real number", backed by the sayso condition.)

(R4′) From ⌜$\alpha = \beta$⌝ and ⌜$\mathbf{O}(\phi(\alpha))$⌝ to infer ⌜$\mathbf{O}(\phi(\beta))$⌝ (since ⌜$\alpha = \beta$⌝ may not be honoured in the story in which ⌜$\mathbf{O}(\phi(\alpha))$⌝ holds true.

(R4″) From ⌜$\mathbf{O}(\alpha = \beta)$⌝ and ⌜$\phi(\alpha)$⌝ to infer ⌜$\phi(\beta)$⌝ (since on an author's sayso a non-modalized falsehood would be provable).

(R5′) From ⌜$\mathbf{O}(\phi \to \psi)$⌝ and ϕ to infer ψ (for obvious reasons).

(R1) is a nonstandard principle of generalization. It does not permit the unrestricted inference from ⌜$\mathbf{O}(\phi(a))$⌝ to ⌜$\exists v \mathbf{O}(\phi v)$⌝. Yet, since some formulas of the form ⌜$\exists v \mathbf{O}(\phi)$⌝ are allowed to hold in our theory, we are espousing recognition of a quantified modal logic a logic that is to say, in which formulas of the form $\mathcal{Q}\mathcal{M}\phi$ are satisfied. Quantified modal logic has not enjoyed anything like the unanimous support of contemporary logical society, but I think it must be obvious that the system of quantified olim-logic is not open to exactly the standard objections. The sketch of an olim-semantics here presented makes it rather unlikely that sentences ⌜$\mathbf{O}(\exists v \phi)$⌝, ⌜$\exists v \mathbf{O}(\phi)$⌝ have *no* coherent interpretation. How well such a treatment will fare depends on many factors, perhaps the more urgent of which is a fully axiomatized development. Such, as we have said, lies beyond the compass of this study, whose main task has been to suggest general strategies by which to pursue a theory of fictionality. Programmatic though our approach has been, it may be worth mentioning that the quantified modal system, whatever its ultimate disposition, holds out a certain not insubstantial promise. For, it is a system that requires only the classical truth values, the semantic rudiments of first order systems, both referential and substitutional, – such items as sets, functions, substitution instances, and the like, a primitive alethic modality, possibility, and another primitive, **O**, which is a very weak modal. Negatively speaking, for a theory of fiction we do not need to depart the classical laws of Non-Contradiction and Excluded Middle; we do not need to postulate the multivocality of 'true' or of 'exists' or of 'is in the world'; we do not need to abandon classical negation for some many-valued interloper; we do not need many-valued composition logics; we do not need history-constitution values, the special predicate '$\mathscr{F}$', or the neutral quantifiers 'Σ' and 'Π'. We can still win and lose bets concerning the whereabouts of Holmes: "**O**(Holmes lived in Baker Street)" wins; "**O**(Holmes lived in Berczy Street)" loses. If all, or most of, what stands in the way of the desirability of developing the theory in a quantified olim-system is that such a system is a quantified modal logic and that quantified modal logic is said to be uninterpretable, we can only return to a point of Chapter I. It is that if a logician says of a formal system of logic that it cannot coherently be interpreted and another logician develops a semantics for that system, which he proves consistent and complete and which answers to intended intuitive interpretations of its logical symbols, then that complaint is dispatched. It is enough, for our purposes, that Kripke and others[23] have vindicated several systems of quantified modal logic from the charge of incoherence to commend details of Sherlock and his exploits to an olim-logic. It is at least worth

---

[23] See, for example, Saul Kripke, "A Completeness Theorem in Modal Logic", *Journal of Symbolic Logic*, 24, 1-14, and A. Bayart, "Quasi-adéquation de la Logique Modale de Second Ordre S5 et Adéquation de la Logique Modale de Premier Ordre S5", *Logique et Analyse*, 2, 99-121.

considering in fine how he might fare there. In fact, it is safely conjectured that in such a system there are good and economical solutions to the contradiction problem and to the quantification problem, and that the property of bet-sensitivity is there explicable without the abandonment of classical epistemology.

BIBLIOGRAPHY OF CITED WORKS

Anscombe, G. E. M., "The Intentionality of Sensation", *Analytical Philosophy*, Series 2, ed. by R. J. Butler (Oxford: Blackwell, 1965), 158-180.
Austin, J. L., *Philosophical Papers*, ed. by J. O. Urmson & J. G. Warnock (Oxford: The Clarendon Press, 1961).
Bayart, A., "Quasi-adéquation de la Logique Modale de Second Ordre S5 et Adéquation de la Logique Modale de Premier Ordre S5", *Logique et Analyse*, 2, 99-121.
Bočvar, D. A., "On a Three-valued Logical Calculus and its Application to the Analysis of Contradictions", *Matématičésky Sbornik*, 4, 287-388.
Church, Alonzo, *Introduction to Mathematical Logic* (Princeton: The Princeton University Press, 1956).
Cresswell, M. J., "The Completeness of S1 and Some Related Systems" (unpublished manuscript, Victoria University of Wellington).
Davidson, Donald, "Truth and Meaning", *Synthese*, 3, 304-322.
Fraassen, Bas C. van, "Facts and Tautological Entailment", *The Journal of Philosophy*, 66, 477-486.
—, "Singular Terms, Truth-value Gaps, and Free Logic", *The Journal of Philosophy*, 63, 481-494.
—, "The Completeness of Free Logic", *Zeitschrift für Mathematische Logik und Grundlagen der Mathematik*, 12, 219-234.
Frege, Gottlob, *The Basic Laws of Arithmetic*, ed. and transl. by Montgomery Furth (Berkeley and Los Angeles: University of California Press, 1967).
Hailperin, T., & Leblanc, H., "Nondesignating Singular Terms", *The Philosophical Review*, 68, 239-243.
Heyting, Arend, *Intuitionism* (Amsterdam: North-Holland, 1956).
Hintikka, Jaakko, "Existential Presuppositions and Existential Commitments", *The Journal of Philosophy*, 56, 125-137.
—, "Transcendental Arguments", *Noûs*, 6, 274-280.
Hughes, C. E. & M. J. Cresswell, *An Introduction to Modal Logic* (London: Methuen, 1968).
Hunter, Geoffrey, *Metalogic* (London: Macmillan, 1971).
Jeffrey, Richard C., *The Logic of Decision* (New York: McGraw-Hill, 1965).
Kaplan, David, "Quantifying In", *Words and Objections*, ed. by Donald Davidson and Jaakko Hintikka (Dordrecht: Reidel, 1969), 206-242.

Kleene, S. C., *Introduction to Metamathematics* (Amsterdam: North Holland, 1952).
Kripke, Saul, "A Completeness Theorem in Modal Logic", *Journal of Symbolic Logic*, 24, 1–14.
—, "Semantical Analysis of Modal Logic II", *The Theory of Models*, ed. by J. W. Addison, L. Henkin, and A. Tarski (Amsterdam: North-Holland, 1965), 206-220.
—, "Semantical Analysis of Modal Logic I", *Zeitschrift für Mathematische Logik und Grundlagen der Mathematik*, 9, 67-96.
Lambert, Karel, "Existential Import Revisited", *Notre Dame Journal of Formal Logic*, 4, 288-292.
—, "Notes on E! III: a Theory of Descriptions", *Philosophical Studies*, 13, 51-59.
—, "Notes on E! IV: a Reduction in Free Quantification Theory with Identity and Descriptions", *Philosophical Studies*, 15, 85-88.
Lejewski, Casmir, "Logic and Existence", *British Journal for the Philosophy of Science*, 5, 104-119.
Leonard, Henry, "The Logic of Existence", *Philosophical Studies*, 7, 49-64.
Lewis, C. I. & C. H. Langford, *Symbolic Logic* (New York: Dover, 1932).
—, "Completeness of Three Logics of Counterfactual Conditionals", Photocopy of typescript (Oxford, 1970).
Lewis, David, *Convention* (Cambridge, Mass.: The Harvard University Press, 1969).
Łukasiewcz, Jan, "On Three-valued Logic", *Ruch Filozoficzny*, transl. in *Polish Logic: 1920-1939*, ed. by Storrs McCall (Oxford: Oxford University Press), 15-18.
Mates, Benson, "Leibniz on Possible Worlds", *Logic, Methodology, and the Philosophy of Science III*, ed. by B. van Rootselaar & J. F. Staal, (Amsterdam: North-Holland, 1968), 507-529.
Plantinga, Alvin, "World and Essence", *The Philosophical Review*, 79, 461-492.
Post, E. L., "Introduction to the General Theory of Elementary Propositions", *American Journal of Mathematics*, 43, 163-185.
Prior, A. N., *Time and Modality* (Oxford: Oxford University Press, 1952).
Quine, W. V., *Word and Object* (New York: Wiley, 1960).
—, *Set Theory and Its Logic*, revised edition (Cambridge, Mass: The Belknap Press, 1963).
—, *The Ways of Paradox* (New York: Random House, 1966).
—, "Three Grades of Modal Involvement", *The Ways of Paradox* (New York: Random House, 1966), 156-174.
—, *The Philosophy of Logic* (Englewood Cliffs: Prentice-Hall, 1970).
—, "Designation and Existence", *The Journal of Philosophy*, 36, 701-709.
Rescher, Nicholas, *Topics in Philosophical Logic* (Dordrecht: Reidel, 1968).
Rose, Alan, "Eight Valued Geometry", *Proceedings of the London Mathematical Society*, Series 3, No. 2, 30-44.
Routley, Richard, "Some Things Do Not Exist", *Notre Dame Journal of Formal Logic* 7, 251-276.
Russell, Bertrand, *Mysticism and Logic* (London: George Allen & Unwin, 1917).

—, "On Denoting", *Mind*, N.S., 14, 479-493.
Schock, Rolf, "Contributions to Syntax, Semantics and the Philosophy of Science", *Notre Dame Journal of Formal Logic*, 5, 241-289.
——, "A Natural Logic without Existence Assumptions" (Address, 1961).
Scott, Dana, "Advice on Modal Logic", *Philosophical Problems in Logic*, ed. by Karel Lambert (Amsterdam: North-Holland, 1970), 143-174.
Shukla, A., "Decision Procedures for Lewis' System S1 and Related Modal Systems", *Notre Dame Journal of Formal Logic*, 11, 141-180.
Smiley, Timothy, "Sense without Denotation", *Analysis*, 20, 125-135.
Sobel, J. Howard, "Utilitarianisms: Simple and General", *Inquiry*, 13, 394-449.
Stalnaker, Robert C., "A Theory of Conditionals", *American Philosophical Quarterly Monograph Series*, 98-112.
—, "Pragmatics", *Synthese*, 22, 272-289.
Stalnaker, Robert C. & Richmond H. Thomason, "A Semantical Analysis of Conditional Logic", *Theoria*, 36, 23-42.
Stroud, Barry, "Transcendental Arguments", *Journal of Philosophy*, 65, 241-256.
Tarski, Alfred, *Logic, Semantics, and Metamathematics*, ed. by J. H. Woodger (Oxford: Oxford University Press, 1956).
Wallace, John, "Convention T and Substitutional Quantification", *Noûs* 5, 199-211.
Woodruff, Peter, "Logical and Truth Value Gaps", *Philosophical Problems and Logic*, ed. by Karel Lambert (Dordrecht: Reidel, 1970), 121-142.
Woods, John, "Subjunctive Conditionals and Middling Modalities", Mimeo (University of Toronto, 1967) (slightly revised version in *Manitoba Modern Languages Bulletin*, 7, 25-31).
—, "Essentialism, Self-Identity and Quantifying In", *Identity and Individuation*, ed. by Milton K. Munitz (New York: New York University Press, 1971), 165-198.
—, "Description, Essences and Quantified Modal Logic", *Journal of Philosophical Logic*, 2, 304-321.
—, "Semantic Kinds", *Philosophia*, 3, 117-151.
—, "Fictionality and the Logic of Relations", *Southern Journal of Philosophy*, 7, 51-63.
—, "The Formal Ontology of Death", forthcoming.
Zino'vev, A. A., *Philosophical Problems of Many Valued Logic* (Dordrecht: Reidel, 1963).

INDEX

Absolute inconsistency, 58, 73, 78
Abstract entities, 20
Adequacy conditions, 38
Alternativeness relation, the, 103, 105
Ambiguity, 127, 129, 130, 131
Amis, Kingsley, 18, 45, 115, 135
Anderson, A. R., 86
Applied physics, 48
Aunt Polly, 24
Austin, J. L., 100
Autobiography, 56
Average man, the, 32
Axiom of Non-Existence, the, 30

Baker Street, 13, 24, 29, 33, 34, 143
Baker Street Irregulars, 25
Base logic, 14, 27
Bayart, A., 143
Beardsley, Monroe, 7
Belnap, Nuel D., Jr., 86
Berczy Street, 13, 24, 143
Berlioz, H., 45
Bet-Sensitivity, 13, 14, 18, 23, 66
Billy the Kid, 30
Bivalence, 58, 59, 110
Bleeker Street, 34
Bočvar, D. A., 110
Boito A., 45
Bombay, 138
Bond, James, 18, 45, 115, 135
Borderline cases, 21
Bunyan, Paul, 30
Buridan, 103, 108

Caesar, J., 40

Campbell, Bryan, 7
Canonical representation, 19, 132
Carnap, R., 56
Category-difference, 31
Cervantes, Miguel, 64
Chambisso, A. V., 45
Chihara, Charles, 7
Chisholm, Roderick, 7
Church, Alonzo, 71
Classical epistemology, 24, 54
Classical negation, 21
Composition Semantics, 119
Compossibility, 103, 105, 106
Compulsion, 85
Condition of material adequacy, 127, 134
Conjunction, 114, 134
Consequence, 61
Contexts, 20
Conventionalism, 95
Conversity, 42
Cook Wilson, J., 42, 116
Copernicus, N., 64
Cresswell, M. J., 105, 106

Davidson, Donald, 129
DeHaven, Steven, 7
Detachment, 142
Deviant Logics, 21, 23, 27
Diffusely being made true, 85
Dimensions, 117, 118
Disjunctive Syllogism, 110
Disraeli, B., 43, 44, 117, 118, 124
Domain, 14, 85
Double negation, 123

Doyle, Sir Arthur Conan, 25, 26, 41, 44, 54, 57, 77, 118, 139

Elementary sayso condition, 133
Ellipses, 34
Ellipsis thesis, 35, 36
Empirical inexactness, 21
Estall, Martyn, 7, 56
Essentialism, 55, 77
Essential kinds, 78, 102
Excluded Middle, 17, 59, 66, 70, 74, 123, 139, 143
Existence-neutral quantifiers, 71
Existential import, 54

F, 114
Facts, 81, 83, 84, 86
Factual truth, 85
Faust, 45
Fictional existence, 31
Fictional names, 138
Fictionalizations, 43, 44, 46, 47, 48, 51, 82, 137
Fictruth, 61, 63
Fill-question, the, 63
First order predicate calculus, 27
Five-valued logic, 96
Fixed worlds, 98
Formal names, 17
Formal pragmatics, 102
France, the present king of, 13, 27, 29, 67, 74, 79, 80, 82, 94, 95, 113, 114, 116, 124
Frege, G., 69
Free logic, 66, 69, 81, 120
Free logic in the wide sense, 68
Freud, S., 18, 25, 40, 61, 62, 65, 93, 95, 135, 136
Functors, n-ary, 15, 17

Garfunckel, Alan, 7
Gauthier, Yvon, 7
Generalization, 142
Geometry, 123
Gladstone, W. E., 41, 43, 47, 48, 55, 56, 73, 77, 115, 125, 135, 137
God, 76
Gödel-number names, 38, 127

Goethe, J. W., 45, 46
Gounod, C. F., 45
Grabbe, C. D., 45
Gradiva, 40, 61, 62, 95, 135, 136
Guardian angel, 56

Hailperin, T., 69
Hamlet, 25, 118
Hatlo, Jimmy, 43
Heintz, John, 7
Heyting, Arend, 59, 60
Hintikka, Jaakko, 54, 69
History constitutiveness, 42, 43, 44, 47, 48, 51, 55
Hobbes, Thomas, 48
Hockey, 82
Holmes, Sherlock, 13, 29
Holmes, Mrs. Sherlock, 27, 81
Hughes, C. E., 105
Hunter, G., 22, 23
Hunter, J. F. M., 7

I, 109
I_1, 113, 116
I_2, 114, 116
Identity criteria, 47
Implication, 71, 114, 134
Impossibilia, 76, 78
Impossibilia logics, 74
Inconsistency, 57
Inconsistency-ω, 57, 93, 112
Independence, of *Sosein* from *Sein*, 78
Indeterminacy, 139
Individuals, 14
Individual variables, 17
Instantiation, 142
Intentionality, 27, 29
Intentional verbs, 135, 136
Interpretations, 85
Intuitions, 18, 59, 60
Irrationality, 137

Jeavons, Lady Molly, 18, 135
Jeffrey, R. C., 104
Jensen, Wilhelm, 25

Kafka, F., 124
Kaplan, David, 37

Kepler, J., 65
Kleene, S. C., 110
Kleene-regularity, 111, 112, 113, 114, 122, 126
Kripke, Saul, 22, 97, 106, 143
Kripke-structures, 103, 106

L^3, 109, 112, 114
L^4, 113, 114, 116, 118
L^8, 119, 120, 121, 122, 123, 124, 126
Lambert, K., 22, 70, 81
Langford, C. H., 50
Language L, of a base logic, 66
Law of Excluded Middle, 58, 114
Law of Non-Contradiction, 92, 114
Laws of nature, 31
Leavis, Frank, 24
Leblanc, H., 69
Legend, 30, 83
Leibniz, G. W., 103
Lejewski, C., 68
Lenau, N., 45
Leonard, H., 69
Lessing, G. E., 45
Lewis, C. I., 50, 97, 105
Lewis, David, 97, 102
Liszt, Franz, 45
Literary corpus, 118
Little Iodine, 43
Logical axioms, 15
Logical consequence, 25
Logical reconstruction, 18
Logical structure, 14, 23
Logical truth, 26
Logic, 4-valued, 113
Logic of relations, the, 42
London, 138
London Mathematical Society, 51
Łukasiewicz, J., 109
Lycurgus, 75

M, 39, 106
Mann, Thomas, 45, 46
Making, 86, 87
Many-sorted quantification, 17
Many-valuedness, 130, 143
Many-valued logic, 109, 126
Marlowe, Christopher, 45, 46

Material adequacy, 38
Mates, B., 103
Maximal consistency, 103
Maximal consistent sets, 104, 105, 107
McCall, Storrs, 109
McKinsey, J., 85
Meaning, c-, 35
Meaning, t-, 35, 36
Meinong, Alexius, 28, 47, 49, 57, 58, 73, 74, 78
Mixed modes of being, 41, 115
Modal logic, 119
Modal operators, 17
Modal system M, 97
Modal system S4, 97
Models, 15
Model-structures, 97
Model theory, 138
Modus ponens, 100, 123
Moravcsik, Julius, 7
Moriarty, Dr., 33, 54, 135
Multiplicity, 46
Multi-sorted quantification, 49, 130
Mythology, 30, 82

Naïve approach, the, 25
Names, 137
Narrowly-free logics, 80, 81
Narrowly-free e-logic, 68, 74
Natural contraries, 32
Natural-kinds, 71
Necessitation, 100
Negation, 71, 114, 133
Nero, C. C., 30, 82, 83
Neutral logics, 71, 74, 75, 81
Neutral quantifiers, 143
Non-Contradiction, 17, 47, 55, 70, 74, 78, 81, 110, 123, 143
Non-entities, 70, 81
Nonesuches, 29, 70, 79, 81, 120
Non-logical axioms, 15, 50, 57
Nonstandardness, 16
Nonstandard objects, 17
Normore, Calvin, 7
Novels, 104, 105, 106, 107, 108
Null-entity, 69

Ockham, William of, 76

INDEX

Olim modality, 131, 141
Olim-operator, the, 40, 135, 137, 139, 140
Ontological indeterminacy, 59
Open-texture, 21
Orthography, 19, 36, 37, 39, 40, 53, 87, 119, 125, 128, 131, 140

Parmenides, 31
Pegasus, 80
Penelhum, Terence, 7
Perfect woman, the, 32
Plantinga, Alvin, 103, 104
Possible totalities, 104
Possible worlds, 77, 101, 102, 103, 105
Possibilia, 75, 77
Post, Emil, 111, 123
Post-inconsistency, 50
Predicate negation, 74, 116, 124
Predicates, n-ary, 15, 17
Primitive states of affairs, 83, 84
Principle of the Independence of *Sosein* from *Sein*, the, 30
Prior, A. N., 123

Quantification, 134
Quantified modal logic, 22, 141, 142, 143
Quine, W. V., 16, 21, 22, 32, 37, 69, 125, 126, 141
Quixote, Don, 64, 65
Quotation, 20, 36, 37

R*, 71, 72, 74, 78, 79, 81
Rational reconstruction, 18, 19, 27
Rawson, Freeman, 7
Reality, 48, 52, 82
Reduction laws, 78
Referential approach to quantification, 63, 89, 130, 140, 143
Regimentation, 18, 19, 120
Relations, 41
Relatively possible worldhood, 106
Relativity theory, 48
Representation question, the, 15
Rescher, Nicholas, 111
Residency, 77
Rose, A., 123

Routley, R., 71, 72, 74, 75, 76, 78, 79 81
Rubicon, the, 40
Russell, Bertrand, 56, 69, 80, 83

S2, S3, 106
S4, S5, 105, 106
Satan, 46
Satisfaction, 132, 133, 134, 140
Satisfaction condition, 141
Satisfiability, 132
Sawyer, Tom, 24
Sayers, Dorothy, 25
Sayso condition, 133, 137, 138
Sayso semantics, 35, 38, 60, 127, 133
Schock, R., 70, 85
Schumann, R. A., 45
Science fiction, 31
Scotland Yard, 41
Scott, Dana, 22, 125
Self-annulment, 113, 114
Self-contradictory predicates, 52
Semantic metalanguage, 14
Semantics, 16
Sentence operators, 39
Sequences, 133
Shafer, Jerome, 7
Shakespeare, Wm., 25
Shandy, Tristram, 56
Shukla, A., 106
Sibyl, 117
Smiley, T., 69
Soames, Scott, 7
Sobel, J. H., 97
Spatio-temporal predicates, 28
Staal, J. F., 103
Stability, 111, 113, 114, 122, 126
Stalnaker, Robert C., 96, 102
Stalnaker-Thomason, 100
Standardness, 111
Stroud, Barry, 54
Structural descriptive names, 38, 127
Structures, 14
Subformula property, 107
Subjunctive conditionals, 96, 100, 108
Substantial change, 55
Substitutional construal of quantification, 63, 88, 130

Substitutivity, 132, 140, 143
Sybil, 43
Symmetry, 42

Tarski, Alfred, 132
Tarski-condition, 24, 127
Tautological entailment, 87, 88
Tertullian's world, 97, 98, 101
Theoretical physics, 48
Thomason, R. H., 96
Three-valuedness, 109
Three-valued logic, 21
Token-reflexivity, 25
t-meaning, 127
Translation, 25, 35, 38
Tremblechin, Henry, 43
Truth-by-convention, 88, 91, 92, 94, 101, 108, 109
True in, 108
True of, 108
Truth conditions, 37
Truth-in-fiction, 34
Truth-predicate, 129
Truth-value gaps, 57, 59, 61, 62
Tunbridge Wells, 117, 119

Tweed, Tommy, 75, 94, 98

Ubiquity, 46
Universal generalization, 80
Unnameability, 137
Urmson, J. O., 100

Validity, 16
Van Fraassen, Bas, 70, 83, 85, 86, 95
Van Rootselaar, B., 103
Verisimitude, 33, 39, 132
Von Wright, G., 97, 106

Wallace, John, 89
Warnock, J. G., 100
Watson, Dr., 41, 51, 75
Welles, Orson, 30
Whitehead, A. N., 80, 83
Wise Man, 59
Woodger, J. H., 132
Woodruff, Peter, 95
Woods, John, 7, 32, 55, 71, 76, 96
World-alternativeness, 97, 106

Zeus, 30, 82

Selected Bibliography on the Logic of Fiction: 1969-2009

Fred Adams, Gary Fuller, and Robert Stecker, "The semantics of fictional names," *Pacific Philosophical Quarterly* 78, (1997), 128–48.

Jody Azzouni, *Knowledge and reference in empirical science*, London: Routledge, 2000.

Jody Azzouni, *Deflating existential consequence: A case for nominalism*, Oxford: Oxford University Press, 2004.

Jody Azzouni, *Talking about nothing: Numbers, hallucinations and fictions*, Oxford: Oxford University Press, forthcoming.

Jody Azzouni, "Partial ontic fictionalism", in Woods (2010a).

Mark Balaguer, "A Fictionalist Account of the Indispensable Applications of Mathematics," *Philosophical Studies* 83, (1996), 291-314.

Mark Balaguer, "Fictionalism in the Philosophy of Mathematics," *Stanford Encyclopedia of Philosophy,* http://plato.stanford.edu/entries/fictionalism-mathematics, 2008.

Mark Balaguer, "Fictionalism, theft, and the story of mathematics," *Philosophia Mathematica* 17, (2009), 131-62.

Mark Belaguer, "Fictionalism, mathematical facts and logical/modal facts", in Woods, (2010a).

Anouk Barberousse and Pascal Ludwig, "Models as fictions". In Mauricio Suarez, editor, *Fictions in Science: Philosophical Essays on Modelling and Idealization,* pp. 56-75. London: Routledge, 2009.

Merri Bergmann, "Metaphor and formal semantic theory". In Woods and Pavel (1979).

H.G. Blocker, "The truth about fictional entities", *Philosophical Quarterly*, 24 (1974), 27-36.

David Braun, "Empty names, fictional names, mythical names", *Noûs*, volume 39, pp. 596-631, 2005.

Alisa Bokulich, "Explanatory fictions", in Suarez, (2009), pp. 91-109.

Daniel A. Bonevac, *Reduction in the Abstract Sciences*. Indianapolis: Hackett Publishing Company, 1982.

Daniel Bonevac, "Fictionalism". In Andrew Irvine, editor, *Philosophy of Mathematics,* pp. 345-394. A volume of the *Handbook of the Philosophy of Science,* Dov M. Gabbay, Paul Thagard and John Woods, editors. Amsterdam: North Holland, to appear 2009.

Stuart Brock, "Fictionalism about fictional characters", *Noûs*, 36 (2002), 1-21.

Otávio Bueno, "Nominalism and mathematical intuition," *ProtoSociology* 25, (2008), 89-107.

John Burgess and Gideon Rosen, *A Subject with No Object*, Oxford: Clarendon Press, 1997.

Alexis Burgess, "Truth in fictionalism", forthcoming in *The Oxford Handbook of Truth*, forthcoming in 2010.

Alexis Burgess, "Metaphysics as make believe", in Woods (2010a).

Tyler Burge, "Truth and singular terms", *Noûs* (1974), 8, pp. 309-325.

Alex Byrne, "Truth in fiction: the story continued", *Australasian Journal of Philosophy*, 71 (1993), 24-35.

Nancy Cartwright, *How the Laws of Physics Lie*, New York: Oxford University Press, 1983.

Hector-Neri Castañeda, "Fiction and reality: Their fundamental connections". In Woods and Pavel (1979).

F.X.J. Coleman, "A few observations on fictional discourse". In *Aesthetics and Language*, edited by B.R. Tilghman, pp. 31-42. Lawrence: University of Kansas Press, 1973.

Mark Colyvan, "There is no easy road to nominalism," *Mind,* forthcoming.

Mark Crimmins, "Hesperus and Phosporus", *Philosophical Review* 107, (1998), 1–48.

Charles Crittenden, "Thinking about non-being", *Inquiry,* 16 (1973), 290-312.

Charles Crittenden, *Unreality: the Metaphysics of Fictional Objects.* Ithaca: Cornell University Press, 1991.

Gregory Currie, *The Nature of Fiction*. Cambridge: Cambridge University Press, 1990.

Newton C. A. Da Costa and Steven French, *Science and Partial Truth: A Unitary Approach to Models and Scientific Reasoning*. New York: Oxford University Press.

P.E. Devine, "The logic of fiction", *Philosophical Studies*, 26 (1974), 389-399.

Lubomír Doležel, "Extensional and intensional narrative worlds". In Woods and Pavel (1979).

Keith Donnellan, "Speaking of nothing," *Philosophical Review* 83/1 (1974), 3-31.

Gareth Evans, "Can there be vague objects?" *Analysis* 38, (1978), 208.

Anthony Everett and Thomas Hofweber, editors, *Empty Names, Fiction and the Puzzles of Existence*. Stanford: CSLI Publications, 2000.

Anthony Everett, "Against fictional realism," *Journal of Philosophy* 102, (2005), 624–49.

Anthony Everett, "Pretense, existence and fictional objects," *Philosophy and Phenomenological Research* 74/1 (2007), 56-80.

Hartry Field, *Science without Numbers*, Princeton: Princeton University Press, 1980.

Arthur Fine, "Fictionalism," *Midwest Studies in Philosophy* 18, (1993), 1–18.

Kit Fine, "The problem of possibilia," in M. Loux and D. Zimmerman, eds. *The Oxford Handbook of Metaphysics*, Oxford: Oxford University Press, 2003, 161-79.

Michael Friedman, "Explanation and scientific understanding", *Journal of Philosophy*, volume 77, pp. 5-19, 1974.

Roman Frigg, "Models and fiction", forthcoming in *Synthese*.

Gottfried Gabriel, *Fiktion und Warheit*. Stuttgart: Fromman-Holzboog, 1975.

Gottfried Gabriel, "Fiction – A semantic approach". In Woods and Pavel (1979), 245-255.

R.M. Gale, "The fictive use of language", *Philosophy*, 46 (1971), 324-340.

Tamar Szabó Gendler and Karson Kovakovich, "Genuine rational fictional emotions". In Matthew Kieran, editor, *Contemporary Debates in Aesthetics and the Philosophy of Art*, pp. 24-264. Oxford: Blackwell, 2006.

Alvin Goldman, "Imagination in responses to fiction". In Shaun Nichols, editor, *The Architecture of the Imagination,* pp. 41-56. New York: Clarendon Press, 2006.

Nicholas Griffin, "Through the Woods to Meinong's jungle", in Kent A. Peacock and Andrew D. Irvine, editors, *Mistakes of Reason: Essays in Honour of John Woods,* pp. 15-32. Toronto: University of Toronto Press, 2005.

John Heintz, "Reference and inference in fiction", in Woods and Pavel (1979).

Robert Howell, "The logical structure of pictorial representation", *Theoria*, 40 (1974), 76-109.

Robert Howell, "Review of John Woods: *The Logic of Fiction, The Journal of Aesthetics and Art Criticism*, 34 (1976), 354-355.

Robert Howell, "Fictional objects: How they are and how they aren't," *Poetics* 8, (1979), 129–77.

Robert Howell, review of Terence Parsons, *Nonexistent Objects, Journal of Philosophy* 80, (1983), 163–73.

Robert Howell, "Essay-review of Walton: *Mimesis as Make-Believe,*" *Synthese* 109, (1996), 413–34.

Robert Howell, "Fiction, semantics of" *Routledge Encyclopedia of Philosophy,* volume 3. New York: Routledge, 1998.

Robert Howell, "La finzione e i suoi oggetti" ["Fiction and its objects"], *Discipline Filosofiche* 15, (2005), 161–79.

Robert Howell, in L. Carlos Baptista and F. Lihoreau, eds., *Fiction and Philosophy*, forthcoming. Frankfurt: Ontos Verlag.

Robert Howell, "Literary fictions, real and unreal", in Woods (2010a).

Jens F. Ihwe and Hannes Rieser, "Normative and descriptive theory of fiction: Some contemporary issues", in Woods and Pavel (1979).

Dale Jacquette, *Meinongian Logic: The Semantics of Existence and Nonexistence.* Berlin: Walter de Gruyter, 1996.

Dale Jacquette, "Animadversions on the logic of fiction and reform of modal logic". In Kent A. Peacock and Andrew D. Irvine, editors, *Mistakes of Reason: Essays in Honour of John Woods,* pp. pp. 49-63. Toronto: University of Toronto Press, 2005.

Mark Eli Kalderon, editor, *Fictionalism in Metaphysics*, New York: Oxford University Press, 2005a.

Mark Eli Kalderon, *Moral Fictionalism.* New York: Oxford University Press, 2005b.

David Kaplan, "Bob and Carol and Ted and Alice". In Jaakko Hintikka, J.M. Moravcsik and Patrick Suppes, editors, *Approaches to Natural Language*, pp. 490-518. Dordrecht: Reidel, 1973.

Saul Kripke, "Naming and necessity", in *Semantics and Natural Language*, edited by Donald Davidson and Gilbert Harman, pp. 253-355, 763-769, Dordrecht: Reidel, 1972.

Saul Kripke, *Reference and Existence,* unpublished typescript of the John Locke Lectures for 1973, Oxford University.

Frederick Kroon, "Was Meinong only pretending?", *Philosophy and Phenomenological Research,* 52 (1992), 499-526.

Frederick Kroon, "Belief about nothing in particular," in Kalderon, (2005).

Peter Larmarque and Stein Olsen, *Truth, Fiction and Literature, A Philosophical Perspective*. Oxford: Oxford University Press, 1994.

David Lewis, "Truth in fiction", *American Philosophical Quarterly*, 15 (1978), 37-46.

Dominic McIvor Lopes, *Imagination, Philosophy and the Arts.* London: Routledge, 2003.

Dominic McIvor Lopes, "The domain of depiction". In Matthew Kieran, editor, *Contemporary Debates in Aesthetics and Philosophy of Art.* Oxford: Blackwell, 2005.

Dominic McIvor Lopes, "Picture this: demonstrative reference through pictures". In Catharine Abell and Katerina Bantinaki, editors *Philosophicl Perspectives on Picturing.* Oxford: Oxford University Press, to appear.

Robert Martin and Peter Schotch, "The meaning of fictional names", *Philosophical Studies*, 26 (1974), 377-388.

Derek Matravers, "The challenge of irrationalism, and how not to meet it." In Matthew Kieran, editor, *Contemporary Debates in Aesthetics and the Philosophy of Art*, pp. 256-264. Oxford: Blackwell, 2006.

Aaron Meskin, and Jonathan Weinberg. "Emotions, fiction, and cognitive architecture", *British Journal of Aesthetics* 43, (2003), 18–34.

Margaret Morrison, "Where have all the theories gone", *Philosophy of Science*, 74 (2007), 195-228.

Adam Morton, "Imagination and misimagination". In Shaun Nichols, editor, *The Architecture of the Imagination*, pp. 57-72. New York: Clarendon Press, 2006.

Bence Nanay, "Taking twofoldness seriously. Walton on imagination and depiction", *Journal of Aesthetics and Art Criticism*, 62 (2004) 285-289.

Bence Nanay, "Is twofoldness necessary for representational seeing?" *British Journal of Aesthetics* 45 (2005) 263-272.

Bence Nanay, "Narrative pictures". *Journal of Aesthetics and Art Criticism* 67 (2009) 119-129.

Terence Parsons, "A Meinongean analysis of fictional objects", *Grazer Philosophische Studien*, 1 (1975), 73-86.

Terence Parsons, "Review of J. Woods' *The Logic of Fiction*", *Synthese*, 39 (1978), 155-164.

Terence Parsons, *Nonexistent Objects*, New Haven: Yale University Press, 1980.

Terence Parsons, "Are there nonexistent objects?" *American Philosophical Quarterly* 19/4, (1982), 365-371.

Thomas Pavel, " 'Possible worlds' in literary semantics", *The Journal of Aesthetics and Art Criticism*, 34 (1975), 165-176.

Thomas Pavel, "Fictions and the causal theory of names", in Woods and Pavel (1979).

Thomas Pavel, *Fictional Worlds*. Cambridge, MA: Harvard University Press, 1986.

Alvin Plantinga, *The Nature of Necessity*. Oxford: Oxford University Press, 1974.

Stefano Predelli, "'Holmes' and Holmes – A Millian analysis of names from fiction", *Dialectica*, 56, (2002), 261-279.

Graham Priest, "Meinongianism and the philosophy of mathematics," *Philosophia Mathematica* 11, (2003), 3-15.

Hilary Putnam, "Literature, science, and reflection," in *Meaning and the Moral Sciences,* London: Routledge & Kegan Paul, 1978.

W.V. Quine, "Goodman's ways of worldmaking," in *Theories and things*, Cambridge, Mass.: Harvard University Press, 96-99, 1978.

Shahid Rahman, "Fiction, creation and their dynamics: First explorations". Forthcoming.

Mark Richard, "Semantic pretense," in Everett and Hofweber (2005a).

Gideon Rosen, "Modal fictionalism," *Mind* 99, (1990), 327-54.

Gideon Rosen, 2005, "Problems in the history of fictionalism", in Kalderon (2005a).

Richard Routley and Val Routley, "Rehabilitating Meinong's theory of objects", *Revue Internationale de Philosophie*, 27 (1973), 224-254.

Richard Routley, "The semantical structure of fictional discourse", in Woods and Pavel (1979), 3-30

Richard Routley, *Exploring Meinong's jungle and beyond: an investigation of noneism and the theory of items*, iterm ed. Philosophy department monograph 3. Canberra: Research School of Social Sciences, Australian National University, 1980.

Richard Routley, *Exploring Meinong's Jungle and Beyond.* Atascadero, CA: Ridgeview Pub. Co., 1982.

Mark Sainsbury, "Why the world cannot be vague," *Southern Journal of Philosophy* 33, (1994), supp., 63-81.

Mark Sainsbury, *Reference Without Referents.* New York: Oxford University Press, 2005.

Mark Sainsbury, *Fiction and Fictionalism.* London: Routledge, 2009.

Nathan Salmon, *Reference and Essence*. Princeton, NJ: Princeton University Press, 1981.

Nathan Salmon, "Existence," in *Metaphysics, mathematics, and meaning* (2005), Oxford: Oxford University Press, 9-49, 1987.

Nathan Salmon, "Nonexistence", *Noûs,* 32 (1998), 277-319.

Nathan Salmon, "Identity facts," *Philosophical Topics* 30, (2002), 237–67; reprinted in Salmon.

Nathan Salmon, *Metaphysics, Mathematics, and Meaning,* New York: Oxford University Press, 2005.

Simo Saatela, "Fiction, make-believe and quasi emotions", *British Journal of Aesthetics*, 34 (1994), 25-34.

Benjamin Schnieder and Tatjana von Solodkoff, "In defence of fictional realism," *Philosophical Quarterly* 59, (2009), 138–49.

Timothy Schroeder and Carl Matheson, "Imagination and emotion". In Shaun Nichols, editor, *The Architecture of the Imagination: New Essays in Pretence, Possibility and Fiction,* pp. 19-40. New York: Clarendon Press, 2006.

Robert A. Schultz, "Analogues of argument in fictional narrative", in Woods and Pavel (1979).

Deena Skolnick and Paul Bloom, "The intuitive cosmology of fictional worlds". In Shaun Nichols, editor, *The Architecture of the Imagination*, pp. 73-86. New York: Clarendon Press, 2006.

B.H. Slater, "The epsilon logic of fictions". In Kent A. Peacock and Andrew D. Irvine, editors, *Mistakes of Reason: Essays in Honour of John Woods,* pp. 33-48. Toronto: University of Toronto Press, 2005.

Nicholas J.J. Smith, "Why sense cannot be made of vague identity," *Noûs* 42, (2008), 1–16.

Scott Soames, *Beyond Rigidity.* New York: Oxford University Press, 2002.

John Stanley, "Hermeutic fictionalism", *Midwest Studies in Philosophy,* XXV (2001), 36-71.

Kathleen Stock, "Fiction and psychological insight". In Matthew Kieran and Dominic Lopes, editors, *Knowing Art*, pp. 51-66. Amsterdam: Springer Netherlands, 2006.

Nomi M. Stolzenberg, "Bentham's Theory of Fictions", *Cardozo Studies in Law and Literature*, 11, (1999). 223-261.

Mauricio Suarez, editor, *Fictions in Science: Philosophical Essays on Modelling and Idealization.* London: Routledge, 2009.

Mauricio Suarez, "Scientific fictions as rules of inference". In Suarez (ed.), 2009, pp. 158-270.

Paul Thagard, *Conceptual Revolutions,* Princeton: Princeton University Press, 1992.

Amie L. Thomasson, *Fiction and Metaphysics*. Cambridge: Cambridge University Press 1999.

Amie L. Thomasson, "Ontological minimalism," *American Philosophical Quarterly*, 38/ 4 (2001), 319-331.

Amie L. Thomasson, "Speaking of fictional characters," *Dialectica* 57, (2003a), 205–23.

Amie L. Thomasson, "Fictional characters and literary practices," *British Journal of Aesthetics* 43/ 2, (2003b),138-157.

Amie L. Thomasson, *Ordinary Objects*. New York: Oxford University Press, 2007.

Amie L. Thomasson, "Existence questions," *Philosophical Studies* 141, (2008), 63–78.

Amie L. Thomasson, forthcoming, "Fiction, existence and indeterminacy," in Woods (2010a).

Giovanni Tuzet, "Cognitive fictions". In Lorenzo Magnani, editor, *Model Based Reasoning in Science and Engineering: Cognitive Science, Epistemology and Logic,* pp. 215-226. London: College Publications, 2006.

Giovanni Tuzet, "How fictions are credible", in John Woods, editor, *Fictions and Models: New Essays.*

J.O. Urmson, "Fiction", *American Philosophical Quarterly*, 13 (1976), 153-157.

Bas C. van Fraassen, *The Scientific Image*, Oxford: Clarendon Press, 1980.

Peter van Inwagen, "The creatures of fiction", *American Philosophical Quarterly,* 14, (1977), pp. 299-308.

Peter van Inwagen, "Fiction and metaphysics," *Philosophy and Literature* 7, (1983), 67–77.

Peter van Inwagen, *Material Beings*, Ithaca, NY: Cornell University Press, 1990.

Peter van Inwagen, "Existence, ontological commitment, and fictional entities," in Loux and Zimmerman, 2003.

Alberto Voltolini, *How Ficta Follow Fiction: A Syncrestic Account of Fictional Entities*. Dordrecht: Springer, 2006.

Kendall Walton, "How remote are fictional worlds from the real world?", *The Journal of Aesthetics and Art Criticism*, 37 (1978), 11-23.

Kendall Walton, "On fearing fictions", *Journal of Philosophy*, 75 (1978), 5-27.

Kendall Walton, *Mimesis as Make–Believe*, Cambridge, MA: Harvard University Press, 1990.

Kendall Walton, "Metaphor and prop-oriented make-believe," *European Journal of Philosophy* 1, (1993), 39–57.

Kendall L. Walton, "Spelunking, simulation and slime: On being moved by fiction." In M. Hjort and S. Laver, editors, *Emotion and the Arts*. Oxford: Oxford University Press, 1997.

Kendall Walton, "Existence as metaphor?" in Everett and Hofweber, (2000).

Kendall Walton, "Restricted quantification, negative existentials, and fiction," *Dialectica* 57, (2003), 239–42.

Timothy Williamson, "Vagueness, identity, and Leibniz's Law," in A. Bottani, M. Carrara, and P. Giaretta, eds., *Individuals, Essence and Identity: Themes of Analytic Metaphysics*, Dordrecht: Kluwer, 2002.

Timothy Williamson, "Vagueness in Reality," in Loux and Zimmerman.

Nicholas Woltersdorff, "Worlds of works of art", *The Journal of Aesthetics and Art Criticism*, 35 (1976), 121-142.

Nicholas Woltersdorff, "Characters and their names". In Woods and Pavel (1979) 101-127.

Nicholas Woltersdorff, *Works and Worlds of Art*. New York: Oxford University Press, 1980.

James A. Woodbridge, "Truth as pretense", in Kalderon (2005a), pp. 134-179.

John Woods, "Fictionality and the logic of relations", *The Southern Journal of Philosophy*, 7 (1969), 51-64.

John Woods, "Meinongean theories of fictional objects", *Journal of Literary Semantics*, 7, (1978), 65-70.

John Woods and Thomas G. Pavel, editors, *Formal Semantics and Literary Theory*. A guest-edited issue of *Poetics*, volume 8, Amsterdam: North-Holland, 1979.

John Woods, "Animadversions and open questions: Reference, inference and truth in fiction", *Poetics*, XI, (1982), 553-562.

John Woods, "God, genidentity and existential parity", *Grazer Philosophische Studien*, 25/26, (1986), 181-196.

John Woods, "Fortress fiction". In C. Mihailescu et al., editors, *Fiction Updated: The Theory of Fictionality and Contemporary Humanities*. Toronto: University of Toronto Press, 39-47, 1996.

John Woods, "The logic of fiction". In Dov M. Gabbay and F. Guenthner, editors, *Handbook of Philosophical Logic*, 2nd revised edition, Dordrecht and Boston: Kluwer, 241-316, 2004, (with Peter Alward).

John Woods, *The Logic of Fiction: A Philosophical Soundings of Deviant Logic*. The Hague and Paris: Mouton, 1974; 2nd edition, with a new Foreword by Nicholas Griffin, London: College Publications, 2009.

John Woods, preface to a volume on fiction to appear in French in the College Publications series *Cahiers de Logique et d'Epistémologie*, Jacques Dubuc and Brian Hill, editors

John Woods, *Paradox and Paraconsistency: Conflict Resolution in the Abstract Sciences*. Cambridge: Cambridge University Press, 2003.

John Woods, "Fictions and their logic". In Dale Jacquette, editor, *Philosophy of Logic*, pp. 1061-1126, volume 5 of the *Handbook of the Philosophy of Science*, edited by Dov M. Gabbay, Paul Thagard and John Woods. Amsterdam: North-Holland, 2007.

John Woods, editor, *Fictions and Models: New Essays.* Munich: Philosophia Verlag, to appear in 2010a

John Woods, *Sherlock's Member: New Perspectives on the Semantics of Fiction,* to appear in 2010b.

Stephen Yablo, "Does ontology rest on a mistake?" *Proceedings of the Aristotelian Society,* supp. vol., 72, (1998), 229–61.

Stephen Yablo, "Go figure: A path through fictionalism," *Midwest Studies in Philosophy* 25, (2001), 72–102.

Stephen Yablo, "The myth of the seven," in Kalderon (2005a).

Robert J. Yanal, *Paradoxes of Emotion and Fiction,* Philadelphia: Pennsylvania State University Press, 1999.

Edward N. Zalta, *Abstract Objects: An Introduction to Axiomatic Metaphysics*, Dordrecht: Reidel, 1983.

Edward N. Zalta, *Intensional Logic and the Metaphysics of Intentionality,* Cambridge, MA: MIT Press, 1988.

Edward N. Zalta, "The road between pretense theory and abstract object theory," in Everett and Hofweber, (2000).

Eddy M. Zemach, *Real Beauty*, University Park, PA: Pennsylvania State University Press, 1997.

FICTIONS AND THEIR LOGIC

John Woods*

1 LOGIC

The logic of fiction came into its own in the 1970s with the publication of a number of seminal works.[1] Fiction has been a stand-alone research programme for logicians only since that time. The logician's interest in fiction had a number of early motivations. However, in a quite general way, the logic of fiction programme arose out of failure. Fictional discourse simply wouldn't fit existing systems. As Richard Routley once put it, "literary phenomena rather convincingly show the inadequacy of most going formal semantics." [Routley, 1979, 3] In particular, the sentences of fiction have not been well-handled in the more traditional theories of nondenoting terms, such as description theory, free logic or supervaluational semantics. On the other hand, fictional discourse appears to be tailor-made for existence-neutral theories of quantification. A third motivation is fictionalism in the philosophy of mathematics. If mathematical objects are to be likened to fictional objects, then it would seem to be incumbent on those who so propose that they give a disciplined account of what it is to be an object of fiction. A fourth consideration is that since it would appear that some fictional truths are inconsistent, this may be some reason

---

*[Woods and Alward, 2002] reflects my thinking about the fictional some thirty years after my original work in the period 1969 to 1974. In writing it, Alward and I brought different inclinations to bear. For Alward, these would be first words in a continuing project on fiction. For me, they would be last words, a kind of valedictory. Alward has turned out to be more prescient than I. He has extended his thinking considerably, and a book will appear in a year or so [Alward, forthcoming]. But, in what can only be considered a surprising turn, I too have continued to think about fiction, and I too have drifted from where I was in 2002. I shall mention just three of the newer developments. The 2002 paper gives no detailed attention to what it would take for fiction to have a *logic*, as opposed to a philosophical analysis of the kind a philosopher could furnish. In the present work, efforts have been made to repair this omission. In the 2002 chapter, stipulationism is flirted with. Here it is embraced fully. In 2002, I leaned toward the theoretical primacy of mathematical stipulationism over fictional stipulationism (with Alward demurring, but not in print.) I have now come to my senses. Mathematical stipulationism is a harder nut to crack than literary stipulationism. Hats off to Alward.

For expository ease, I have in a few places drawn modestly upon [Woods and Alward, 2002], with Alward's and Kluwer's kind permission. Aside from these expository matters, the present chapter is a considerable departure from earlier work. Errors are mine alone. Alward bears no responsibility for them. He will make his own in [Alward, forthcoming].

[1]These include in chronological order [Woods, 1969; Gale, 1971; Routley, 1973; Coleman, 1973; Crittenden, 1973; Woods, 1974; Devine, 1974; Martin, Schotch, 1974; Blocker, 1974; Howell, 1974; Pavel, 1975; Gabriel, 1975; Parsons, 1975; Wolterstorff, 1976; Howell, 1976; Urmson, 1976; Lewis, 1978; Walton, 1978a, 1978b; Parsons, 1978; Woods and Pavel, 1979]. In addition to works expressly designed to accommodate the analysis of fictional discourse, various other contributions of the period bear on the issue somewhat tangentially, but with interesting and influential things to say about fiction [Kripke, 1972; Kaplan, 1973; Plantinga, 1974].

to construe logic dialetheically. Other motivations concern philosophy of language and epistemology rather more centrally, but some of these also have a bearing on modal logic, especially theories that postulate fictive operators. A case in point is the apparent inability of widely received theories of reference and of knowledge to account for our capacity to refer to fictional objects and to know something of them. Such theories are causal in their orientation, and they to give rise to problems not unlike Benacerraf's Dilemma in the philosophy of mathematics [Benacerraf, 1973], which offers us — so it is said — a difficult choice between "easy epistemology for unbelievable objects or implausible epistemology for constructed objects". [Thomas, 2002, 19].[2] We shall return to these pre-existing logics in §3.5 below

The first issue for the aspiring logician of fiction is what a logic of fiction would be. What would it be like for fiction to *have* a logic, and in what sense of the word 'logic'? Bearing on this is a distinction adumbrated — albeit not under this name — in the writings of Frege. It is the distinction between a *mathematical* and a *philosophical* logic. What we find in the *Begriffsschrift* [1967] is mathematical logic. What we find in "Sense and Reference" [1952] is philosophical logic. A philosophical logic investigates properties such as reference, truth and inference in natural languages. Accordingly, there is a substantial overlap between philosophical logic and the philosophy of language.

Reference figures significantly in Frege's mathematical and philosophical logics alike. In his mathematical logic, it is a simplistic and rather naïve concept. The reference of names is represented by a primitive notion of object-designation. The reference of individual variables is relativized to countable sequences of arbitrary objects; a variable v_n bears this primitive relation of denotation to the object occupying the nth place in that sequence, where 'n' is the variable's index. Predicate symbols are taken to denote sequences of abstract objects. Plural reference is seen as the quantificational binding of variables.

In reading Frege's papers on the philosophy of language, one is struck at once by the sophistication of its treatment of reference. While the theory retains a denotational cast (in which referring, crudely speaking, is like labelling), considerable attention is paid to semantic constraints, that is, to the role played by (something like) a referring term's meaning. Frege's analysis of these semantic constraints focuses on the notion of *Sinn*. But there is no place for *Sinn* in Frege's mathematical logic.

PROPOSITION 1 (Underdetermination). *Frege's mathematical logic of reference underdetermines his philosophical logic of reference.*

Underdetermination as such is nothing to get over-excited about. Even our best formal models always leave some things out of account. What matters is whether reference is well-enough handled to enable the logic to elucidate its own target properties, such as

---

[2]It is widely held that the best theory of knowledge to date is one in which knowledge arises from the knower's causal contact with the object of his knowledge (albeit, on occasion, a quite complex sort of causal contact). It is also widely held that the best theory of truth to date is one in which the truth of a sentence, e.g., "Harry is a man" consists of the object denoted by "Harry" being an element in the class of objects denoted by "is a man". Similarly, "2 is a prime" would be true if and only if the number two were a member of the set of prime numbers. The gist of Benacerraf's Dilemma is this: If the causal theory of knowledge is right, it is difficult to see how mathematical knowledge is possible. For we seem not to have causal contact with such objects.

entailment and logical truth. Another way of saying this is that reference is not a primary objective for standard approaches to mathematical logic. It is more an instrumental necessity. One has to say *something* about reference in order to be able to say what one *wants* to say about entailment. If we wished to have a full-blown conceptual analysis of reference, it is clear that we would not find it in Frege's mathematical logic. We would need to explore the relevant options in the philosophy of logic. If we came to be satisfied that the right account could be found there, a further possibility would present itself. We might return to some preferred mathematical logic in an effort to determine whether, under suitable adaptation, the philosophical account of reference could be accommodated by the logic's formalisms, or some natural enrichment of them.

Mathematical logics put a premium on mature and coherent formalization. The devil is in the details, of course, but in a general way it can be said that formalizations are well-specified uninterpreted languages on which a proof theory is definable and a model theory is constructible. Formalizations are always formalizations *of*. In the case of mathematical logic, what is sought for is a formalization of its primary or target properties — entailment, logical truth, consistency, and so on. A formalization is *coherent* to the degree that it has a comprehensive metatheory. A system's metatheory is comprehensive to the extent that it allows for nontrivial consideration of the standard metatheoretical issues. Is the system consistent? Is it sound and complete? Are its target properties decidable? Is its entailment relation compact? Does it have a deduction metatheorem? Is it extrapolative? And so on. A formalization is *mature* to the extent that its answers to these questions are well-developed and rigorous. Coherence and maturity are what one would expect to find in what Joke Meheus calls "decent logics" [Meheus *et al.*, forthcoming].

A useful one-line summary of what has been said so far is that mathematical logic is conceptual formalization, whereas philosophical logic is conceptual analysis. As we have said, one question that the contrast gives rise to is whether a formalization of a property underdetermines its correct conceptual analysis. If it does, a second question arises. Does the underdetermination matter? Throughout the history of logic, there are numbers of cases where it has been asserted that it matters very much, that it amounts to severe conceptual distortion. (As Quine once said about the dialetheic approach to inconsistency, it makes negation "unrecognizable.") A case in point is the dispute between relevant and classical logicians.[3] In classical logic, entailment does not require that antecedents be relevant to consequents. Against this, relevantists argue that, in the absence of a relevancy connection between S and S', it cannot be the case that S entails S'. Here we meet with a question in the philosophy of logic. Naively put, it asks, "What is the true nature of entailment?" Like most philosophical controversies, the present dispute has not been graced with a definitive resolution. However, a kind of holding pattern can be mentioned in passing. It involves a presumed pluralism in logic, according to which "entails" is *ambiguous* as between classical entailment, which first-order logic gets right, and relevant entailment, which first-order logic gets wrong.[4]

---

[3] And modal and intuitionistic logicians, as well as some paraconsistent logicians.
[4] Not to overlook intuitionistic entailment, (non-relevant) paraconsistent entailment, many-valued entailment, dialetheic entailment, and so on.

We can see a certain strategic cunning in the pluralist manoeuvre. It keeps options for the formalization of entailment open as long as the issue remains unresolved. It is as if the mathematical logician is saying, "Look, if entailment is actually classical, then we have a logic for it, namely, classical logic. On the other hand, if entailment is actually relevantist, then we have a logic for it, namely, relevant logic. Until things settle down philosophically, it is best to keep an open mind." As a response to unresolved conceptual conflict, undoubtedly this has a certain attractiveness. But there is also a down-side. The extent to which formalizations can proceed apace and succeed as mathematical constructions in the absence of settled and mature conceptual constraints, they risk promiscuous ambiguation, in which *any* coherent formalization of a notion captures a "sense" of it.[5] Consider, for example, the sheer number of modal logics. They are more or less interesting as mathematical structures (and wonderfully interesting things to study), but it strains belief that corresponding to each different modal system is a different meaning of "possible" in English. So we might have here a case in which, collectively, modal logic *over*determines conceptual adequacy. Of course, there might be many more concepts of possibility than are discernible in the give-and-take of natural language usage. But it is not obvious that there are. This is a matter for the philosophy of language.

It is instructive to take note of two quite different emphases that drive the work of contemporary logic. One is abstract and experimental. It involves building mathematical structures with a view to discovering the logical concepts that can be made to "fall out" of it. It is an adequacy condition on such logics that they have a mature and coherent formalization. In its most extreme form it is *not* a condition on their success that they get even their target concepts "right".[6] "Right" is for philosophers.

The other option *is* philosophical. It takes seriously Eddington's jape that theories are "put-up jobs" (and Quine's that they are "free for the thinking up"). They seek to constrain this latitude by imposing conditions of conceptual adequacy. In actual practice, there is ample evidence that both these forces are in play and that they operate under more or less successful conditions of equilibrium. So in order to get your target concepts *quite* right, it is necessary to get your ancillary or instrumental concepts *somewhat* right; that is to say, right enough. Even so, *in extremis* the two emphases are miles apart.

It is easy to see these contrasts at work in analyses of fictional discourse. Logicians whose interests are primarily mathematical might see a logic of fiction as any mature and coherent system of mathematical logic, in which referring terms and quantifiers for objects of fiction, and truth and closure conditions for fictional sentences are dealt with as part of the logic's overall handling of reference, truth and inference. The mere fact that the theory is mature and coherent would count to some degree in favour of its provisions for its fictional elements. For what is wanted here is not just an *account* of the fictional, but an account that deserves the name of logic. But what really counts depends on what the theory's *primary* targets actually are. If, for example, the logic is chiefly concerned with

---

[5] Left unchecked, we would soon be met with "Anything Goes-Pluralism" (with apologies, in order, to Cole Porter and David Stove [1999].

[6] The impulse to experiment abstractly resembles what drove non-Euclidean geometry before the comforts of an empirically confirmed relativity theory. Here, too, there was no intention of getting space right. That Riemannian geometry did get (big) space right was an inadvertence, and a lucky break for physics.

giving an account of entailment and logical truth, it might well achieve a formalization of those concepts under a number of different conditions, including the following:

1. The account it gives of entailment and logical truth is mature and coherent and conceptually adequate.
2. The account it gives of these notions is mature and coherent but conceptually inadequate.
3. The account it gives of entailment and logical truth for fictional sentences is conceptually adequate, but fails to provide a conceptually adequate representation of still other features of fictional discourse, an understanding of which is essential for a philosophically adequate representation of it.[7]

Needless to say, this trio is neither exhaustive nor strictly disjoint.

Perhaps we have said enough provisionally to identify three levels of logical treatment of the fictional.

> *Level 1 (Mathematical).* A mathematical logic of the fictional is a first-level logic to the extent that it is an adaptation of an existing logic without principled regard for the conceptual adequacy of the adaptations. What counts at level 1 is that aspects of the fictional are taken *some* note of and the resultant system is a coherent and mature mathematical logic.

> *Level 2 (Conceptual).* A philosophical logic of the fictional is a conceptual analysis of the concept of the fictional. It would stand to a mathematical system as Frege's philosophy of language stands to his formal logic. Although the nature of entailment and logical truth for fictional sentences would be among the theory's targets, there would be an even greater emphasis on reference, quantification and (nonlogical) truth, considered now not as an instrumental necessity but as target properties in their own right. The logic might also engage further parameters of the philosophy of language, including a role for context and user-agency. Accordingly, the theory would take on a pragmatic dimension.

> *Level 3 (Conceptually Purpose-Built Formalization).* At this level, a logic of fiction is a mathematical structure whose primary target properties involve all those features of a conceptually adequate account of the fictional, as well as the traditional targets of entailment and logical truth. Such a logic is governed by two kinds of adequacy condition. As a mathematical logic, it must produce a mature and coherent account of its target properties. As a logic sensitive to conceptual nuance, the treatment it affords its further target properties must be philosophically adequate.

Some of the virtues and drawbacks of this trio are readily apparent. Counting for level 1 approaches is their comparative familiarity and their known strengths prior to adaptation. Counting against is the likelihood that their adaptive accounts of the fictional will not be conceptually adequate. Level 2 presents us with all the difficulties attaching

---

[7] For example, are fictional beings incomplete? Are they ever *impossibilia*? What non-deductive inferences are required for a reader to understand a fictional text fully?

to unresolved disputes in philosophy. Level 3 raises questions as to where the limits of mathematical modelling lie. Even so, difficulties and challenges aside, we are now in a position to lay down a corresponding three-step *investigation-procedure* for the logic of fiction. *First step.* Attempt to find an existing mathematical logic which gives a mature and coherent account of its primary properties. Check for conceptual adequacy under fictional adaptation. *Second step.* Whether it is found to be conceptually adequate or not, verify this finding in a conceptual analysis of the fictional. *Third step.* Take what you take to be the best conceptual account of the fictional and try to find a mature and coherent mathematical model for it. To the extent that this proves possible, we will have a mature, coherent and philosophically adequate logic of fiction.

Before bringing this section to a close, it would be useful to introduce the idea of *minimal adaptations*.

PROPOSITION 2 (Minimal adaptations). *Let Σ be a system of mathematical logic. Let Σ be extended by adding to its vocabulary fictional terms and to its grammar fictional sentences. Let Σ^f be the result of these changes. Then Σ^f is a minimal adaptation of Σ if the model theory and proof theory pass to Σ^f unchanged except for input constraints.*

COROLLARY 2(a) Clearly, if Σ itself does not count as a logic of fiction, then Σ^f is at best a level 1 logic of fiction.

In a number of ways, the three-step investigation procedure embodies a rather naïve idealism. There is ample evidence that success at step two sometimes inhibits success at step three. It is not difficult to see why. The success of a conceptual analysis of a property might well bring to the fore parameters that resist formalization. They might be conceptually too rich for any extant or foreseeable symbolic representation to digest. Of course, this is an important possibility. It presents us with two options. One is to throw in the towel now. The other is to throw in the towel only after our best efforts have failed. (It is called the principle of best evidence).

2 TARGETS FOR A LOGIC OF FICTION

In considering whether the logic of fiction even has a chance, it is necessary, as I say, to reflect on the *target properties* it is reasonable to suppose that such a logic would seek to elucidate. We turn to that task now.

Systems of mathematical logic routinely set their sights on entailment and logical truth. Should these be considered primary targets of a logic of fiction? Let us begin with entailment. It certainly needs to be determined whether, and to what extent, fictional sentences are deductively closed under the standard logical operations. More basically still, we should want to know something of the conditions under which fictional sentences entail one another, and the conditions, if any, under which a fictional sentence entails a non-fictional sentence. Mainstream systems of mathematical logic also embed certain standing assumptions about *inference*. In a system's proof theory, any deduction of S from $\Sigma = \{S_1, S_2, \ldots, S_n\}$ is taken to licence the inference ⌜If Σ, then S⌝. If $S_1,\ldots,S_n$ are theorems, then the inference to S itself is mandated. Similarly, if the system's model theory determines that ⌜$S_1 \wedge S_2 \wedge, \ldots, \wedge S_n$⌝ entails S, the conditional inference ⌜If $S_1 \wedge S_2 \wedge, \ldots, \wedge S_n, S$⌝ is sanctioned. If the S_i are logical truths, then the inference of S itself is sanctioned. No one doubts that this is naïve and rather unrealistic approach to inference. It mandates that there be no extensional difference between the consequence a set of sentences *possesses* and the consequences it is permitted (or required) to *draw* from those sentences. It is easy to see that part of what logic of fiction should try to sort out is the extent to which this view of inference holds water for fictional discourse.

Although entailment and its associated notion of deductive inference make the cut as target properties of a logic of fiction, it should be noted that comparatively little of what makes for a conceptually adequate account of the fictional will show up in the theory's provisions for these notions. The same applies to its logical truths. To the extent that the logic caters for entailment, it will also cater for the associated logical truths. Apart from that, the status of two such truths in particular will require special attention. The law of excluded middle is challenged by accounts in which fictional beings are incomplete, and the law of noncontradiction is challenged by approaches in which fictional entities have logically inconsistent natures or perform logically impossible deeds. Overall, however,

PROPOSITION 3 (The marginality of deduction). *Not a great deal of what is distinctive about fictional entities and their goings-on is captured by the strictly deductive apparatus of their logic.*

COROLLARY 3(a) *In particular, the consequence relations that are most distinctive of fictional discourse are not truth-preserving.*

We saw that in classical approaches to mathematical logic, the concepts of reference and (ordinary, nonlogical) truth are not so much primary targets as instrumental necessities. Classical logic needs *some* kind of story about reference and truth in order to get the main story of entailment and logical truth right, but you can be completely right about entailment and logical truth without having to be completely right about reference and truth. Similarly, you can be completely right about entailment without having to be completely right about deductive inference.[8] As we have said, by the lights of his own philosophical logic, the treatment of reference in Frege's mathematical logic is deficient. But it is adequate, he thought, for the attainment of the mathematical logic's primary targets.

This is very much *not* the case with fiction. Reference and truth are of central importance, both conceptually and formally. In the logic of fiction, reference and truth are not instrumental necessities. They are theoretically primary. It is the same way with inference. The question of what can be inferred from a literary text is fundamental to what [Parsons, 1980] calls the "maximal account" of it, in relation to which the written text is a kind of extended enthymeme.

Doubtless there will be features of a comprehensive conceptual account of fiction, e.g., matters of style or the literary significance of irony, that exceed the reach of anything that could reasonably be called a logic. However,

---

[8]Similarly, a theory might produce a wholly credible analysis of entailment and logical truth, based in part on counterintuitive treatments of, say, negation (in, e.g., a logic of first-degree entailment).

PROPOSITION 4 (Target properties). *Since entailment, logical truth, reference, (ordinary) truth and inference are squarely within any logic's ambit, we shall, as a first pass, make these the target properties of a logic of fiction.*

3 INTUITIONS

The targets proposed by Proposition 4 are well-supported by the more basic of our pre-theoretic intuitions about literary fictions. The following five appear to be centrally important [Woods, 1974]:

A. Reference is possible to fictional beings even though they do not exist.

B. Some sentences about fictional beings and events are true.

C. Some inferences about fictional beings and events are correct.

D. These three facts are made possible in a central way by virtue of the creative authority of the authors of fiction. Indeed, the primary and originating criterion of truth for fictional sentences is the author's sayso.

E. It is also possible for a fictional truth to make reference to real things. For example, "Sherlock Holmes lived in London" is true and refers to the actual capital city of England.

If we wished to exploit an analogy with the axioms of naive set theory, we could speak of these as axioms of intuitive theories of fictionality or the *intuitive axioms for fiction.*

No one should think for long that the intuitive axioms are problem-free. It is true that axiom *A* appears to take on a degree of corroboration from the structure of quantification in natural languages. In classical logic, "There are things that don't exist" is an inconsistent (or in some versions a non-well-formed) sentence. In English, it is well-formed, consistent and *true*. Nevertheless, philosophers have long struggled to produce accounts of how we manage to achieve reference to existing objects. As I write, the leading such theory — the causal theory — cannot be extended (or so it would appear)[9] to putative references to the nonexistent. If the causal theory of reference gives our best account of reference, it is disappointing that reference to the nonexistent lacks as good a theory, if any at all.

Perhaps the biggest problem that besets axiom *B* is that for well over a half-century of tightly focused attention by philosophers of language and model-theoretic logicians, truth is tied to reference. So if reference to the fictional cannot be reconciled to our best theory of reference (if any), neither can truth about the fictional be handled by our best theory of truth (if any). A second problem for *B* can be loosely described as follows. Let *S* be any sentence from a story. Then the world is such that *S* is not true. In some cases, the contradiction is more direct. For example, *B* allows us to say that we know that Holmes lived in London. But what we know of London allows (indeed requires) us to say

---

[9]As witness e.g. [Kripke, 1972; Kaplan, 1973] and [Plantinga, 1974].

that he did not. One possibility is that these are only apparent contradictions, that they disappear once the ambiguity of such sentences is duly noted. But *where is the ambiguity*? The sentence, "Holmes lived in London", gives no sign of lexical or syntactic ambiguity. Perhaps it is an ellipsis of some kind. But if so, care needs to be taken in unpacking it lest unnecessary damage be done to the axioms.[10]

Axiom *C* tells us that sound and accessible inferences exist from sets of fictional sentences. But if there are difficulties in deciphering what, if anything, they are about, and linked difficulties in making out the conditions, if any, under which they could be true, it is hardly surprising that similar uncertainties would afflict the matter of what inference rules are correct for fiction. For example, if '*a*' is "Prime Minister Blair" and '*b*' is "Sherlock Holmes", then

$$Fa$$
$$\therefore \exists x Fx$$

is a classically good inference, whereas

$$Fb$$
$$\therefore \exists x Fx$$

is problematic. Of course, in this case the variable of quantification may range over the nonexistent as well as the existent. But this subjects inference to the same uncertainties as attach to *A*.

Philosophers of language are familiar with Austin's notion of a *performative utterance*. It is widely agreed, for example, that in uttering, "I promise to wash the car" I have, in the absence of particular reasons to the contrary, created a promise. I haven't just said that I promise; I've actually promised. Performative utterances have attracted some successful attention in theories of speech acts [Austin, 1975; Searle, 1970; Grice, 1989]. There would be a clear advantage if the creative aspect of an author's sayso could be modeled in a speech-act pragmatics. The trouble is that the statements by virtue of which fictional objects and events are created seem not to have the character of performatives.[11]

A further puzzle is whether, and how, an author's sayso can make contradictions true. Even if were able to deal with the kinds of contradictions mentioned above, this would not help with the problem of directly authored contradictions such as the case in Ray Bradbury's *A Sound of Thunder* in which Keith both is and is not elected president in one and the same election in 2055. One might think that such sentences could be accommodated in a dialetheic logic. Dialetheic logics aren't particularly congenial to the providence of axiom *A*, but perhaps this might be fixed.

3.1 Pretense and make-believe

To date, the logic of fiction research programme has concentrated on literary fictions, as opposed to legal and mathematical fictions, to name just two. Important as this focus assuredly is, there is a potential drawback. It lends encouragement to the idea that a logic

---

[10]See here [Woods, 1974, chapter 2].
[11]This is disputed in [Åqvist, 2003].

of literary fictions is somehow basic, or canonical, for fictions of all types; in other words, it appears to assume *The Literary Primacy Thesis*. Upon reflection, however, it is worth pausing to consider whether we might be better served by thinking the opposite, namely, that

PROPOSITION 5 (Fiction as generic). *It might turn out to be the case that there is a generic logic of fiction of which the logic of literary fictions is a special case.*[12]

I shall not at this stage attempt to decide the correctness of Proposition 5, or of *The Literary Primacy Thesis*. For the time being I shall concentrate on theories of literary fictions, returning to Proposition 5 towards the end of the chapter.

Let us now supplement our intuitive axioms with some further commonplaces. A fictional fact is not a real fact. A fictional person is no person at all. No fictional event ever occurred. Fictional properties don't exist. These and other like features of the fictional are a natural setting for an intuition of broad appeal.

PROPOSITION 6 (The Pretense/Make-Believe Model). *Fictional objects and facts are the subjects (or contents) of pretense.*

COROLLARY 6(a) Discourse that is nominally about fictional objects and facts is a form of make believe.[13]

The tug of the pretense/make-believe (*PMB*)-intuition draws emphatic attention to the intuitive fact that when it comes to fictional entities *there is nothing there*. It lays corresponding emphasis on the intuitive fact that fictional discourse *leaves no metaphysical footprints*.

A difficulty with the *PMB* approach is that it suggests a certain general playfulness. Doubtless some pretendings — children in a game of Cops and Robbers for example — are the sheerest play. How close the *PMB*-intuition drives the philosophical logic toward these paradigms is something we shall have to consider with due care. This task is taken up in §4.1.

3.2 Can't help it realism and the impulse to reify

Against the *PMB*-intuition something equally strong countervails. For lack of a better name, we'll call it the *objectual intuition* (the *O*-intuition). It embeds the idea of axiom *A*:

PROPOSITION 7 (The O-model). *In some nontrivial sense fictional beings are indeed objects and fictional goings on are indeed events.*[14]

Underwriting the *O*-intuition is the fact (or apparent fact) that unlike terms such as "the present king of France", which have no denotations at all, terms such as "Sherlock Holmes" are genuinely denoting, albeit not of existent objects. Accordingly, as [Woods, 1974] points out, statements about Sherlock Holmes, unlike those "about" the present

---

[12]This is the position adopted by [Woods and Alward, 2002].

[13]An early example of authorial pretense analyses is [Searle, 1975]. See also [Scruton, 1974]. The leading reader-appreciator analysis is [Walton, 1990]. [Lewis, 1983] is also a pretense theory.

[14]*O*-approaches include [Kripke, 1973; Routley, 1980; Woltersdorff, 1980; Lewis, 1983; Zalta, 1983; Deutsch, 1985; Lamarque and Olsen, 1994; Thomasson, 1998; van Inwagen, 2000] and [Zalta, 2000].

king of France, are *bet-sensitive*. There is a bet to be won or lost as to Holmes' place of residence. "221B Baker Street" wins. "2237 W. 14th Avenue" loses. Concerning the present king of France all such bets are lost (vacuously).[15][16]

The *O*-intuition seems to be grounded in the kind of cognitive being the human animal is. The human animal is a "can't-help-it realist."

PROPOSITION 8 (Can't-help-it realism). *Whether by nature or by nurture, the human cognitive agent is rigged so as to take the realist stance, that is, to experience the world realistically.*

Perhaps it all has to do with survival, since the world is dangerous and realism is an efficient way of paying attention. In our Kantian moments, we might think that experiencing the world realistically is a condition of there being experiences at all. Smart skeptics (of whom Hume was one and Sextus not) fully well know that scepticism is not a livable truth if indeed true, that one could no more experience the world as acausal, or as wholly interior, or as mindless except for me, than jump over the moon.

PROPOSITION 9 (Smart scepticism). *Smart sceptics, therefore, allow that even though they may concede that realism is false, the human animal is a can't-help-it realist.*

Our can't-help-it realism gives us natural occasion to reify. When seized by an on-rushing tiger experience, we take it that a tiger is rushing on. Of course, this is no ordinary postulation. It happens automatically and in a blink. Reifications elsewhere take longer. A case in point is the reification of *ZF* sets. When in 1902 Russell conveyed to Frege the news that killed intuitive set theory dead, a philosophical crisis ensued. The critical question was whether set theory could be rehabilitated and, if so, under what conditions. Russell answers this question in *The Principles of Mathematics* [Russell, 1903]. In one way, says Russell, set theory could not be rehabilitated. The paradox that bears his name rendered it impossible to generate the axioms of sets by a *philosophical analysis* of the idea of set. On the other hand, Russell supposes that a kind of rehabilitation could be achieved by what he called *mathematical definition*, which he sees as a form of nominal definition. In other words, the project of revealing the true natures of what sets actually are was pole-axed by the Russell contradiction, but it remained possible to re-introduce sets by *stipulation*. Russell was fully aware that stipulated objects are not free for the asking. Stipulations were also invitations to use. Their mathematical legitimacy would be decided by the mathematical research community. Russell's own contributions to this competition fell by the wayside, and in time *ZF* became the theory of choice (actually, *ZFC* if the pun might be forgiven). *ZF* arose in the axiomatic stipulations of Zermelo as early as 1908, but with the passing decades it came to be regarded as the authoritatively correct description of the intuitive idea of set. It was a remarkable transition, from fiction

---

[15] Consider a case. If the present king of France is the king of France, then where does he live? Does he live in Paris or Versailles? Or possibly in Avignon? Perhaps he's in exile in Atlantic City? These are transparently silly questions. All bets are off.

[16] In [Woods, 1974] the contrast between bet-sensitive and bet-insensitive terms is also reflected in the contrast between *nonesuches* and *non-existents*. Whereas there is no such thing as the present king of France, there is such a thing as Sherlock Holmes albeit not a thing that exists. The present king of France is a nobody. Holmes is a somebody, albeit a nonexistent one. For doubts about these contrasts see [Griffin, 2005].

to fact. It was occasioned by impulse to reify that flows unstoppably from our can't-help-it realism.

Can't-help-it realism doesn't settle the question of whether realism is true. It calls to mind the distinction between strong and weak AI. According to strong AI computers (or computer programs) have minds in just the way that humans do. Weak AI allows that strong AI may be false, but holds that the study of mind is methodologically advantaged by the assumption that it is true. We might draw a similar distinction between strong and weak realism. Our own can't-help-it realism is pairwise compatible with each. But it is *like* weak realism. It suggests that, all things considered, we get a better appreciation of how things are by experiencing the world realistically and of yielding to the impulse to reify.

3.3 Modalities de dicto *and* de re

It is natutal to think of the tug between *PBM* and *O*-models as paralleling that between *de dicto* and *de re* modalities. This has something to do with the interplay between quantifiers and the syntactic devices that betoken the fictional. One of the founding data of most accounts of fiction is that, while it is true that none of it happened, there are nevertheless well-individuated entities of which it is true. The *PBM* and *O*-orientations incline their respective supporters to different formulations of this fundamental insight. *PMB*ists see it on the model of

1. It is true in the story that $\exists x(\ldots x \ldots)$.

Those of the *O*-persuasion are more drawn to

2. $\exists x$ (it is true in the story that $\ldots x \ldots$).

If we put T^F as short for "it is true in story S that", the *PMB*-formulation becomes

3. $T^F \exists x(\ldots x \ldots)$

whereas the *O*-formulation comes out as

4. $\exists x T^F(\ldots x \ldots)$.

If we also followed the practice of a good many theorists of fiction in regarding T^F as a kind of *modal* operator on sentences, then the *de dicto/de re* parallelism is quite clear. In (3) the fictive modality is *de dicto*, having no occurrence within the scope of the quantifier. In (4) the modality is *de re*; it occurs in the scope of x. It is a virtue of (3) that its truth leaves it undisturbed that the fictional leave no metaphysical footprints.[17] One of its drawbacks is that it trifles with the intuition that there are well-individuated objects of which the goings on in fiction are true, as well as the kindred intuitions that they are also subject to truths emanating from us rather than from the story.[18]

---

[17] As Kendall Walton once remarked to me in conversation, it is of central importance to a correct account of fiction that, while there may be objects of fiction, no *object* is an object of fiction, or could be.

[18] Richard Routley, also in conversation, once pointed out that, given that Agatha Christie admired Sherlock Holmes, not only was there some object of which that is true, but that it is something made true by Christie, not by Conan Doyle.

On the face of it, the O-interpretation is more accommodating. That Holmes is a well-individuated object of which certain things are true is indicated by the quantifier of (4) in *de re* position. That the things that are true of it (or him) never happened — to him or anyone — is flagged by the fictive operator on the scope of (4)'s quantifier.[19] It also bears on the advantages and disadvantages of (3) and (4) that it is much more natural for us denizens of the world to speak of Holmes and his ilk, and on their to-ing and fro-ing, in the manner of (4); whereas (3) is held in reserve for when (4) is under *philosophical* challenge of the sort pressed by no-object theorists such as Walton. In natural speech under normal circumstances, quantifiers show a marked tendency to poke to the left. Doing so gives syntactic expression to our fondness for reification. Our leanings towards reification find a safe harbour in attributions *de* re. Reification is *de re*-ification. We might say that in speech and thought we are predisposed to handle quantification in modal contexts in conformity to the Barcan formula. So conceived, quantifiers have a preference for the left. As we are presently characterizing the presumed tension between (4) and (3), if we found reason to doubt (4), then (3) would be the only alternative. We should reconsider this. A further attraction of the O-model is the promise it holds out for reconciling the two, roughly as follows:

5. For any interpretation under which (4) is true, (3) is also true.

6. There are interpretations under which (4) is true.

An interpretation under which both (4) and (3) are true is one in which, for the values of the quantifier in (4) objecthood is assured but actuality is not. I shall return to this point in §§4.2 and 4.3.

The transition of *ZF* sets from fictions to facts, reminds us of the necessity to recognize a third intuition about fictions. This is reflected in the S-model.

PROPOSITION 10 (The S-model). *Fictional objects arise from stipulations and, in the first instance, fictional truths are made true by stipulation.*

The S-model brings into consideration a certain way of making of our can't-help-it realism (and the embedded disposition to reify) not only states of mind forced upon us by nature and circumstance, but states of mind having genuinely objectual content. This is precisely what they would be were it the case that stipulations that meet certain minimal constraints are metaphysically *creative*. This was Hilbert's view of mathematics, for whom any consistent stipulation of a mathematical entity produced that entity, brought it into being. Of course, there is something weaker to say about creative stipulations. It is that stipulations aren't creative in fact, but that our can't-help-it realism induces us to see them as such. So there is an important question to be considered. Do stipulated beings leave metaphysical footprints or are they metaphysically more ephemeral than that? Here too we see the *de dicto/de re* distinction. In purely instrumental versions, stipulations verify sentences in the form $\ulcorner T^F \exists x(\ldots x \ldots) \urcorner$ but not in the form $\ulcorner \exists x T^F(\ldots x \ldots) \urcorner$. In objectual versions it is the other way round.

---

[19] (4) does not however seem to capture Christie's admiration of Holmes, in as much as her admiration is a fact of the world, not of fiction, and seems not to belong in the scope of the fictive operator. I return to this question in §5.4.

This would be a good place to make the present point more generally and to note that

PROPOSITION 11 (A slack trichotomy). *Our three models are not all on a par, and are not entirely disjoint.*

It is easy to see why the *PMB*-model leaves no metaphysical footprints. But the same might also be said of some versions of the *O*-model. If so, the model could postulate genuine objects that nevertheless "aren't there." On the other hand, some versions of the *S*-model have it that stipulated objects are indeed there (it's just that they weren't there prior to stipulation.) Similarly, we might find theories in which the objects are stipulated yet their subsequent adventures are a matter of make-believe. If this is right, the *PMB*-model is itself a hybrid. So there is some slack in the space occupied by the *PMB*, *O* and *S*-models.

In the large literature that has grown up around these issues, perhaps [Walton, 1990] is the purest expression of the view that there are no fictional objects in any sense of "are" or "object", as are [Parsons, 1980; Jacquette, 1996] and [Griffin, 2005] the purest expression of a strong realism towards the fictional.[20] Virtually everything else lies somewhere between these extremes, with the majority of these intermediate positions clustering around a loosely structured notion of weak realism.

3.4 *Fictional discourse*

It is necessary to distinguish three distinct sort of fictional discourse, all of which require elucidation in a conceptually sensitive logic of fiction. Following [Currie, 1990] we will say that *fictive* discourse consist of those sentences which constitute fictional texts [Doyle: 1981]:

- Holmes was sitting with his back to me, and I had given him no sign of my occupation (p. 7).
- 'Good!' said Holmes. 'Excellent!' (p. 7).
- Sherlock Holmes waved our strange visitor into a chair (p. 12).
- Holmes stretched out his hand for the manuscript and flattened it upon his knee (p. 14).

Metafictive discourse consists of sentences that are not fictive, but which may be inferred or surmised from literary texts.

- Holmes was a detective
- Holmes lived in London
- Holmes solved the Case of the Speckled Band
- Holmes patronized Watson

---

[20] See also [Parsons, 1975], [Routley, 1979; Castañada, 1979] and [Zalta, 1983].

- Holmes was a marvellous reasoner.

Such sentences appear to make claims true of the stories, yet false of the world, to speak loosely.[21] For example, it appears to be true of Holmes that he lived in London but not true of London that Holmes lived there [Woods, 1969].

Transfictive discourse consists of sentences are also used to make claims about the characters and events that occur in works of fiction, but they make particular claims about their relations to things external to the works in which they occur.

- Holmes was admired by Agatha Christie

- Holmes was appropriated in a later novel, *A Monstrous Regiment of Women*, by Laurie R. King

- Jeremy Brett caught nuances of Holmes' personality better than any other actor to date

Such sentences might be said to make claims that are true of the world, yet false of the stories, still speaking loosely.[22]

A principal part of the logician's task is to set forth the production rules of stories' maximal accounts. Here the concept of presumption plays a key role. There is a widely held intuition that the full story of, for example, *The Hound of the Baskervilles* is not exhausted by the totality of the lines constituting Conan Doyle's printed text, that is to say, by the fictive sentences to be found there. There is much there that it is left to the reader to "fill in" by way of metafictive sentences. This, too, is a kind of closure exercise, but it is closure under weaker consequence relations than that of deductive implication. So a further requirement of the logic of fiction is to specify these consequence relations and determine their closure-conditions. A case in point: It is nowhere recorded that Sherlock Holmes had an aliamentary canal. Should we presume, metafictively, that he did have one? If so, on what basis? Do we repose our trust in the generalization that aliamentary canals are standard equipment for people? Or should we allow that since fictional people *aren't* people, what characteristically holds of people may well not hold of Holmes? In that case, should we try to locate Holmes' aliamentary canal in the generalization that all fictional people have them? The trouble is that it is precisely *this* that is in question here.

Consider a second case. With regard to transfictive or mixed sentences, such as "London was the city of Holmes' residence", the quite general question arises as to what London (and the world, for that matter) would have to have been like for that sentence to be true. For example, do Holmes' city and the world in which it resides obey the laws of physics? Varying the example, it happens Cervantes' *Don Quixote* was published in two parts, one in 1605 and the other in 1615. Kepler's first two laws of planetary motion were published in 1609; the third in 1619. Does this mean that the heavenly bodies under which Don Quixote slept in the first part described circular orbits, yet those of the second part described elliptical orbits? [Woods, 1974, 65].

---

[21] Of course, a sentence of metafictional discourse containing the name of a real person might turn out be true of the world as well.

[22] A sentence of transfictive discourse might also turn out to be true of the story.

3.5 Difficulties with pre-existing accounts

3.5.1 Descriptivism

Many philosophers are of the view that Russell's motivation in developing the theory of descriptions [Russell, 1905] was as a means of handling the problem of negative existentials [Cartwright, 1960]. If this is right, it is natural to look to Russell for instruction in matters fictional, since one of the problems thrown up by fiction is the nonexistence of its objects. How, then, are we to express this negatively existential fact? As developed by Russell and extended to names by Quine [1939], sentences about Holmes are false, just as sentences "about" the present king of France are false, and the intuitive difference between these referring expressions is wholly erased. In that regard, descriptivism won't do at all for fiction. It might also be remarked in passing that, although Russell was interested in the problem of negative existentials, this was not in fact the motivation for "On Denoting". What Russell wanted the theory of descriptions for was to elucidate the contrast between knowledge by acquaintance and knowledge by description. This is also a question of direct salience for fiction. Given that we cannot be acquainted with him, how is our knowledge of Holmes structured? "On Denoting" embeds a relevant question for fiction, but gives the wrong answer. Accordingly,

PROPOSITION 12 (Minimal adaptations of the theory of descriptions). *Since they are minimal adaptations of conceptually inadequate logics, description logics are at best level 1 logics for fiction.*

3.5.2 Free logics

A free logic in the narrow sense is a quantificational system whose domain of interpretation can be empty and whose individual terms need not denote (but when they do they denote actual objects). Sentences containing nondenoting terms are classically truth-valueless, thus violating axioms A and B. A narrowly free e-logic is a free logic with a dedicated existence predicate [Lambert, 1963; 1963a; 1964] and [van Fraassen, 1966; 1966a].[23] Such logic fails to preserve the contrast between terms for nonesuches, such as "the present king of France", and terms for somebodies that don't exist, such as "Sherlock Holmes" So these logics violate axiom A.

Free logics were purpose-built for nondenoting terms. The question here is whether they can be adapted to include fictional terms as a special case. Such a view of fiction is conceptually inadequate, never mind its formal virtues. Accordingly,

PROPOSITION 13 (Minimal adaptations of free logics). *Since they are minimal adaptations of conceptually inadequate logics, free logics are at best level 1 logics for fiction.*

Let us also add that a logic is a free logic in the broad sense if it admits nondenoting terms without paraphrase or whose terms may denote non-actual individuals. (An exception is Lejewski [Lejewski, 1954], which — rightly in my view — doesn't tolerate empty singular terms such as "the present king of France".) Routley's existence-neutral

---

[23] [Hailperin and Leblanc, 1959] is also a narrowly free e-logic. [Hintikka, 1959] is not, despite some similarities. [Smiley, 1960] too resembles, without quite being, a narrowly free logic.

quantification theory [Routley, 1966], is a broadly free e-logic. But such logics cannot accommodate mixed sentences such as "Holmes lived in London"; hence they disconform to axiom E.

3.5.3 Supervaluational logics

A supervaluation logic is a logic in which there is a way of assigning truth values to sentences of a formal language which allows that some sentences are classically nonbivalent and yet none of the standard theorems is lost [van Fraassen, 1966; Bencivenga, 1980; 1991]. But here too the intuitive contrast between "the present king of France" and "Sherlock Holmes" collapses.[24] However, non-bivalence approaches to fiction persist. See, e.g., [Taylor, 2000; Adams *et al.*, 1997], and [Slater, 2002].

PROPOSITION 14 (Minimal adaptions of supervaluational logics). *For reasons cited above, supervaluational logics are at best level 1 logics for fiction.*

3.5.4 Epsilon calculi

Of note here are [Slater, 1987] and [Slater, 2002], in which it is proposed that the inducements of many-valued and supervaluational approaches to the logic of fiction can be obviated by way of epsilon terms. In an epsilon calculus — which is a conservative extension of the predicate calculus — there corresponds to every predicate 'F' the epsilon term '$\varepsilon x Fx$', which denotes a given F provided there are some Fs, and "has an arbitrary reference otherwise" [Slater, 2002, 181]. Epsilon calculi have the resources to explain how it can be the case that something is the one and only F even though there is no such thing. As Slater observes, this is a feature that makes the epsilon approaches an attractive way of handling fictional discourse. For although there is no such person as Holmes, it was he and only he who solved *The Case of the Speckled Band*. Even given that Holmes is the one and only person who is Holmes, the epsilon calculus offers us the good advice not to try to book an appointment with him, yet without having to give up on the question of who solved *The Case of the Speckled Band*. A crucial test, as always, is whether the epsilon approach preserves the distinction between the present king of France and Sherlock Holmes. The answer is that it doesn't and it does. At the level of reference, "the present king of France" and "the solver of *The Case of the Speckled Band*" are at par. At the level of truth things are different. The truth of e.g., Holmes' residency is conveyed by a map from {"Holmes lived in Baker Street", i} to the truth-value 1. Here 'i' denotes the stories that make this true. As for the residency of the present king of France, there is nothing to be known; this is because there is no authorizing i for the present king of France. Some readers will think that the requisite contrast is not deeply enough drawn here. If we have it that he who presently reigns in France is the one and only who does, and yet that there exists no one who presently reigns in France, and that he who solved *The Case of the Speckled Band* is the one and only person who did, and yet there exists no one who solved *The Case of the Speckled Band*, the difference between them is that

---

[24]We note in passing that neither free logic nor supervaluation semantics has had the legs intended for them if we are to judge by, e.g., [Everett and Hofweber, 2000].

there are stories about the latter, and none so far about the former. As with Meinongian approaches, the subjects of fictions precede their fictionalization. This is tantamount to a violation of axiom D — that fictional beings originate with their ficationalizations. The distinction between "Sherlock Holmes" and "The present king of France" is also lost here. Accordingly

PROPOSITION 15 (Minimal adaptations of epsilon calculi). *These too are at best level 1 logics for fiction.*

3.5.5 Meinongian logics

Meinongianism also runs afoul of axiom D — the author's sayso axiom. On this view, all objects, fictional or otherwise, *are* by virtue of their corresponding sets of properties. Thus fictional objects "were objects before they were written about; they were so to speak only identified, or perhaps discovered, by the author, and writing about them did not confer objecthood upon them" [Parsons, 1975, 79]. The requirement that fictional objects be run-of-the-mill Meinongian objects precludes it being the case that in a rather deep and somewhat literal sense fictional objects have a literary paternity; i.e., that they are created by their authors.[25]

Particular note should be taken of Jacquette's [1996]. It is a good example of a mature and coherent mathematical logic. It has a well-specified formal language, and the requisite proof and model theories. The system is sound and complete. It has deduction, compactness and interpolation theorems. It is a three-valued logic in the manner of Łukasiewicz. It is undoubtedly a "decent" logic in Meheus' sense. It is inspired by a conceptually mature metaphysical theory. It was purpose-built to accommodate Meinong's theory of objects, which notwithstanding the slurs of Russell is an intellectually robust rival of the timorous ontologies of classical logic. Of special note is its satisfaction of axiom A. In Jacquette's hands, the logic of objects adapts in an apparently natural way to the logic of fiction. It is a fair approximation of a level 3 logic of *Meinonge*. And while it handles fictional language with all the formal adeptness it affords to Meinongian language, it cannot be regarded as a level 3 logic of fiction. It is not adequate for the conceptual demands of fiction. Its adaptation to the demands of fiction is minimal. I recur to this point in greater detail in §4.2 to follow.

3.5.6 Theories of partial objects

Theories of partial objects [Landman, 1986] permit the introduction of formal objects with out identity criteria in *ATMS models* that are designed to consider hypothetical objects in the context of alternative abductions of bodies of evidence or data [de Kleer, 1986]. Informally, the basic idea is that in a criminal investigation, various possible theories of the case are often considered. In an incriminating theory, an account of the findings is predicated of some determinate individual. In a non-incriminating theory, an account

---

[25][Kivy, 1993] argues that musical works are discovered and not created. Presumably similar arguments could be mobilized on behalf of the thesis that fictional characters pre-date authorial creative activity. Levinson, however, has offered reasons for balking at such arguments [Levinson, 1980].

of the case is predicated of some merely possible object. The theory of partial objects develops a semantics for the sentences of such accounts that purport to refer to such "objects".

The partiality of hypothetical objects squares well with any theory of fiction in which fictional objects are incomplete. Even so, lost in the partial objects approach is the intuition that fictional beings, whether incomplete or not, are well-individuated by their maximal accounts. So, here too, partial objects logic of fiction could at best be only a level 1 logic.

3.5.7 Paraconsistent logics

The principal feature of paraconsistent logics is that they are contradiction-tolerant [da Costa, 1998; Schotch and Jennings, 1989; Brown, 2000; Batens, 2000; Meheus *et al*, forthcoming; Jacquette, 1998]. Paraconsistent consequence does not satisfy the classical provision that a contradiction implies every statement. To the extent that axiom D — and also axiom E — allow for intended contradictions to hold in a work of fiction, it is certainly arguable that deductive closure in fictional discourse is subject to paraconsistent constraints. However, as they stand, such logics make no provision for axioms A, or for B, C, D or E. Accordingly, any successful minimal adaptation would be at most a level 1 logic of fiction.

Here, too, we meet with strongly competing theoretical intuitions. Meinongians such as Jacquette are at ease with the idea of nontrivial reasoning from inconsistent data-bases, which they effect with the device of predicate complementation. Theorists, such as Lewis, who abjure the very idea of "allowable" inconsistencies, preclude nontrivial inferences from inconsistencies by imposing severe constraints on fictional reasoning as such. It falls to the logician of fictional to adjudicate these rivalries. Lewisen insights are further explored in §4.1.

3.5.8 Dialetheic logics

Dialetheic logics are paraconsistent, with a difference. Whereas paraconsistent systems are contradiction-tolerant, dialetheic logics are contradiction-*affirming* [Routley and Meyer, 1976; Priest, 1979; 1987; Armour-Garb; 2005; Woods, 2005]. If we persist in the view that D and E have the force of verifying fictional contradictions, deductive closure in fiction would have to be dialetheic, except as otherwise provided by their author's fictive sentences. But notwithstanding [Heintz, 1979], dialetheic logics are not, as they stand, especially congenial to fictional objects and fictional truths. Consequently, here too, minimal adaptation would at best provide a level 1 logic of fiction.

With the dialetheic turn, we appear to lose the sympathies of virtually anyone who has attempted an analysis of fictional discourse. In fact, it is a dispute in which dialetheists have a certain tactical advantage. Why, they will ask, if it is inferentially harmless to admit contradictions to literary texts, what *further* harm would flow from their sometimes being true? All paraconsistentists agree that, whatever else, it should not be allowed that from an inconsistency everything be inferred. But apparently it is possible to avoid the disaster of *ex falso quodlibet* without forbidding the very idea of true contradictions.[26] That being so, it remains an open question in the logic of fiction as to whether a fictional truth might be a contradiction.

3.5.9 Substitutional quantification

We come now to an early attempt to move beyond level 1. Sentences containing quantifiers are usually interpreted by assigning a value to a contained variable. Values are construed as objects from the theory's domain of discourse. However, when considered substitutionally [Woods, 1974], *terms* (not objects) are assigned to quantified variables.[27] By these lights, "Someone solved the Case of the Speckled Band" would be true just in case, for some name N, "N solved the Case of the Speckled Band" would also be a true sentence. If N were the name of Sherlock Holmes, the sentence would indeed be true. One of the attractions of the substitutional approach to fiction is that it offers an engaging solution to the problem of negative existentials; it frees quantifiers from the burden of existential import. Accordingly, "There are things that don't exist" could turn out true on the strength of the truth that Sherlock doesn't exist, without the embarrassment of the embedded name "Sherlock"'s having to denote an existent object. But there are problems. One is to find the right link between the reference of "Sherlock" and the truth of "Sherlock solved the Case of the Speckled Band". As mentioned above, it would appear that these objectives can't be met in the standard (and best to date) theories of reference and truth. An alternative might be to fashion a theory of truth in the manner called for by C, and leave fictional names without referents. Doing so, however, would violate axiom A.

[Woods 1974] is purpose-built for fiction. It is a nonstandard modal extension of classical logic. Apart from the trouble occasioned by its failure to fit axiom A, additional problems threaten. One is that it might fail to be mature and coherent mathematical logic. This is, in effect, precisely what the criticisms of [Howell, 1976; Parsons, 1978] and [Routley, 1979] claim. A further difficulty might be that the conceptual model that [Woods 1974] takes pains to articulate is underdetermined by its own mathematical logic. Such indeed is the case. For example, Woods' formal logic makes no provision for inference relations peculiar to the construction of maximal accounts.

3.5.10 A methodological reflection

As our brief examination of pre-existing logics makes clear, there is a natural tendency among investigators to assimilate their findings to what is already known. We see in this the guiding presence of the *Can Do Principle*. *Can Do* helps regulate the cognitive economies in which scientific and other forms of enquiry occur. It is a principle of methodological conservativism, bidding the researcher to transact his business with tools he already commands and to repose his results in theories that are well-understood and have stood the test of time. At bottom, *Can Do* is stout discouragement of re-inventions of the wheel. It is a motivating force behind reductionism in most of its varieties and it is a

---

[26]This issue is explored in greater detail in [Woods, 2005].
[27][Pavel, 1986; Doležel, 1979] and [Currie, 1990].

presupposition of many attempts to unify knowledge. Like many good principles, *Can Do* has a degenerate case. At its most extreme, *Make Do* is *Can Do* run amok. At its least extreme, *Make Do* abuses the perfectly reasonable principle that often it is better to have an imperfect theory than no theory at all. In the hands of *Make*-Do, *wrong-headed* theories tend also to make the cut. *Make Do* inclines the theorist to employ tools that don't fit his present task and to seek a home for his results in theories that cannot justifiably accommodate them, on the grounds that the appropriated tools and borrowed theories are well-understood and have scored impressive successes in their rightful spheres of influence. Accounts fashioned in this way suffer from what [Toulmin, 1953] calls *procrusteanism*.

It is an abiding difficulty of theoretical analysis that degenerate cases of *Can Do* are so often not self-announcing and that they make themselves known only after the fact, if at all. Similarly, some of the most fruitful reductions, as with Descartes' algebraic reworking of plane geometry, have been considered wildly implausible before the fact. In general, we do not have a particularly reliable working command of the *Can Do – Make Do* distinction. So one does the best one can and waits to see what happens. The logician's desire to get a handle on the fictional is wistful occasion to bear these difficulties in mind. Like it or not, he is caught in the tug of two forces. To the extent possible, he should assimilate the account of fiction to what he already knows how to handle. To the extent possible, he should also avoid the excesses of *Make Do*.[28] Readers sympathetic to this line will likely agree with Penelope Maddy on a similar issue.

> ... philosophers seem occupationally disposed to analogies: mathematics is like a game, or mathematics is like fictional story-telling, or mathematical language is like metaphorical language ... Let us imagine that [a philosopher of mathematics] instead undertakes to characterize mathematics *directly, as itself*; instead of trying to understand mathematics by analogy with something more familiar, she tries to make mathematics *itself* more familiar. [Maddy, 2005, 364], emphases added).[29]

As we see, the usual run of pre-existing logics seem not to work convincingly for fiction. Perhaps this was only to be expected. Perhaps a happier outcome will be achieved by a logic that has been wrought with the imperatives of a conceptually adequate appreciation of the fictional firmly in mind. In the section to follow, we shall examine in some detail the dominant conceptual models of the fictional. Of the three, as we shall see, only the *S*-model evades the depredations of *Make-Do* although, even there, not everything is clear sailing. So we shall now flag a negative thesis.

---

[28] *Can Do* and *Make Do* are discussed at greater length in [Woods, 2006]. But we might here note further variations. As we have it so far, *Can Do* and *Make Do* are about the appropriation of existing *theories* in an effort to bring the analytical task at hand to heel. The same processes are also at work with regard to one's choice of an *analytic vocabulary* for a problem. Two quick examples will give the flavour of this. First, it is common among modal semanticists to analyse possible worlds as maximal consistent sets of propositions. Modal sceptics such as Quine complain that the analyzing idiom of "proposition" is no better-understood than the *analysandum* "possible world". Secondly, it is still widely accepted to define "analytic sentence" as one that converts to a logical truth upon the replacement of terms by synonyms. Intensionality sceptics (Quine again) complain that the analyzing idiom 'synonym' is no better-understood than the *analysandum* 'analytic'. In each case, the sceptic is pressing a version of the *Make Do* complaint. (I cite these examples without prejudice.)

[29] Cf. Michael Oakeshott on what the poet does: he imagines *poetically*.

PROPOSITION 16 (PMB, O and Make-Do). *The dominant versions of the PMB-model and the O-model suffer, in varying degrees, from the debilitations of Make-Do.*

4 EXAMINING THE BASIC CONCEPTUAL MODELS

The upshot of the forgoing discussion is that existing logics have not responded well under minimal adaptation to the requirements of a logic of fiction. Even logics such as [Woods, 1974], which was specifically constructed for fiction, fail to formalize a number of conceptually significant features. In effect, it too is a minimal adaptation. In the present section, we turn our attention to the various ways in which fictions have been conceptualized, with particular reference to our three paradigms – the *PMB*-model, the *O*-model and the *S*-model. If our objective is to have an account of fiction that is mathematically mature and coherent, as well as conceptually adequate, it is necessary to begin with the issue of conceptual adequacy, which is prior. It bears remarking that to date most of the conceptual work on fiction has been produced independently of attempts to develop formal structures in the manner of a level 3 approach.

4.1 PMB approaches

PMB approaches invoke a pair of inequivalent notions. One is pretense and the other is make-believe. In some variations of the model, the two concepts are hand in glove. Even so, as we shall later see, their disjointness should not be overlooked. Most examples of the *PMB* approach arise from what we might call a *propositional attitude* orientation towards the analysis of fiction.[30] Here the basic idea is that fundamental to the creation of fictions and to their being responded to as fictions is the role of the imagination, where imagining is construed as a propositional attitude. Not all propositional attitude approaches conform to the *PMB*-model, but *PM*-approaches are all propositional attitude approaches.

By far the currently dominant *PMB*-theory is that of Kendall Walton in his widely acclaimed *Mimesis as Make-Believe* [Walton, 1990]. There is also something to be said for the stronger claim that Walton's is widely considered the best conceptual account of fiction — the best of the *PMB*-type and better than what is on offer in any of the competing models. My interest here is with Walton's theory as a paradigm of the *PMB*-model. Since Walton is to some extent anticipated by John Searle's paper, "The logical status of fictional discourse" [Searle, 1975], it is best to begin our discussion there.

4.1.1 Authorial pretense

According to Searle, pretense is the characteristic *authorial* attitude towards the sentences they pen in story-telling. When Doyle first wrote "'Good!' said Holmes. 'Excellent!'", he made no assertion. Rather he pretended to assert that this is what Holmes said. Similarly, when Doyle produced the sentence, "Holmes stretched out his hand for the manuscript and flattened it upon his knee", he pretended that there existed and that he had referred

---

[30] Other propositional attitude approaches include [Smith, 1978; Gabriel, 1979; Oversteegen, 1982; Currie, 1990; Mooij, 1993] and [Everett and Hofweber, 2000].

to a real Sherlock Holmes. What makes this possible is that by "pretending to refer to people and recount events about them, the author creates fictional characters and events." [Searle, 1975, 33]. It should be noted that here Searle's way of being a *PMB*-theorist takes on aspects of the *O*-model. For, unlike Walton, who holds that Sherlock Holmes is an object of no kind, Searle allows that Holmes is an object of some kind, namely, the fictional kind. Equally, whereas Walton holds that pretending to refer is reference of no kind, Searle's view is that in pretending to refer we do refer, albeit to something of a kind different from the pretended referent of the pretend-reference. This gives us what we might call

PROPOSITION 17 (Searle's Principle). *Suppose that x doesn't exist and yet pretending to refer to x as real succeeds. Then in pretending to refer to x, one is in fact referring to an unreal x.*

Searle himself does not explicitly proclaim *Searle's Principle*. But he is committed to it. This being so, it is especially awkward that nowhere in [Searle, 1975] do we find a discussion of the principle's putative truth conditions.

If *Searle's Principle* leaves the ontological status of the fictional Holmes in the dark, also problematic is the following pair of issues.

- What is the *reader*'s role? Do readers engage in pretense? Is it the same pretense as authors are involved in? If so, what explains this remarkable concurrence? If not, how is co-reference possible?

- What is the *critic*'s role? When someone says that Jeremy Brett captured Holmes' character better than Basil Rathbone, is the critic engaging in pretense? If so, what is he pretending? If not, then must we not concede that pretense is not a condition on reference to fictional beings.

4.1.2 Appreciator make-believe

[Walton, 1990] is a more developed propositional attitude analysis than Searle's. While there are clear similarities between the two accounts, there is a notable difference. Searle concentrates on an author's attitude towards the sentences he produces. Walton emphasizes the attitudes of the reader. In so doing, Walton takes himself to have adapted the model of a child's game of make-believe. Accordingly, in reading a story, readers are *playing games*. As in various kinds of games (but not all), in playing the game of reading, readers make use of special kinds of *props*. What is more, the props of which readers avail themselves are those that are (tacitly) *authorized* by the type of game that story-reading is.

Walton sees games of make-believe as governed by rules. In the case of the games that constitute the reading of a story, the associated rules allow that certain propositions can be imagined. These are the fictional truths of the game. Walton also thinks that a prop in a game of make-believe is, as provided by the rules of the game, an object that *generates* these fictional truths. In the case of the game of fiction, the role of prop is played by the work on the text of the story. Accordingly,

PROPOSITION 18 (Waltonian works of fiction). *A work of fiction is an object whose function is to serve as a prop in a game of make-believe of the requisite type.*

What is more,

> A thing may be said to have the function serving a certain purpose, regardless of the intentions of its maker, if things of that *kind* are typically or normally meant by their makers to serve that purpose [Walton, 1990, 52].

Walton allows that stories make-true sentences in the form "It is true-in-t that S", where t is a fiction and S a fictive sentence. He gives their truth conditions as follows:

PROPOSITION 19 (Waltonian truth). *A sentence of the form "It is true-in-t that S" is true iff fiction t is such that one who engages in pretense of kind K in a game authorized for it makes it fictional of herself that she speaks truly.* [Walton, 1990, 400].

An authorized pretense is a pretense of the requisite kind. But what is a pretense of the requisite kind? As Walton sees it,

PROPOSITION 20 (Requisite pretense). *A speaker displays the requisite kind of pretense when in pretending to assert a fictive or metafictive sentence he actually asserts the Waltonian paraphrase of it.*

COROLLARY 20(a) Speakers producing such sentences other than in the "spirit of pretense" fail to display a pretense of the requisite type, but only go through the motions of so doing [Walton, 1990, 402-404].[31]

Walton's account is shot-through with obscurity. The problem is so bad that it calls it sharply into question as to how *Mimesis and Make-Believe* could have attained and preserved its status as the leading conceptual account of fiction. The obscurity problem arises as follows. Central to Walton's account are the terms *pretense, make-believe* and *prop*. As used within the theory, it is arguable that not one of these terms retains its customary meaning, yet their nonstandard, theoretical, uses are unexplained. Central as they are to the Waltonian analysis, they give rise to

PROPOSITION 21 (Walton's dilemma). *Concerning the terms "pretense", "make-believe" and "prop", one of two things is true. (1) In their application to Walton's theory, they lack their ordinary meanings, and their theoretical meanings are unexplained. (2) They have ordinary meanings incompatible with the claims of the theory.*

Let us begin with *make-believe*. Make-believe is what actors do to audiences (and children, in certain of their games, do to one another). Christopher Plummer *plays* John Barrymore in ways that get the audience to experience the action on stage as Barrymore's own. Plummer *gets* his audience to *believe* that this is happening to Barrymore. Hence *make*-believe. One must not gainsay the genuine complexity of the relationship between Plummer and his audience. In getting his audience to experience his behaviour on stage as Barrymore's and to care about it as Barrymore's, something quite remarkable has occurred. We might say that something similar occurs between Doyle and his readers. Doyle's sentences get readers to experience the events described as happening to Holmes

---

[31] Are they then pretending to pretend?!

and to care about them as affecting Holmes. Yet not a word of *Mimesis and Make-Believe* suggests that this is what Walton means by make-believe.

In a further of its common uses, "make-believe" carries connotations of the unreal. It ranges from Plummer's state of mind (make-believe grief), to models (make-believe markets), and from them to props (a make-believe gun). But there is nothing here that comes close to elucidating Walton's idea of fiction as a game of make-believe. Of course, there *are* games of make-believe. Cops and Robbers is a game of make-believe. But it is folly to liken the reading of a story to Cops and Robbers. In playing a game of Cops and Robbers it is not essential to its success (indeed it may be fatal to its success) that spectators be doxastically and affectively engaged — there is nothing here like being *convinced* that Hamlet is a homosexual or *hating* Iago's guts.[32] Fiction stands apart from this in two respects. One is that *readers* play no role remotely similar to that played by any of the parties to a game of Cops and Robbers. The other is that a story fails if it fails to engage its readers doxastically and affectively.

Another vexation is Walton's appropriation of the idea of a *prop*. "Prop" is a theatrical term. It is short for "properties". A prop is an object from the company's properties department. The task of the Royal Shakespeare Company's properties department is to dress the stage and equip the players with the objects and other physical wherewithal required by the play. In most cases these are not only real objects, but real cases of the type of object that the play calls for. When the play calls for a dinner table to be set, the props department sets it with real plates. Similarly, curtains are usually real curtains, chairs real chairs, beds real beds, and so on. There is in the idea of a prop not the shred of a presumption of type-unreality.

Sometimes the objects called for by the play are too big, too heavy, too expensive or too dangerous for use on stage. In that case, the props department will furnish stands-in for the objects not present. An object stands in for an object not present by virtue of various similarity relations, but also by virtue of its place in what is played out on stage. So a cap-pistol can also be a prop, standing in for a .45. Equally, the stool that is broken over the actor's head can be a prop, standing in for the real thing, which, had it been present, would have surely ended the performance. Although some props are pretend-objects, such is only a contingent and occasional connection. Most props are not pretend-objects of any kind. This makes Walton's appropriation of the term rather perplexing.

Walton thinks that *The Hound of the Baskervilles* is a prop. Like the .45, it is a real object. Like the .45, its "function" is to generate truths. In the performance of a play, the actor playing Spike might be brandishing a .45, thus helping to engender the truth that *Spike* is brandishing a .45. The text of *The Hound of the Baskervilles* also engenders a truth. In Walton's telling, it is true-in-*The Hound of the Baskervilles* that Holmes was a detective because the prop, *The Hound of the Baskervilles,* is such that one who engages in pretense of the requisite kind in a game authorized for it makes it fictional of himself that he speaks truly. Now whatever this might actually mean, it isn't a jot necessary or helpful to invoke the concept of prop. Of course, it can't be ruled out that Walton has a theoretically loaded sense of prop in mind. If so, he might have let us in on the secret.

---

[32]There is a large literature on fictionally induced emotions. See, e.g., [Radford, 1975; Slater, 1993; Walton, 1990] and [Alward, forthcoming].

Pretense is central to Searle's account of the author's role, and to Lewis' as well [1978; 1996]. Pretense is central to Walton's account of the reader's role. According to Searle and Lewis, authors are taken to be pretending to be reporting the actual truth of what they are writing about. Upon reflection however, there isn't the slightest reason for thinking that this is so. What *is* true is that when an author pens his lines, he is writing a story, and that writing a story is a *special* kind of make-believe. The author writes the story in the hope that its readers will be made to believe that what it ascribes to its characters is actually happening to them. It is, again, exceedingly difficult to fathom the mechanics of such make-believe, but there is no denying its efficacy or its power. People argue with the greatest intensity about Hamlet's character and motivation, and are reduced to tears at Little Nell's brutal death. If the *ordinary* meaning of "pretend" is to have any sway here, we should have to accept that if these make-believes arose from the author's pretense, then it would have been the case that in creating the story, the author was intent on deceiving us. If he was pretending to report the actual facts of the case, he would have been deceiving us; and, for this to be true, we would have to think that he was reporting what actually happened. It matters greatly that authorially intended make-beliefs succeed wildly even in the face of his readers' knowledge of what he has done, namely, write a story. So, for the present sense of "pretend", the last thing that the author is doing is pretending to do what he is not doing in fact.[33]

Of course, other senses of "pretend" might also be considered. When, in a game of Cops and Robbers, little Harry pretends to be Dick Tracy, he is not trying to deceive his playmates that he is indeed that pointy-chinned sleuth. He is play-acting. He is playing the role of Tracy. It is a condition of his doing this well that his playful behaviour be somehow indicative of Tracy's behaviour (he can't play him as the Virgin Mary).[34] When Sir Arthur Conan Doyle sat down to write *The Case of the Speckled Band*, he was not pretending to be reporting to his readers the adventures of Holmes. This is not to say that in this story the adventures of Holmes are not reported at all. In fact, they are reported by Watson. Somehow Doyle gets it to be the case that the events recounted by Watson are true of Holmes;[35] but, however this was done, it was not done by Doyle pretending to report those doings as fact, as Lewis expressly claims. Neither was it done by Doyle play-acting that he is reporting the actual fact that Watson is reporting the actual facts about Holmes (and about himself; these stories are Watson's memoirs).

Pretense, in both of the two senses under review, leaves no metaphysical footprints. What Doyle was doing was writing the Holmes stories. He was making them up. Doing this also leaves no metaphysical footprints. In writing his stories, Doyle constructed narratives. It is quite common to use narratives to deceive people, to lie to them. It is not uncommon to use narratives for make-believe. But it is a massive disanalogy to equate

---

[33] Still, Walton is in celebrated company. Plato makes the same mistake in the *Republic*, in making the case for the exclusion of the dramatic poets from the perfect civil society. Plato was entirely right to notice in the arts a propensity to corrupt, but was entirely wrong in identifying the corruption as a form of lying.

[34] Perhaps he might play Tracy as *Tracy* pretending to be the Virgin Mary, but little Harry would have to be one sophisticated little kid to do that.

[35] This is challenged by Holmes himself in the successor novels of Laurie R. King. An interesting complication.

story writing with pretense in either of these two senses, just on the grounds that the narratives of fiction don't leave metaphysical footprints.

The idea that authors are pretenders, in either of its two senses, has nothing to recommend it. The kindred suggestion that readers also play such a role is, if anything, even less worthy of a gentle reception. Readers might misread a work of fiction, taking it as an historical narrative, although such confusions are much rarer, and harder to fall into, than one might think. But when a reader reads a work knowing it to be a work of fiction, there is a certain psychological state that it is necessary for him to be in, a certain mode of concomitant susceptibility. He must be moved to take the story's claims as true of its characters and he must be capable of being affectively engaged by those characters and the events that befall them. No doubt the full story of this psychological complexity is a long way from being told. But we know its rudiments. The appropriate response of a reader to a work of fiction is one in which he accepts the story's attributions as true recognizing all the while that the events attributed and the subjects to which they are ascribed are not real. (Hence, "the *willing* suspension of disbelief.")

Another leading *PMB*-theorist is Lewis.[36] Lewis is equivocal about fiction. He produces two accounts, whose differences are apparent in the following two truth definitions. First,
PROPOSITION 22 (Lewisean truth I). *A sentence in the form 'In fiction f, ϕ' is non-vacuously true iff some world where f is told as known fact and ϕ is true differs less from our actual world, on balance, than does any world where f is told as known fact and ϕ is not true (1983, 270].*[37]

Second,
PROPOSITION 23 (Lewisean truth II). *A sentence of the form. "In fiction f, ϕ" is non-vacuously true iff whenever w is one of the collective belief worlds of the community of origin of f, then some world where f is told as known fact and ϕ is true differs less from the world w, on balance, than does any world where f is told as known fact and ϕ is not true (p. 273).*

The idea of a *collective belief world* plays an important role in the specification of maximal accounts, and we shall have occasion to return to it later. Suffice it to say for now that collective belief worlds are populated by background beliefs. A background belief is one which more or less everyone in the author's community accepts, virtually everyone believes that everyone accepts, and so on. Lewis also requires such beliefs to be jointly consistent.

It is easy to see that for Lewis, too, pretense is essential to the analysis. A fictional story is one told as known fact, but storytelling is pretense; the story-teller pretends that he is recounting a story he knows to be true. Lewis' approach is also a heavily *consistentist* one. It may be that in f, S and that in $f, \sim S$, but it cannot be true of any f and S that in $f, S \wedge \sim S$. On the face of it, this cannot be right. In *A Sound of Thunder*, Keith both is and is not elected president in the same election.

---

[36]Critics of Lewis include [Byrne, 1993; Currie, 1990; LePoidevin, 1995; Phillips, 1999; Priest, 1997; Jacquette, 2001]. Of the favourably-minded camp, [Hanley, 2004] thinks better of Lewis' account than Lewis himself does.

[37]Note the similarity between "true in f" and "T^F".

Even so, Lewis won't have it. What is true in *A Sound of Thunder* is some subset of its fictive sentences. Lewis considers two ways in which flat-out sentential contradictions might be disabled. One is the *method of intersection*, and the other the *method of union*. Much of the criticism that Lewis' theory attracts is directed at this refusal of authorially validated in-fiction contradictions. This, too, is an issue that I'll take up later. Here it is enough to emphasize the point that for Lewis authors of fiction are pretending to tell the truth, and when, in fact, there isn't the slightest reason to think that this is what they themselves think that they are doing. If it *is* true that this is what they are doing, is it not surpassing strange that David Lewis would know it but Miguel Cervantes would not, and that Kendall Walton would know it, but Henry James wouldn't have had a clue? Of course, here too there is a possible explanation of these affronting asymmetries. There is a sense of "pretense" known to Lewis and Walton but unknown to Cervantes and James (and, we may suppose, virtually everyone else) for which it is indeed the case that what Cervantes and James were doing is pretending to tell the truth. But what sense of "pretense" *is* that?

Whatever we are to take them to mean, Walton's notions of pretense, make-believe and prop are embedded in an overarching concept of *game*. It is true, of course, that some games are games of pretending and make-believe, and that some such games involve the use of pretend-objects used as props. The concept of game has achieved a high importance in Anglo-American philosophy since the 1950s. Wittgenstein's likening of the speaking a language to the playing of a game has attracted enormous philosophical attention [Wittgenstein, 1956; Kripke, 1982]. Contractarian approaches to ethics and political theory also brim with the game theory of von Neumann and Morgenstern [1944] and Nash [1950]. Logic itself has taken on a game-theoretic character, beginning with the pioneering work of Hintikka [1974][38]. It would not be going too far to say that games are by now the objects of detailed, carefully refined and rather powerful theories. Not that the analysis of games is entirely a *fait accompli*. As I write, it is still a work in progress and a growth industry.[39] The sheer importance of the philosophical analysis of games embeds a twofold attraction. To the extent that it is considered a safe harbour, it invites the working researcher to repose his own theories there, to try to effect a kind of reduction of the issues he is working on (say, the analysis of X) to the theory of games. To the extent to which the theory of games is still a work in progress, it invites the reduction of (say) the analysis of X to the theory of games also as a contribution to the theory of games (in the manner, for example, of the Stone Representation Theorem [Stone, 1937]). There is much to commend in such assumptions. If the theory of X is indeed subsumed by the theory of games, then locating X within the theory of games is an efficient way of achieving genuine elucidations of the structure of Xhood. But if, by chance, X doesn't reduce to the theory of games, then a game-theoretic analysis of Xs is at best a conceptual distortion and at worst a profound mistake.

---

[38]In [1974] Hintikka mentions that he first presented the idea of a logic as a game in his 1964 John Locke Lectures at Oxford.

[39]In November 2005, at King's College London, the prestigious De Morgan Conference on Logic was devoted entirely to game-theoretic logic.

In Proposition 16 we flagged a negative thesis about some widely received analyses of the fictional. In this regard, Walton's contributions to this approach, as indeed are all pretense theories, is a disappointment. There is straighter way of saying this.

PROPOSITION 24 (Games and Make-Do). *The employment within the PMB-model of the notion of game shows indications of Make-Do.*

There is nothing in Walton's writings to suggest that any such reduction was ever in his mind. And certainly, it would be a considerable stretch to represent *Mimesis as Make-Believe* as a contribution to the philosophical analysis of games. Still, games *are* at the centre of Walton's approach to fiction. So it cannot be dismissed out of hand that he might have been drawn to this assimilation unawares. (After all, weren't we just now considering that Cervantes and James were *pretending* unawares?) What really counts, of course, is whether the concept of game plays any kind of load-bearing role in the logic of fiction. It takes little reflection to see that there is nothing good to be said for assimilation. In none of the ordinary meanings (*pace* Wittgenstein) of "game", is what an author is up to in writing a story a game and what a reader is up to in reading a story (knowing it to be one) a game. Some philosophers are of the view that Wittgenstein greatly overplayed the similarities between games and language-use. In this they may well be right. But it cannot seriously be doubted that in conceiving of story-telling and story-reading as games, Walton has transgressed every ordinary meaning of "game". It is possible, of course, that he intends an unordinary or technical sense of this word. If so, he would have done well to tell us about it.

A further sense of "pretense" can now be considered, at the juncture where the *PMB*-model and the *S*-model converge. Given the sense now in play, pretense arises from one person's proposal to *say* and another person's *acceptance* of it. Its natural idioms are "let us say that …", "we put it that …", "we take it that …" and the like. Such expressions are the common currency of working mathematicians, especially when introducing concepts by nominal definition (or what [Russell, 1903] calls mathematical definition, as opposed to philosophical analysis). Such sayings, puttings and takings are stipulative. In mathematical contexts, stipulation is subject to a two-phase process. First there is the form of words and the speech acts that bring the stipulated object into view. Second, there is a judgement by the intended audience (here, it is the relevant research community) as to whether this is a usable stipulation, whether it integrates with what is presently known and facilitates the unearthing of new theorems. Hilbert appears to have thought that phase one was primary and autonomous. Russell appears to have thought that in the absence of phase-two communal acceptance, whatever had been wrought at phase one would atrophy and eventually die out. The idiom of *taking* gives us occasion to re-visit the *de dicto/de re* distinction. We remarked earlier that in our own discourse about the fictional the *de re* mode of expression is the more natural. If we allow that what an author's stipulations make true is that

3. $T^F \exists x(\ldots x \ldots)$,

we nevertheless find it natural to *take it that*

3. $\exists x T^F(\ldots x \ldots)$

When we turn to a more detailed discussion of the S-model in §4.3, it will be important to re-acknowledge the dual character of mathematical stipulationism — its objectual or quasi-objectural orientation and its purely instrumental orientation. Even so, the present take on taking is worth keeping in mind.

4.2 Meinongian logics

One of the basic approaches to the O-model of fiction is to treat fictional objects as a special subclass of *Meinongian objects*. Roughly speaking, a Meinongian object is anything that might be the object of someone's thought. Such objects are separate from the content of the thoughts that "intend" them. Those that inhabit space and time are said to exist. Those that have an abstract character, such as numbers or the propositional contents of sentences, are said to subsist. But there are also objects, such as Sherlock Holmes, that neither exist nor subsist. Some objects, such as Berkeley's round square are impossible. Some objects are incomplete ("... there is no fact of the matter about Inspector Lestrade's blood type." [Lewis, 1983, 270].) Some impossible objects are also incomplete, (the round square, again, which is neither blue nor not blue.) Meinongian ontologies are of considerable interest to O-minded logicians of fiction. Two of the best Meinongian logics are [Parsons, 1975, 1980] and [Jacquette, 1996, 2006].

4.2.1 Parsons' logic of fiction

Parsons invokes a central distinction among actual objects, or things that *are*, between those that are *existent* and those that are *nonexistent*. In this approach, correlated with each nonempty set of properties there is a distinct, specific object in [Parsons, 1975, 75]. Uniquely correlated with the set of properties $\{p:$ Madame Curie has $p\}$ is Madame Curie, and uniquely correlated with the set {goldenness, mountainhood} is the golden mountain. In the case of both existent and nonexistent objects, the set consists of those properties that the correlated object has. If no restrictions are placed on the properties that can be members of the sets correlated with objects, severe difficulties arise. In addition to the golden mountain, a nonexistent object, there would be a nonexistent object correlated with the set {goldenness, mountainhood, being existent}. And in addition to the round square, an impossible nonexistent object, there would be the possible round square. To avoid such difficulties, Parsons restricts the properties of sets with which objects, existent and nonexistent, are correlated to what he calls *nuclear* properties. Nuclear properties are ordinary properties of objects such as roundness and being red, whereas *extranuclear* (or nonnuclear) properties are special properties such as being existent, being possible, and being thought of by Meinong. Fictional objects — objects "native" rather than "immigrant" to fiction — are, on Parsons' view, a subclass of the class of nonexistent objects. They are the objects correlated with sets of the following sort:

$\{p:$ according to (the 'maximum' account of) the Conan Doyle stories, Sherlock Holmes has $p\}$ [Parsons, 1975, 80].

More generally, where x is a fictional object:

x = the object correlated with $\{p$: according to the relevant body of literature, x has $p\}$.

One final feature of Parsons' view worth pointing out concerns the relations that hold between nonexistent objects native to fiction and existent objects that are immigrants to fiction. Parsons concedes that when a fictional objects stands in relation to an existent objects, the existent object does not stand in the corresponding relation to the creature of fiction. Even if Holmes has the property of having had tea with Prime Minister Gladstone, Gladstone will lack the property of having had tea with Holmes [Woods, 1969; Parsons, 1980, 60].

Parsons' assumption that a distinct, genuine and well-individuated object is correlated with each nonempty set of nuclear properties is problematic. Some readers might find this an over-generous criterion of objecthood, and others could wonder whether, say, *unit* sets of properties are ever property-rich enough adequately to individuate. Not only is there no particular reason to think that there is just one object that is red and has no other (nuclear) properties — corresponding to the set {being red} — it is dubious that redness alone ever makes a substantive enough contribution to its bearer so as to confer genuine individuality upon it. What is more, when imported into Parsons' account of fictional objects, this assumption implies that characters who receive identical descriptions in a given work of fiction are the same character in that work [Howell, 1983, 170].[40]

A further difficulty concerns Parsons' claim that fictional objects are ontically incomplete[41]. For all properties such that neither they nor negations are in Holmes' representing set, Holmes is indeterminate with respect to those properties [Parsons, 1975, 84]. But on the face of it, it is not credible to say that Sherlock Holmes neither lacked nor possessed an alimentary canal, a liver, ten toes, two elbows or a mother; that he neither went to school nor not, that he neither did nor did not comport himself with Watson and the world in ways not expressly chronicled by Doyle. A view that rendered the indeterminacy of

> Holmes had a mole on his back

and

> Holmes lacked a mole on his back

in ways compatible with the *truth* of

> Holmes either had or lacked a mole on his back

might well be acceptable. But Parsons' account fails to meet even this weaker condition [Howell, 1979, 136].

Roughly speaking, nuclear properties are constitutive properties, such as a thing's physical attributes. Nonnuclear properties do not fix the object's kind. These include

---

[40]There is also the question of whether Parson's luxuriant ontology isn't occasion of unintended consequences, such as confirmation of the ontological argument for God's existence [Woods, 1986].

[41]Similarly, while it is true that Holmes lived in London, it seems not to be true of London that Holmes lived there. The idea of objectual incompleteness originates with [Meinong, 1915]. It is also a theme developed in [Ingarden, 1931] and, quite recently in [Akiba, 2000]. *Cf.* [Parsons, 1982; Lear, 1982; Simons, 1999].

self-identity, existence, possibility and the like.[42] So, whether numbers exist or not is something that leaves it undisturbed that the kind of thing they are is numbers. The nuclear-nonnuclear distinction is important for characterizing impossible and incomplete objects. An object is said to be impossible when it has a nuclear property and its complement. An object is said to be incomplete when it lacks a nuclear property and its complement. The distinction itself is not clearly determined[43] and it is a matter of controversy as to whether some of the properties Parsons counts as nuclear really are ordinary properties of objects at all [Howell, 1983, 167-168].

Additional difficulties arise as a result of the asymmetries Parsons posits in relations that obtain between existent and nonexistent objects. Although in a fictional work the very same properties may be attributed to an immigrant object as are attributed to an object native to the work, the latter will have but the former will lack these properties [Howell, 1983, 171]. These asymmetries pose intractable problems for an adequate account of transfictive discourse — claims about the relations of characters and events that occur in works of fiction to existent things external to the works in which they occur.

In certain respects Jacquette's is an improvement on Parsons' treatment of *Meinonge* (after all, Parsons has broad shoulders). A particular advantage is that Jacquette offers a formal definition of nuclear and nonnuclear properties. He also furnishes the reader with a plausible, though informal, means of making the distinction between them recognizable. The formal definition draws on a distinction between sentence negation, represented by $\sim$ and predicate complementation represented by *neg*. If S is a sentence, its negation $\ulcorner \sim S \urcorner$ is a sentence. If Q is a predicate, its complement *neg* Q is a predicate. If Q is a nuclear-property predicate, then negation and complementation are irreducibly different. If κ is a nonnuclear predicate, then sentence negation and predicate complementation are everywhere interdefinable. [Jacquette, 2006, section 5.1]. A property is nonnuclear if any only if it is definable via logical operators and uninterpreted predicate symbols and nothing else. A property is nuclear if and only if it is not nonnuclear.

Jacquette's Meinongian logic is a quantificational extension of the basic Łukasciewicz 3-valued system. As remarked earlier it is consistent, sound and complete. Compactness, deduction and extrapolation theorems are provable. Much of classical logic is preserved. The set theory of the logic's semantics is nonstandard and paradox-free, notwithstanding that it has an unrestricted comprehension axiom.

4.2.2 Jacquette's logic of fiction

> Fictional objects arise from the creative endeavors of their authors. As a story is created, the author determines by free assumption the nuclear properties of its characters. These are what John Woods in *The Logic of Fiction* calls the characters' 'sayso' properties. [Jacquette, 1996, 256].

---

[42]The nuclear-nonnuclear distinction originates with Mally, not Meinong. See [Rapaport, 1978] and [Zalta, 1983, xi-xii].

[43]Another hard case: the property of being fictional. How plausible is it that being fictional or real is immaterial to whether Holmes is or is not a man?

What is more,

> The author is the primary and often the only source of what nuclear properties characters do or do not have. (p. 257)

On the face of it, this is rousing endorsement of axiom D, the author's sayso axiom. But appearances to the contrary, nothing remotely like axiom D is sustainable in a Meinongian theory of objects. Let Σ the set of all and only the nuclear properties of male human beings. Holmes, as it happens, is constituted by a particular subset of those properties. But since Doyle did not create those properties, and those properties constitute Holmes, it cannot in any strictness be said that Doyle created Holmes. Given the way that Meinongian truth works can it be the case that whereas the objects of fiction precede an author's creative intervention, the truths about those objects are precisely what are conferred by it. Every truth about Holmes is fixed by the properties he has and the relations he bears to others, and others to him. Not only do the properties constitutive of Holmes precede authorial intervention, so do the properties constitutive of Holmes' history. So a Meinongian logic of fiction violates D, the sayso axiom.

[Woods, 1969] draws attention to the previously remarked apparent asymmetry in relations that normally one would have taken as symmetric. If it is true of Holmes that he lived in London, why would it not also be true of London that Holmes lived there? But surely it is *not* true of London that Holmes lived there. Certainly "... a stake-out on Baker Street would have obtained no trace of Holmes" [Routley, 1981, 563]. Jacquette cites with approval Routley's own proposed solution, which he calls "contextualism". The sentence, "Holmes lived in London" is analyzed as "According to the detective stories of Arthur Conan Doyle it is true that Holmes lived in London", and the sentence "London was where Holmes lived" is analyzed as "According to the detective stories of Arthur Conan Doyle it is true that London is where Holmes lived". Routley's intuitions tell him that the first paraphrase is true and that the second paraphrase is false. Jacquette's intuitions confirm this solution. I can only say that I am at a loss to understand these intuitions.[44] Here is why.

Routley's device of contextualization takes many forms in the literature. One of the most prominent of these is the postulation of the fictive operator T^F carrying essentially the Routleyian meaning "it is fictionally the case in story F that" or "it holds in story F that". Routley's paraphrases are meant to elucidate our pre-theoretical impressions that "Holmes lived in London" is true and "London is where Holmes lived" is false. But "According to the detective stories of Arthur Conan Doyle it is true that Holmes

---

[44][Woods, 1969] proposes a different solution, by invoking a distinction between what is *true* of an object and what is *true and history-constitutive* of it. Accordingly, that he lived in London is true and history-constitutive of Holmes, whereas that this is where Holmes lived is true but not history-constitutive of London. The two sentences are true together and false together but they differ with respect to history-constitutiveness. Symmetry is preserved in the first instance, but not in the second . Looking closely at Routley's example of the false member of the pair, we see that he blurs this very distinction. "According to the detective stories of Arthur Conan Doyle it is true *of* London that it was lived in by Holmes", equivocates as between "it is true that London was lived in by Holmes" and "it is history-constitutive of London that it was lived in by Holmes". The distinction is pre-figured in Frege's notion of *Sinn*. Roughly speaking the *Sinn* of 'r' gives that part of its history that individuates r. Accordingly, "was lived in by Holmes" is not part of 'London's' *Sinn*.

lived in London" is no warrant that Holmes *did* live in London unless Doyle's sayso is authoritative. It would be authoritative if Doyle's sayso *made* it true that Holmes lived in London. But, as we have seen, that is the last thing that Doyle's sayso can do if the Meinongian theory of objects is correct and Holmes is a Meinongian object.

This leaves wide open the question of how to interpret the authorial role of Doyle. Doyle may be the primary source of *information* about Holmes, but, on the Meinongian account, he cannot be the source of the *truths* about Holmes. Properly understood, the author is reporting facts that the antecedently present Holmes already has. Yet it seems equally essential that whatever else might be the case, the author not take himself to be doing this; rather that he take himself to be satisfying the sayso axiom D. It is not impossible that this is what happens. Perhaps literary authorship is indeed a kind of delusion in which, in thinking that he is making it all up, an author chances upon a set of antecedently constituted facts, which deluded readers, in their turn, take as facts constituted by the author. The delusional theory of literary creativity cannot be dismissed out of hand. For one thing, it is almost certainly the only safe harbour for Meinongians. However, perhaps one might be permitted to observe that, true or false, the delusional theory must be the most rococo theory of literary creativity on record.[45]

The nuclear-nonnuclear distinction is fundamental to the Meinongian approach to *fictional* impossibilia. What is wanted is a conception of the logically impossible whose positive instantiation does no violence to the law of noncontradiction. Accordingly, that the round square is both round and square implies that it is both round and not round and square and not square. But "x is round and not round" is formalized not as "x is round and $\sim x$ is round", but as "x is round and *neg* x is round". Since "x is round and *neg* x is round" does not imply "x is round and $\sim x$ is round", the round square may safely be constituted with no disturbance to the law. Since fictional objects are special cases of Meinongian objects, they too are subject to these same constraints. While some fictional objects are *impossibilia*, the law of noncontradiction remains intact.

As we have seen, other theories of the fictional allow for logically impossible fictional objects without the necessity to call upon a distinction between sentence-negation and predicate-complementation. In these cases, a preferred device is the fictive sentence operator T^F ("It is true in story F that ... "). T^F operates somewhat like a modal operator. It allows not only chat

$$T^F(S)$$

and

1. $T^F(\sim S)$

but also that

2. $T^F(S \wedge \sim S)$

---

[45]When we were considering pretense theories in the manner of Walton and Lewis, we reflected on the possibility that in writing *Don Quixote*, Cervantes was deluding himself that he was not pretending to tell the truth. The delusionality posited by the present case is oppositely directed. What is now under the glass is whether, by Meinongian lights, Cervantes was deluding himself in thinking that he *wasn't* telling the truth.

none of which violates the law of noncontradiction. It will not have escaped notice that Meinongians such as Routley and Jacquette are also drawn to a device something like the fictive operator, expressed by the clause "According to the story [ies] of so-and-so it is true that ... ". With this at hand, it is difficult to see why fictional *sentence*-contradictions cannot also be allowed, since they are expressible in the form

4. According to the story [ies] of so-and-so it is true that $S \wedge \sim S$.

On the face of it, sentences embodying the Routley modality are sentences that acknowledge the authority of axiom D, the author's sayso axiom. If that were actually so, then sentential contradictions are true *in fiction,* and are so without disturbing the repose of the non-ontradiction law. Certainly such would be the dominant view of the contradiction about Keith being elected and not elected President in one and the same election. But in the hands of Meinongians, Keith is an item subject to whatever constraints are imposed on all objects by Meinong's theory. One is that in *no* sense does any object violate the law of noncontradiction. So it is pre-determined that if indeed Keith is a Meinongian object, Keith was not concurrently elected and not elected President, notwithstanding that precisely this is what happened in *A Sound of Thunder.* Accordingly, the truth of "According to Bradbury's story it is true that Keith was elected and not elected President" is wholly irrelevant to what Keith did or did not do. But if that is so, the Routleyan device "according to the story [ies] of so-and-so, it is true that ..." is *also* inert in the context of symmetrical relations that lose their symmetry in fictional contexts. This takes us back four-square to the sayso axiom. Not only do authors not validate contradictory goings-on among the fictional, there is nothing whatever that they make true of them. What, then, is to be said about the asymmetry between it being true of Holmes that he lived in London, yet not true of London that this is where Holmes lived? The original intuition of [Woods, 1969] comes close to being right for Meinongians. For, by Meinongian lights, Holmes is constituted by his properties, and London by its properties. Holmes is constituted in part by the relational property of living in London, but London's counterpart property is not that of having been lived in by Holmes. It is rather the property of having been *represented* as having been lived in by Holmes. There appears to be a general rule for this.

PROPOSITION 25 (Asymmetries). *For any x and y, if x is a fictional object and y a real object, then if it is constitutive of y that it is represented as bearing R to x, then it is constitutive of x that it does bear R to y.*

As was originally surmised, we now have the wherewithal to represent in a natural way the intuition that, whereas Holmes lived in London, he really didn't. True by the author's sayso are

5. Holmes lived in London.

6. London is where Holmes lived.

History-constitutive by the author's sayso is

7. Holmes lived in London.

History-constitutive by the *up-shot*[46] of the author's sayso is the sentence

7. London is represented as the place where Holmes lived.

But what is *not* history-constitutive by the author's sayso or its upshot is

8. London is where Holmes lived.

4.2.3 What authors create

The Meinongian ontological constraints have the force of restricting an author's creative wherewithal to making stories rather than making true the propositions which the story advances. So constrained, authors create neither their objects nor the truths about them. Authors create *stories* about such objects in which various such truths are *told* of them. Accordingly,

PROPOSITION 26 (Meinongian creativity). *Given that fictional objects are Meinongian objects and that what is true of them are Meinongian truths, an author's creative endeavour is wholly restricted to making fictions of such objects by the telling of such truths.*

COROLLARY 26(a) Fictional creativity has neither ontological nor alethic import. Therefore, it is necessary to read "T^F" more on the model of "according to the Associated Press" rather than on the model of "according to the Supreme Court".

With Proposition 26 in hand, Meinongians would appear to have the wherewithal to answer the objection that in their failure to satisfy axiom D, Meinongian theories are just wrong. For it now be rejoined, with some plausibility, that, as we presently have it, there is something quite right about D and yet also something wrong. What is right about it is that there is something that the author freely creates. What is wrong about it is the presumption that what it creates are objects and truths about them, when in fact all that it creates are *stories*.

This is a powerful suggestion. It has an unmistakable strategic appeal, and it generalizes in interesting ways. Not only does it offer a principled basis for rejecting the intuition embedded in axiom D, it also tells equally against what many regard as the foundational contrast for a logic of fiction, the contrast between non-existents and nonesuches, and the allied distinction between bet-sensitivity and its bet-insensitivity. On the present suggestion there *is* indeed a distinction between the present king of France and Sherlock Holmes. In the old way of thinking, the contrast was ontological. Nothing whatever is denoted by "the present king of France", whereas Sherlock Holmes is a somebody who happens not to exist. What is more, rooted in these ontological arrangements are explanations of additional epistemic and semantic commonplaces. We *know* who Holmes is and what he did and suffered, but concerning the present king of France, there is nothing to *be* known. Sherlock Holmes is a *well-individuated* entity, whereas with the present king of France, there is nothing that begins to count as individuating. Sherlock Holmes manages a brisk

---

[46]Upshot is transfictive. The sentence, "London is represented as the place where Holmes lived" neither occurs in the text of any Holmes story nor is inferable from the sentences that do. It is inferable, in fact, from our knowledge that Doyle borrowed London for a guest-appearance in his stories.

trade with the truth values, *truth* and *falsity* (both of them), whereas the present king of France is paradigmatic occasion of truth-valuelessness.

Might there not, however, be another way of explaining these contrasts without the necessity of positing an ontic chasm between Sherlock Holmes and the present king of France? As Slater suggests (also Griffin), the chief difference between the two lies in the *contingent* fact that there are stories about the one and, so far, none about the other. They are the source of what is known (and knowable) about Holmes, they are what makes for Holmes' individuation, and they are what constitutes what is true of him. If there are explanations that we were prepared to accept, then a number of previous criticisms would lapse. In particular, it might now be possible to rehabilitate accounts of fiction in whose base logics the ontic contrast between Holmes and the rootless monarch is not honoured — whether free logics, epsilon calculi, supervaluational logics or Meinongian logics. True, the distinction between the two would have to be drawn somewhere; but presumably this would be taken care of once the story component is folded into the base logic.

Axiom A embodies the powerful intuition that what sets Holmes part from the present king of France is that "Holmes" refers to Holmes and "the present king of France" refers to nothing. Accordingly, there is such a thing as Holmes, but no such thing as the present king of France. If this is so, if this is indeed the difference we are questing after, it certainly *looks* like an ontic difference. There *are* things that don't exist. Holmes is one of them. The present king of France (if the *façon de parler* may be allowed) is not. If the explanations presently proposed were allowed to stand, it would appear that axiom A has lost its moorings. Whether this is actually so is a matter to which we shall return. Suffice it to say for now that

PROPOSITION 27 (Doubting the axioms). *As the conceptual account of the fictional evolves and deepens, the idea that the intuitive axioms are somehow sacrosanct loses some of its original luster.*

4.2.4 Worlds

[Jacquette, 1996] contains a general account of mixed sentences, in which Parsons' contrast between "native" and "immigrant" objects is put to good use. Migrancy is a considerable occurrence in fiction. Examples abound.

> We may think of Socrates in Aristophanes' *The Clouds*, Napoleon and the Battle of Borodino in Tolstoy's *War and Peace*, De Soto and La Salle and the conquest of New Spain in Edward Dahlberg's *The Sorrows of Priapus* (p. 258).

A further example is Democritus of Abdera, confined by Dante in the *Inferno* to an upper circle of hell. Migrants are objects depicted in fiction. It is the real Democritus, rather than a fictional character of the same name, who occurs in Dante's poem. Being thus depicted is one of the real Democritus' nuclear properties, as proposed in [Woods, 1969].

Democritus has the converse intentional nuclear property of being supposed by Dante (and Dante's readers) to occupy an upper circle of hell [Jacquette, 1996, 259].

According to Jacquette, we must say that

In creating a work of fiction, the author freely invents an alternative incomplete so-being for immigrant existent and native or immigrant nonexistent objects relative to a particular story-context or fictional world (p. 259).

Fictional worlds? A story is a fictional world? Perhaps when speaking in the casual ways of light conversation this can be said. Can it also be said with deliberate philosophical intent? No. Jacquette's logic for *Meinonge* contains a modal fragment, and rightly. If the golden mountain is golden and a mountain, then we may safely presume that it is possibly golden and possibly a mountain. If something is possibly golden, then we may safely suppose that it is not the case that it is necessarily not the case that it is golden. Jacquette adapts a standard Kripke semantics for the modal expressions of his logic. It is a semantics in which the modalities are conceived of in Abelardian fashion. Something is possibly true at a world when it is true in at least one world possible with respect to it. Something is necessarily true at a world when it is false in every world possible relative to it. At the core of this treatment is the primitive concept of possible worlds and an alternativeness relation varying through the standard relational properties of reflexivity, symmetry, transitivity and extendability. In some treatments of fiction, the careers of fictional characters play out in fictional worlds. For some theorists, fictional worlds are proper subsets of possible worlds. For others they are disjoint from them. On this latter view, what distinguishes a possible world from a fictional world is that fictional worlds can accommodate *impossibilia*, and possible worlds cannot. In some approaches, fictional worlds overlap with what modal logicians call *nonnormal* worlds. Nonnormal worlds are worlds in which everything is possibly possible and nothing is necessary (and the necessitation rule fails).

As a technical device, the notion of possible worlds has proved all but indispensable for the mathematical logic of the alethic modalities of necessity and possibility. It is well to bear in mind that giving a conceptually adequate elucidation of the idea of possible worlds is *not* a prime target of any known — or foreseeable — modal mathematical logic. Modal logicians have the same *primary* targets as classical logicians. They too, want to know what entailment is, and logical truth and consistency. Their difference is that modal logicians want to know how these properties fit languages enriched by the addition of modal expressions. It comes as no setback to these ambitions that the very idea of a possible world is the centre of a vigorous philosophical dissensus. In a recently published primer on nonclassical logics, Graham Priest touches on the several points of contention in this debate. He allows that

The preceding considerations hardly settle the matter of the nature of possible worlds. There are many other suggested answers (most of which are some variation on one or other of the themes that I have already mentioned); and there are many objections to the suggestions I have raised, other than the ones I have given, as well as possible replies to the objections I have raised; philosophers can have hours of fun with possible worlds. This will do for the present though [Priest, 2001, 32].[47]

Of course it will *do*. The mathematical logics of the modals are logics of entailment and logical truth, and the like. Since these properties are now definable for modal languages, *some* attention must be given to how modal expressions might be interpreted. But the treatment of modal terms has in such logics about the same importance as the treatment of reference in the *Begriffsschrift*. In both cases they are there rather more as instrumental necessities than full-bore, conceptually adequate analyses. There is another way of saying the same thing. No one wanting to have a rich and conceptually robust analysis of reference would dream of finding it in the *Begriffsschrift*. Equally, no one wanting a rich and conceptually robust analysis of possible worlds would dream of finding it in S5 (or worse, S2).

We have been at some pains to argue that what is urgently required for a credible logic of fiction is a logic that embeds a conceptually adequate — a rich and robust philosophical analysis — of the concept of fictionality. Any attempt at achieving such an analysis by way of the philosophically half-baked mathematician's device of possible worlds is asking for trouble. It is trouble born of an over-careless fondness for devices that chance to be lying about. It suggests the menacing presence of *Make-Do*.

According to Jacquette,

> The semantic device of fictional world-indexing in modal Meinongian logic implements the story-contextual interpretation of a fictional object's nuclear properties, so that by Kripke-style stipulation Democritus [according to Dante] languishes in the inferno, not in the actual world, but in an accessible fictional Meinongian world [1966, 259].

He adds,

> The same world-indexing requirements for transworld identity of existent and nonexistent native and immigrant Meinongian worlds of the modal Meinongian semantic model [1966, 259].

Actually, I think not.

PROPOSITION 28 (Good-bye to worlds). *All going possible worlds semantics leave a conceptually adequate logic of fiction significantly underdetermined. This being so, a number of our better-regarded candidates will have to be re-considered.*[48]

COROLLARY 28(a) If Proposition 28 is right, the disinclination to invoke a worlds semantics for fiction might well be attended by a corresponding inclination to reconsider the value of conceptualizing T^F as a modal operator.

---

[47]For the present? No; for the whole book, as it turns out.

[48]Not only Meinongian approaches but those of [Plantinga, 1974; Kaplan, 1973; Gabriel, 1979] and [Lewis, 1983]. The same is true of fictional worlds treatments in the manner of [Howell, 1979; Pavel, 1986] and [Woltersdorff, 1980]. In [Woltersdorff, 1980] fictional worlds are conjunctions of possible states of affairs and fictional characters, considered as kinds rather than individuals.

4.2.5 The incomplete and the impossible

It is clear from the literature that intuitions differ about the incompleteness and impossibility of fictional entities. But it may safely be said that anyone drawn to the view that fictional objects are incomplete should make a case for it, and that such a case would be at its most strong if it proceeded from an analysis of the concept of a fictional object. As even a casual review of the problem of maximal accounts makes plain, a good many of the attributes that readers ascribe to fictional characters are ascribed neither by fictive sentences nor by sentences in their deductive closures. So it is not just that either Holmes had an alimentary canal or lacked one; he *had* one (also ten toes, a mother and a brain stem). The problem begins to bite with properties that have no place in the maximal account, such as having had a tummy ache following Holmes' third-year birthday party. Of course, it might actually be the case with beings such as Holmes neither to have had nor to have been spared such unpleasantness. But what would be lost if we treated these cases in more familiar ways, in the way for example that we do with Julius Caesar? Here we haven't the slightest difficulty in representing his incompleteness as epistemic rather than ontic. Of course, we say, either Caesar had such a tummy-ache or was spared it, but which it is we'll never know. What is it about the nature of the fictional that obviates this same kind of epistemic explanation? It cannot, for one thing, be that by their very natures, fictional objects are resistant to familiar inferences or, roughly, inferences from what Lewis calls "collective belief worlds" [Lewis, 1983, 273]. This cannot be, since familiar inference is precisely what maximal accounts brim with. So Holmes has an alimentary canal, since Holmes is a human animal and that's what human animal's have.

However we resolve to handle this question, we should again note that it is *pre-settled* in the logic of Meinongian objects. If we allow that fictional objects are Meinongian, then the incompleteness of the fictional is established. But it was settled by what Meinong thought objects could and could not be, not by what he thought fictional objects had to be. In choosing a Meinongian account of objects as our base logic for fiction, we risk miring the logic of fiction at level 1. For while the logic of *Meinonge* is backed by a rich conceptual analysis of objecthood (and so makes a claim on level 3), the analysis of *Meinonge* might not suffice for the *fictional*. For this reason it is insufficient to have the ontic incompleteness of the fictional settled by what is not, after all, a theory of fictions.

Another notable constraint which a Meinongian logic also predetermines precludes even the fictional violation of the law of noncontradiction. Virtually everyone who writes about the logic of fiction is a *consistentist*. For them, it goes without saying that the law of noncontradiction is unbreachable. It is not in the slightest degree unusual that this should also be Meinong's view. Dialetheism (the doctrine that some contradictions are true as well as false) is the furthest thing from Meinong's mind. Equally, however, many who write about the logic of fiction are open to examples of the Keith kind, and ready to allow that Keith's concurrent election and non-election is a sentential contradiction that is true *in fiction*. As we have noted, one of the prime motives for introducing fictive qualifiers T^F into the analysis of fiction is to accommodate just such a possibility. So, whereas

$$\text{Keith was elected} \land \sim \text{Keith was elected}$$

cannot be true,

T^F (Keith was elected $\wedge \sim$ Keith was elected)

is true and was *made* true by Bradbury's story. Meinongians such as Routley and Jacquette appear to give the nod to fictive qualifiers. Routley's "According to the stories of so-and-so" seems clearly to function as T^F does. Jacquette is even more emphatic, apparently.

> As a story is created, the author determines by free assumption the nuclear properties of its characters ... The author stipulates what is supposed to be true of the people, places, and events of the narrative, which by the Meinongian [principle of the] independence of so-being *makes it true that these fictions have the nuclear properties bestowed on them by their creator.* (p. 259. Emphasis added.)

We have already noted the ambiguity of this claim. For those drawn to axiom D, the author's sayso axiom, Jacquette's words invite the interpretation that authors create the objects that their stories are about, and that authors make the sentences that are true of them true. On the contrary, as we have seen, Jacquette is a Meinongian. Holmes is constituted independently of Doyle's stories, as were whatever is true of him. Doyle's "free assumption" does not extend to any object that isn't already available — or to any proposition not already true of it. And it is this, precisely, that explains why neither Doyle nor Bradbury nor whomever else can make it true by free assumption that T^F(Keith was elected $\wedge \sim$ Keith was elected.) In fact,

PROPOSITION 29 (The concurrence of T^F-truth and truth). *In a Meinongian logic of fiction, for all sentences S, $\ulcorner T^F(S)\urcorner$ is true only if S is true.*

COROLLARY 29(a)   Accordingly, in Meinongian logics of fiction the operator T^F is semantically inert, which is a further reason not to construe them as modal operators.

Here, too, we are met with the problem of which is the tail and which is the dog, and which wags which. If sentential contradictions are to be barred from fiction, it is natural to prefer that this be justified by how fiction is rather than by how Meinongian objects are. Meinong's view is that if we allow contradictions to be true in fiction, we must allow them to be true without qualification. Proposition 26 tells us quite generally that this is precisely what a Meinongian theory of fictional truth does require. So we have two options in our quest to accommodate Holmes. We can capitulate to the Meinongians. Or we can look elsewhere.

We have come to a point at which Jacquette's, Walton's and Lewis' quite different positions (see [Jacquette, 2001], acquire a degree of convergence. It is a consequence of Walton's position that only real objects can be fictional (e.g., London), whereas no object whatever is Holmes. Likewise, it is a consequence of Jacquette's position that the only truths that can be fictional truths are non-fictional truths. A further point of convergence involves Lewis. Like Jacquette, Lewis is adamant that no sentence of the form $\ulcorner T^F(S \wedge \sim S)\urcorner$ is ever true. It is easy to see what draws Jacquette to this view. It is entirely a matter of his pre-commitments. Jacquette commits the analysis of the fictional to the already standing logic of *Meinonge*. The logic of *Meinonge* is a consistentist logic; hence no sentence of the form $\ulcorner S \wedge \sim S \urcorner$ is true there. By Proposition 26, for any S

such that ⌜$T^F(S)$⌝ is true, S itself must be true. Anyone thinking that the exclusion of ⌜$T^F(S \wedge \sim S)$⌝ from a theory of fiction is just a mistake can pin the blame of Jacquette's mistake on his having insufficiently adapted the logic of *Meinonge*. In Lewis' case, it is not so clear as to where the blame should be laid. Lewis proposes to handle the problem of apparently true contradictions in fiction in one or other of two ways. By the method intersection, let F be an inconsistent fiction and R a consistent revision of it. Then ⌜$T^F(S)$⌝ is true if and only if S occurs in every R of F. Where this method employs the device of revision, the *method of union* pivots on fragmentation. Where t is an inconsistent story, C is some consistent part of it. Then ⌜$T^F(S)$⌝ is true if and only if S occurs in it at least one C of F.

A good many of Lewis' critics see the expulsion of contradictions by these methods as *ad hoc* [Currie, 1990, 69]. Others complain that it mangles our concept of the fictional to insist on these exclusions [Byrne, 1993, 26]. In his agile defence of Lewis against these charges, Richard Hanley allows that

> If it's possible for it to be fictional that a contradictory-proposition is fictional, then it *might* by Lewis' own analyses be possible for a contradictory proposition to be fictional [Hanley, 2004, 120].

Hanley considers whether this possibility might be confirmed by a thought-experiment in the manner of [Currie, 1990, 69], in which we suppose that there is a story in which someone refutes Gödel's theorem. Currie thinks this example is decisive against Lewis. Who would not agree? Not Hanley. He thinks that in imagining that there might be such a story, it is as likely that one is begging the question against Lewis in calling it a story as it is that in that imagined story a contradiction is true. What Hanley demands is an *extant* story in which contradictions are made true.

Hanley's charge of question-begging is hardly to be credited. There is no known account of it in which that is what Currie is up to. In its most general sense one party X begs the question against another party Y if and only if X adopts as a premiss in his argument against Y a proposition P in fulfillment of the following four conditions.

1. P is damaging to Y's case.

2. P is unconceded by Y.

3. P is not a consequence of what Y does concede.

4. P cannot be attributed to Y as a default.[49]

Hanley is here standing in for Lewis. He represents Lewis as holding that it is a condition on storyhood that no contradiction is true in it. For Currie simply to say, "Well here's a story with a true contradiction in it", would indeed be to beg the question. But suppose Currie's reasoning were, "There is a proposition that is in the presumptive closure of other

---

[49]For example, P is not in the collective belief world of X and Y, P is not a matter of common knowledge, P is not in the presumptive closure of propositions that Y expressly concedes.

things you have said about fiction, namely, the "story" imagined in the Currie thought-experiment is actually a story. And since it is a story in which a contradiction is true, it cannot be the case that contradictions can't be true in stories."

It is true, of course, that determining what is the presumptive closure of David Lewis' concessions is not an exact science. Far easier to determine what is in the presumptive closure of Hanley's beliefs. Hanley concedes that Lewis' no-contradiction policy might well fail should there be an actual piece of fiction in which someone refutes Gödel's theorem. Hanley considers a number of candidates: *Flatland, Peter Rabbit, At Swim-Two-Birds, Sylvan's Box*, the Holmes stories themselves.[50] One could reflect on these rejections with profit. But there is no need. Hanley makes it clear that if there were an extant story in which Gödel's proof is refuted, then Lewis' constraint would be imperiled. This is extremely helpful. It tells us how to proceed against Lewis.

PROPOSITION 30 (Contra Lewis). *Find an author who will make it the case that there is an extant story that executes the story-line of Currie's thought experiment — that is, making it the case that such a story exists by writing it.*

Suppose Hanley (or Lewis) were now to say, "But you've begged the question". Perhaps that would be the point to move on to other things.

Incompleteness is a further point of convergence between Jacquette and Lewis. Consider the sentence, "Inspector Lestrade has blood type O". Both authors allow that it might be the case that "T^F(Lestrade has type-O-blood)" is false and that "T^F (Lestrade does not have type-O blood)" is false. But they won't allow that "T^F (Lestrade has type-O blood ∨ ~ Lestrade has type-O blood)" is false. Both are sufficiently classical logicians to want it left undisturbed that if $\ulcorner T^F(S \vee \sim S)\urcorner$ is always true then $\ulcorner T^F(S \wedge \sim S)\urcorner$ is always false. We have surmised that Jacquette's refusal of true contradictions in fiction flow from his pre-commitment to a Meinongian ontology. We have complained that this is an arrangement in which the tail of the receiving theory wags the dog of fiction. Perhaps this was wrong. Perhaps there is another explanation that applies to Jacquette and Lewis alike. They are determined that Lestrade's indeterminancy of blood-type not overturn to the law of excluded middle, and they are sufficiently classical about logic to want the tie between excluded middle and noncontradiction to stand. Whatever we might think of such an explanation, we now find ourselves at a point at which the convergence of the two accounts blows apart. Jacquette negotiates the problem of indeterminacy without loss of excluded middle by the device of predicate complementation. Lewis shuns the device (or anyhow does not avail himself of it) and makes do with restrictions on closure, betokened by the operator T^F. There is a marked difference between the two. That the falsity of $\ulcorner T^F(S)\urcorner$ and $\ulcorner T^F(negS)\urcorner$ does not overturn $\ulcorner T^F(S \vee \sim S)\urcorner$ is made intelligible by the semantics of *neg* and ~. That the falsity of the same pair does not overturn the law is also said to lie in the providence of T^F. Perhaps it does. But it is unclear as to how.

---

[50]Also to be considered is "The Mischief of Ricardo Bosque", by Djaitch da Bloo, reprinted in [Woods, 2003] at pages 226-227.

4.3 The S-model

The earliest published version of stipulationism in the Western tradition is *Genesis*. In it the Almighty *speaks* the world into being. In the beginning was the Word. No other creation story comes so close to making it literally the case that the Creator is the author of our being. In the holy writings it is also said that humans were created in the image of God. Nearly all theologians agree that, whatever the details, the fact of mankind in God's image is constituted by the sharing of certain attributes which, in the first order of things, would be considered distinctive of the divinity. Perhaps we might think that the authorship of truths is one of those similarities. Well, this is theology, and what is wanted here is logic.

Mathematics is a good place to start. Mathematicians are dab hands at speaking things into being. This, anyhow, is a fact of such presumptive weight as to stand as a pre-analytic datum for philosophical theories of mathematics. As such, it must receive the endorsement of theory or cause must be shown as to why it should be over-ridden by it. In the century just past, perhaps the most aggressive sponsor of this view is Hilbert. Hilbert famously proposed that "if it can be proved that the attributes assigned to a concept can never lead to a contradiction by application of a finite number of logical processes, I say that the mathematical existence of the concept ... is thereby proved."[51] By the existence of a concept K of something x, Hilbert means the existence of that thing *as conceived of as falling under* K. While there is room to interpret these lines in the manner of Meinong — in which case every (consistent) descriptive term would be guaranteed a denotation — it lies closer to Hilbert's actual practice to take to heart the qualification, "the attributes assigned [by the mathematician] to the concept".[52] In that case, Hilbert's view is that when a mathematician asserts or presupposes the existence of a mathematical object, it is necessary and sufficient for the truth of that assertion or that presupposition that the purported object be provably consistent. On this non-Meinongian interpretation, it is clear that stipulation plays a central role in Hilbert's philosophy of mathematics. A mathematical object exists if a mathematician consistently says so or if what he says consistently presupposes it.

Fictionalism in the philosophy of mathematics has a larger literature than can be done justice to here. Some commentators see [Vaihinger, 1935] as providing a general philosophical background, but this is far from a universally held position. Among more or less contemporary investigators, one could mention, among several others, [Balaguer, 1996; Bunge, 1997; Field, 1980; Hodes, 1984; Korner, 1967; Resnik, 1997; Tharp, 1989; Tiles, 1998; Torretti, 1981; von Freytag-Loringhoff, 1951; Wagner, 1982; Wang, 1986] and [Thomas, 2000; 2005]. It is sometimes held by mathematical fictionalists that the way to proceed with a fictionalist theory of mathematics is to appropriate, and, if necessary, adapt, a good theory of literary fiction. This, again, is the *Literary Primacy Thesis,* called into question in Proposition 5, and to which we shall return in due course.[53]

---

[51] Quoted in [Davis, 2000, 90-91].
[52] Quoted in [Davis, 2000, 90].
[53] See, for example, [Hoffman, 1999]. See also [Resnik, 1997, 184ff]: "Positing mathematical objects involves nothing more mysterious than the ability to write novels ...".

As we have said, truth-by-stipulation lies open to varying degrees of ontological audacity. At its most careful, stipulating that P is making it the case that P is *true in some system* Σ within which the theorist makes his stipulation. Thus P is Σ-true and correspondingly describes objects that exist-in-Σ. Hyphenation is a wholly natural way of marking the stipulator's ontological caution. It is also much the standard way of sparing the teeming pluralism of present-day logic from the inconsistencies that would flow from the unhyphenated truth of all their contending inventions.

Still, as any student of even the recent history of mathematics knows full well, it is not uncommon that a portion or entire branch of mathematics might originate with a body of hyphenated truths sanctioned by stipulation together with their consequences under agreed proof procedures, only in the fullness of time to lose their hyphens en route to an established canonicity. The suppression of hyphens is facilitated by two conditions in particular. One is the omnipresence of *the realist stance*. The other is acceptance by the research community, driven by the dynamic of *epistemic integration*.

Re-visiting our earlier example, in the immediate aftermath of the death of naive set theory, Russell sought for a consistent rehabilitation of it [Russell, 1903]. Essential to his purpose was a distinction between philosophical and mathematical analyses. Russell thought that the paradox of sets that bears his name made a philosophical analysis of sethood impossible. This was because the paradox demonstrated that the very concept of set was inconsistent. This left mathematical analysis, which is what Russell actually resorted to. In its most basic sense, mathematical analysis is nominal definition, which is a form of stipulation.

Russell, in effect, saw that stipulations produced hyphenated truths, and that communal acceptance eliminates them. When this happens, as appears to have been the case with ZFC, the theory in question is, or approximates to being, a received theory. A *received theory* is a set of stipulated truths, and others proved from them, whose acceptance by the appropriate disciplinary community or disciplinary culture, induces in such groups hyphenation-blindness. Typically, community-acceptance embeds a successful attempt to integrate the hypthenated truths in an established branch of knowledge. Also integral to this blindness is the sheer psychological allure of the realist stance, abetted by the conditions under which later generations are *introduced* to such truths (they are introduced to them as objective mathematical facts). It is a powerful leaning. Stipulated truths are hyphenated truths. If, as sometimes happens, these become received truths, those who see them so fail to see their hyphens; in fact, fail to see their hyphens even if they are made aware of the received theory's stipulative origins. In this some may detect grave defections from rationality and honesty. We see the psychological dominance of the realist stance.[54] Realism, we said, is an especially efficient way of paying attention. Beings like us find it as natural as breathing to experience the world as external; and even when, in particular ranges of cases, it is experienced internally, the internalities are experienced as occurrences in a more capacious and embracing externality. Can't-help-it-realism is not

---

[54]Hyphenation-blindness generally comes in degrees. From the stipulatively bold "true-in-S" (e.g., "true-in-intuitionistic logic"), there is a further stage, which we might call adverbilization (e.g., "intuistionistically true"), thence to adjectivism ("an intuitionistic truth"), and finally, in the absence of rival abjectivisms, we have substantiation (e.g., "true").

a metaphysical theory. It is a habit of mind. Judging from its historical circumstances, its mathematical influence is often more extreme than in fictional cases. In each case, we tend to be Barconists; that is, given truths in the form

3. $T^F \exists x(\ldots x \ldots)$

we find it natural to reformulate them as truths in the form

4. $\exists x T^F(\ldots x \ldots)$.

In one good meaning of the term, we *take* (3) as (4). But if the actual evolution of ZFC is anything to go on, truths in the form

3'. $ZFC\ \exists x(\ldots x \ldots)$

are now taken as

4'. $\exists x(\ldots x \ldots)$

in which one finds no occurrence of the *ZFC*-operator or of *ZFC*-hyphenation. Twice-over this should give us pause. Even in the case of something as settled and mainstream as *ZFC*, perhaps (4Σ) is a bit much. It is more than a bit much for fiction.

There are two main ways of being a Hilbertian stipulationist. One can hold that stipulations give rise to *bona fide* objects. Or one can make the lesser claim that stipulations make *reference* possible. Roughly speaking, the first way embeds a *de re* fondness for (4). The second holds back in the *de dicto* manner of (3). Each possibility has something to be said for it. In the first instance, except for their discursive origins, stipulated objects are on a par with any other created thing, whether widget or skyscraper. If pressed to explain how speaking such objects into existence is possible, the stipulationist may plead that it lies in the nature of (certain kinds of) mathematical objects to be created thus. Of course, in so saying he sets himself for Molière's dormitive virtue riposte. But aside from that, there is something rather impressive about his position. He can attach his stipulationism to the dominant view of reference, the causal theory. If reference to a thing depends on one's being an element in a chain of events, preceding links of which have had causal contact with it [Kripke, 1980], the condition is met here. For this is a view on which the object in question has a causal origination, and whose creation is a directly witnessable event.

The second is a more circumspect alternative. It imbibes the ontological caution of something like substitutional quantification. It preserves the intuition that mathematical fictions leave no metaphysical footprints. And, in seeking to preserve the intuition that sentences ostensibly about such objects can nevertheless be true, it tries to have the very cake that it eats.[55] In effect, it shifts the Hilbertian emphasis from objects to sentences, decreeing that anything provable about them is true. As a bonus, it also attaches itself to a Fregian notion of reference, according to which the reference of a term is determined

---

[55]Cf. Azzouni's *thin posits x*, concerning which 'there are *x*s' can be true without there being *x*s [Azzouni, 1994; 2004].

by its *Sinn*, its sense, and it does so in ways that encourage a needed refinement of the general doctrine. Let '*a*' be a purported mathematical object, and let *P* be the set of its provable sentences. Let *j* be the point at which *a* and *P* make their way into working mathematics. Then at *j* the sense of '*a*' is fixed by some subset of *P*. If sense determines reference, the reference of '*a*' is set by *P*.

One of the complaints made by causalists against Frege's account of reference is that it leaves it inadequately unexplained as to how it can be that referring terms actually pick out objects. Frege thinks that one doesn't understand a referring term '*r*' unless one understands who (or what) *r* is, where *r* is whatever, in the context at hand, '*r*' uniquely denotes. If the task is to know what the reference of the term is, it is clearly insufficient to understand the ordinary meaning of it (if it has one). One perfectly well understands the meaning of "the present king of France" even though it is a referential disaster. What *Sinn* contributes is, in the context at hand, are bundles of true sentences which, if simultaneously satisfiable at all, could only be uniquely satisfied. Thus those sentences make it possible to know who or what the reference of '*r*' is. Since there are no true sentences about the present king of France, there is nothing to constitute the reference of "the present king of France". So it is the lack of such truths, not the lack of an object, that makes "the present king of France" a referential wipe-out. It is the same way with "Elizabeth II". Knowing who its reference is made possible by relevant chunks of her biography — her *Sinn*. It may be directly necessary for the existence of those particular truths that the reference of "Queen Elizabeth" be a real object, but it is not *directly* necessary to knowing who the reference of "Elizabeth II" is that Elizabeth II be a real object. It is precisely this that the present, more circumspect, form of stipulation exploits. In providing a common explanation of knowing what the references of, say, "the smallest transfinite cardinal" and "Elizabeth II" are, it places the question of the criterial importance of objecthood where it belongs, in the theory of truth.

On Frege's approach, reference is likened to a function, with terms as arguments and objects as values. The theory is meant to answer two questions.

1. What does it take to understand '*r*''s reference.

2. What does it take for '*r*' to pick out *r*?

A common part of the answers to these questions is *Sinn*. Concerning 1), it is insufficient that I understand the meaning of '*r*'. It is also required that I be acquainted with '*r*''s *Sinn*. Concerning 2), it is insufficient that '*r*' has an understandable reference (*Sinn*) in order that '*r*' refer to *r*. I know what the reference of 'Sherlock Holmes' is and I know that no object is denoted by it. The *Sinn* of '*r*' does not suffice for it to be true that *r* is the object '*r*' denotes. *Sinn* is necessary for it to be the fact that '*r*' denotes *r*, *if* indeed *r* is the object '*r*'denotes. By these lights, knowing '*r*''s reference is one thing, and knowing '*r*''s referent is another. In Frege's treatment the distinction is overlooked. Frege wanted to preserve the intuition that '*r*' lacks a reference if it lacks a referent, i.e., and object which '*r*' picks out. One of the valuable byproducts of the problem of fictionality is the ease with which it makes the present distinction a useful one to have. For we now have the wherewithal to make a threefold contrast between 'the present king of France', 'Sherlock Holmes' and 'Saul A. Kripke'.

1. 'the present king of France' lacks *Sinn* and therefore lacks reference and therefore lacks a referent.

2. 'Sherlock Holmes' has *Sinn* and therefore has reference, but, given its *Sinn*, lacks a referent.

3. 'Saul A. Kripke' is a triple-threat. It has *Sinn*, reference and a referent.

Does this beg the question against Frege? Frege thought that reference was functional and that values had to be well-individuated objects. On a quick reading, it may seem that it is precisely this feature that our present suggestion over-runs. The appearance is misleading. In Frege's theory, whenever '*r*' refers, it must be true that

- $\exists ! x$ ('*r*' refers to x).

Reference for Frege is quantificationally rooted, and uniquely so. The same, however, is true for fiction. It is part of the *Sinn* of 'Sherlock Holmes' that it refers to a character generated by a fictional text. Accordingly,

- $\exists ! x T^F$ ('*r*' refers to x)

We see in this trichotomy reason to invoke the distinction between objectual and substitutional quantification. In the standard case, the quantification gives an object *to which* '*r*' refers. In the fictional case, the quantification gives an object *in which* '*r*' refers. So in both cases, objects are essential to reference, albeit objects of a markedly different kind.

It is easy to see that substitutional quantification also extends a welcoming hand to all forms of *de re* discourse about the fictional. In

4. $\exists x T^F(\ldots x \ldots)$

we have *de re* attribution without the objects. Instantiation restores T^F to left-most position. Every truth about the values of (4)'s quantifier is a truth *de dicto*.

For good or ill, substitutional quantification gives a theory of truth without objects. It is not everyone's cup of tea, needless to say. But is very far from being dismissible out of hand; there is a lot that counts in its favour. (See, e.g. [McKeon, 2005]). It is at least a theory with legs, and as such is streets ahead of any logic of fiction yet devised.

Earlier we mentioned the perplexing fact that beings like us are capable of believing things we know to be false to be true of the fictional and of being emotionally stirred by things that we know didn't occur. There is a tendency among literary theorists to liken these phenomena to delusions or other forms of mental relapse. It takes little reflection to see the inadequacy of such assumptions. If in watching a performance of Christopher Plummer as King lear, I slip into the delusion that this is all actually happening I cannot be said to be following the play. If, in the grip of the excitement at Reichenbach Falls, I lose all sight of its literary origins, I cannot be said to be understanding the story. It is true that an expertly performed play or an expertly crafted story is something that we can lose ourselves in. It is a condition of this happening that we understand the work that absorbs us. It is a condition on such understandings that in having them the works retain their recognizable fictionality. Interacting with a work of fiction is doing two things at once. It is believing things that one knows to be untrue and it is being moved by things that have not happened. So we speak of the things that we believe as holding in the story and of the things that move us as occurring there. Let us call such beliefs and such affects *double-aspected*. Accordingly,

PROPOSITION 31 (Essential double-aspectness). *It is a condition on one's understanding a work of fiction that the beliefs and emotions to which it gives rise are double-aspected.*

As it happens, it is an advantage rather than a liability, that a fictional name's *Sinn* should embody some sign of fictional origination. What this tells us in simple English is that you cannot know who Holmes is unless you know that he is fictional. Since this is tantamount to saying that you cannot know who Holmes is without knowing that he isn't anything, then

PROPOSITION 32 (The double-aspectness of *Sinn*). *Our understanding of the* Sinn *of fictional names is likewise double-aspected.*

Something like the distinction between the objectual and the referential senses of stipulationism attends the distinction between idealism and instrumentalism in the foundations of mathematics. The first term of the latter contrast is in play in the early debate over the philosophical legitimacy of the axiom of choice.

> On the one hand, metaphysical elements tinge the famous debate between Hadamard and French School of Baire, Borel and Lebesque — do sets exist objectively, independently of us, or do they exist only insofar as they have been defined or constructed by us? — in other words, there was a conflict between something like Robust Realism and a version of Idealism [Maddy, 2005, 355-356].

On the idealist approach, the objects of mathematics — sets, for example — are ideal objects, the fruit of the mathematicians' definitions. In one variation, sometimes called "conceptual realism", these are objects in the theorist's mind. It is possible in principle to be one or other of two kinds of mathematical idealist, or conceptual realist (shades of Kant). One might be an across-the-board idealist, holding that all mathematical objects are human intellectual artifacts. Or one might also take a realist position with regard to parts of mathematics and reserve one's idealist leanings for the more *recherché* bits. For instrumentalists, something like this latter distinction is mandatory. Some part P of mathematics is taken as privileged in some way, and some further part I — the instrumental part — is justified solely by the contributions it makes to proofs in P. One way of instantiating the $P-I$ divide is by taking P as finitistic mathematics in the sense of [Tait, 1981]. Thus finitism is number theory formalized in primitive recursive arithmetic PRA.[56] It is possible to proceed to I from P in two ways, instrumentally or idealistically.

> [W]e can add stronger arithmetical principles, which seems to amount to adding more induction, or we can first expand the language with variable for

---

[56]Either as an *equational* rendition or a *first order* theory. See here [Caldon and Ignjatovi, 2005].

new types of objects (e.g., sets) and then add new arithmetical principles for these objects [Caldon and Ignjatović, 2005, 779].

The second way is the way of idealism. It also flags an ambiguity in the word "instrumentalism." The second way is also the way of instrumentalism to the extent to which the contributions of its postulated objects to its I-rules is justified by the I-rules yield in *PRA*, the privileged part of mathematics. The first way is also the way of instrumentalism, but in a purer sense. Proof rules are mere instruments. If the contributions they make to *PRA* justify their use in I, then, since the rules introduce no new objects, their use is entirely as proof instruments. So, roughly speaking, the difference between an idealist instrumentalism and a pure instrumentalism in extending *PRA* to I is the difference between instrumentally successful rules that supplement the objects of *PRA* and instrumentally successful rules involving no objects not in *PRA*.

It is well to keep in mind that both idealistically instrumental and nominalistically instrumental sets of proof instruments are judged solely on the basis of their contributions to *PRA*. While it is possible to assimilate the stipulations of the S-model of fiction to either strand of this instrumentalism, there is nevertheless an over-arching dissimilarity that might tend to count against the S-model generically. In both forms, idealist or pure, the stipulations of I are justified by the extent to which they facilitate the demonstration of new facts about *PRA*. For this analogy to hold in the case of literary fictions, the stipulations of *The Hound of the Baskervilles* would be legitimized only by the extent that they facilitated the production of new facts about the world. Now it is quite true that the world is made different by the fact that Arthur Conan Doyle penned *The Hound of the Baskervilles*, as well as by the fact that it has had legions of readers and critics. But, in the general case, the truths that hold in *The Hound of the Baskervilles* don't hold in the world, and those that do hold in the world were not made so to do by *The Hound of the Baskervilles*. So a question for the S-theorist of fiction is wherein does the "justification" of the truths of *The Hound of the Baskervilles* lie?

Perhaps the dissimilarity might be discounted through judicious generalization. I is justified by the contribution it makes. What matters most is that it is a contribution, not where it is made. No one in his right mind thinks that the truths of *The Hound of the Baskervilles* make a contribution to our knowledge of the world (to the history of Dartmoor, for example). But they do make a story. *That* is their primary contribution; that is what they are *for*. As with mathematics, there are two ways in which one might be an instrumentalist about this. One might opt for idealism and ascribe to the author's stipulations not only the truths of *The Hound of the Baskervilles* but also some new objects to serve as their subjects. Alternatively, one might elect the course of pure or nominalistic instrumentalism, plumping for the idea that whereas *The Hound of the Baskervilles* is constituted by its author's stipulated truths, these are truths that — in the manner of substitutional quantification — require no objects other than names. Here again we see some convergence. In Waltonian versions of the *PMB*-model, there are no fictional objects. The same is true of purely instrumental versions of the S-model. In these variations, fiction leaves no metaphysical footprints. With regard to a story's characters, there is nothing there.

Unless the present discussion has been seriously wrong-headed, it would appear that we have ample grounds for proposing that

PROPOSITION 33 (Giving the nod to the S-model). *Of all the going approaches, there is a version of stipulationism that is best for literary fictions.*

PROPOSITION 34 (Quantification as substitutional). *In the variation that works for fiction, the S-model allows for* de re *quantification into fictional contexts, provided that quantification is substitutional.*

PROPOSITION 35 (Reference without referents). *In this same variation, the S-model is (as it were) tailor-madet for the distinction between a term's having a reference and its having a referent, and for the allied notion that a term's reference is set by its* Sinn, *and its referent, too, but only if it has one.*

5 MAXIMAL ACCOUNTS

Maximal accounts when adjoined to a text's fictive sentences give the full story that it tells. In most of the work done to date, conditions on maximality are usually thought of as given recursively by closure clauses on sets of fictive sentences. We are now in a position to see that this is a duly restrictive way in which to construe maximality, much in the way that the lingering preference for deductive closure is an unduly restrictive way to construe fictive closure. It goes without saying that maximality owes a good deal to what follows from what in fictional settings. It owes at least as much to background assumptions. Sets of background assumptions are what Lewis calls collective belief worlds. Its beliefs are those that everyone in the community shares, more or less everyone believes everyone shares, and so on. A community's background assumptions encompass what is "common knowledge" there, including its accumulated store of lore about what things are actually like. It includes the belief that Saul A. Kripke has an alimentary canal, because it is known that Saul A. Kripke is a human and that having alimentary canals is part of what humans are like. The beliefs in a community's background assumptions come in varying degrees of strength, but over all they reflect an interesting epistemic division. By and large the generalizations are held with greater confidence than its instantiations. This is as it should be, epistemically speaking.

These observations are designed to capture the following kind of situation. We know very well that it is generally (though not universally) true that Americans are not flat-earthers. We know every bit as well that Saul A. Kripke is an American. It does not follow that Kripke is not a flat-earther, but it is something that we may safely presume on sufferance. In other words, it is a *default* that Saul A. Kripke is not a flat-earther, whereas it is a *fact* that he is a human and a *fact*, albeit a *generic* one, that Americans aren't flat-earthers.[57] So we may say that "Saul A. Kripke is not a flat-earther" is in the *presumptive* closure of a beliefs shared by readers of this chapter, and many others besides.

---

[57]Concerning genericity, [Carlson and Pelletier, 1995] is required reading. See also [Gabbay and Woods, 2005, chapter 7]

A further feature of background assumptions is that they are largely tacit. No one thinks that it is realistic for anyone whose background is that of the readers of this chapter to set out to produce a complete inventory of it. At a certain level, therefore, it is true to say that it is epistemically indeterminate as to what the contents of one's background are. Hence an ambiguity in "know" presents itself. All sorts of things that I know (by common knowledge) I cannot enumerate or specify on demand, or perhaps ever. For those cases, I do not know what I know by common knowledge. To a degree, the tacitness of common knowledge is off-set by the efficacy of retrieval-to-surface mechanisms in beings like us. A cognitive economy of tacit knowledge is like a manufacturing or retail economy run on the principle of just-in-time. But even here elements of taciticity persist. In forming the belief that, Saul A. Kripke is presumably no flat-earther, the presence of the genericization that Americans aren't flat-earthers may itself be tacit, and usually is.

Background assumptions are an attempt to carve out a portion of a usually much larger set of background *facts*. Roughly speaking, the background facts of anything I chance to know about the world is how the world actually is, whether I know it or not. Common knowledge, therefore, is knowledge of a proper subset of background facts. As measured by our own common experience, both sets are vast — well-beyond our capacity for specific direct-command manipulation. In our common experience, we haven't the slightest difficulty in acknowledging their existence and their salience. In particular, we have little inclination to ontologize their epistemic indeterminacies, or to confuse, as mediaeval philosophers would say, *ordo cognescendi* with *ordo essendi*. Accordingly,

PROPOSITION 36 (The parasitism of fiction). *Except where the contrary is indicated by a story's fictive sentences, authors tacitly include in their maximal accounts (a) the background facts, e.g., facts as to how the world actually is, and (b) background beliefs, i.e., common knowledge shared by author and reader. What this shows is the extraordinary degree to which fiction is parasitic on the world.*

COROLLARY 36(a)   In making their respective passages from the world to the story, background sentences become true-in-the-story, hence also T^F-true in the world.

COROLLARY 36(b)   Just as the epistemic indeterminacies of backgrounds are not ontologized (in the world), neither need they be in fiction. Thus fictions incorporate complete worlds, and incomplete, though large, epistemic subworlds of them.

Maximal accounts arise from recursive interplay between and among fictive sentences, background facts, background beliefs, and consequences thereof. Maximal accounts subsume the closures of such sentences. We have already laid the stage for recognition of a four-fold ambiguity in the notion of the closures in fictional texts. Corresponding to the distinction between the consequences a story has and the consequences that should be drawn from it is a distinction between a story's *propositional* closure and its *inferential* closure. Within this contrast are the various grades of closure, corresponding to the various grades of consequence: deductive, inductive, statistical, abductive, presumptive, plausibilistic and so on. Let $L_1, \ldots L_n$ be logics for these consequence relations. The question is whether to embed them in the logic of fiction. There is no strategic advantage in not doing so. Let the sentences of the maximal account imply whatever they will. It suffices that they not be given a free-ride into it. In other words maximality should not be closed under consequence. This is tantamount to saying that only inferential closures should be seen as involved in the construction of maximal accounts. This is entirely the right way of seeing things, at least as an approximation. [58]

Even so, a second distinction now presses for attention. *Whose* inferences belong in the inferential closures of a story? As with the requisite collective belief worlds of a given text, Lewis thinks that it is those shared by author and reader alike. There are two things wrong with this. One is that it leaves it undetermined as to how conflicting inferences might be decided. In *Faust* it is true that Faust makes a pact with the devil. It may also have been the case that Goethe believed that the world was such that human beings could make pacts with the devil, literally. As such, this goes into the maximal account of Goethe's poem as a background consideration — as part of how the world is. Yet for many readers of the poem, this is at best a dramatically interesting superstition, never mind that they would concede that just this actually occurred in the poem. There is an answer to this. Goethe doesn't get to decide theological questions *except fictively*, just as Cervantes doesn't get to decide astronomical questions *except fictively*. Whatever Cervantes or anyone else may have thought, the motion of the heavenly bodies of part one of *Don Quixote* are elliptical, not circular, unless otherwise provided by the sentences of the text. This notwithstanding that part one was published prior to Kepler's breakthrough and only part two afterwards.

There are two questions about inferential closure, not one. Of course, we want to know what inferences we as readers and critics should draw from a text's fictive sentences and its background considerations. But there is also the question of what inferences Holmes and his ilk draw about the events of the story. In some respects, Holmes is better placed than we to fill in the maximal account. He knows more about late-Victorian London that we do, and about the myriad facts of his own life. This being so, Holmes will be privy to consequences of such facts that can only escape us. On the other hand, the fictive sentences of stories are often arranged so as to give the epistemic advantage to readers. Readers of *Oedipus* can see the trouble coming from miles away, but Oedipus has no clue until the madly bitter end. Intuitively, we want to count inferences that Oedipus doesn't make or that contradict those that he made mistakenly. To this end the nod goes to the reader. But in light of the first difficulty, it can only be a qualified nod. The best compromise would be that the requisite inferences are those drawn by anyone combining the advantages of readers and of characters within the fiction. A good, though not perfect approximation to this is the third-person narrator of stories in which reader and author are near-contemporaries.This can't be all there is to it, needless to say. Some narrators, often in first-person cases, are mistaken in various ways. In very old stories, the Homeric poems for example, there is much that I will miss that (even) Achilles will not. These are difficulties of a sort that commend themselves to the device of the ideal observer. An ideal observer is someone in the world who has mastery of a text's fictive sentences and who is counterfactually present in the story and positioned there in ways that facilitate his drawing the appropriate inferences. Because both reader and fictional character are

---

[58] Of course, don't the facts of the world have their own consequences independently of whether we have the resources or occasion to draw them? Yes, but we may take it that the facts of the world include the facts of their closures.

differentially disadvantaged, readers and characters will draw different subsets of the inferences that the ideal observer is able to draw. But, for all that, these will in the general case be a substantial overlap.

5.1 Contra ideal observers

Some readers will take the resort to ideal observers as a retrograde step, if not a *cri du coeur*. Fiction is a hard enough problem (they will say) without the added burden of counterfactual in-fiction observers. For anyone still drawn to a worlds approach to fiction, the present strategy presents us with two levels of modality, one made necessary by the fictional and the other made necessary by the counterfactual, the upshot of which is that we are now required to chart the connections between non-fictional possible worlds and fictional worlds. I am myself rather sympathetic to this complaint. I have tried to say why the worlds approach to fiction is misbegotten. I admit to having similar doubts about the conceptual (as opposed to mathematical) adequacy of a worlds approach to counterfactality. Running a possible worlds account for counterfactuals in fiction involves running a fictional worlds account of the possible worlds account that takes care of counterfactuality. This is not to say that such interactions are beyond us; but, as Quine would say, the returns had better be good. Upon reflection, it is better to be realistic. There is a great deal that is true in fiction that we shall never know. There is a great deal in the world that we shall never know. In particular, there are lots of inferences that Holmes and his ilk do (and should) draw from whatever it is that they have knowledge of. Since in lots of cases what they have knowledge of extends to what we lack knowledge of, we will not know how to infer what inferences it was right for them to draw from such knowledge. This is nothing to be over-concerned about. It is just another patch of epistemic indeterminacy in our understanding of Holmes and his doings. Nor need this indeterminacy leave a gaping hole in our appreciation of the kind of man Holmes is and the nature of his doings. For in all things, Holmes is as much like us in his nature and his actions and passions as is compatible with the fictive sentences of the stories and his status as a fictional being.

We have already seen that a stipulationist approach allows for, but does not demand, a substitutional account of quantification. Here, too, it is essential to distinguish between the quantifications we ourselves make and those made by Holmes and his ilk. Bearing on this is the parasitism of fiction on the world. To the extent that its fictive sentences allow it, quantification there should be like quantification here. There is no particular reason to attribute to Holmes substitutional quantifications except for those cases in which Holmes is trying to quantify over what he has trouble in recognizing as real. Like us, Holmes too is subject to nominalistic provocation. When this happens, we should not deny him the utility of substitutional quantification.

Holmes is a nominalistic provocation for us. Although we know who he is and what he did, we also know that he is not there and that none of what has ever happened happened to him. This is an interesting duality, for which the truth of "There are lots of things that don't exist" is a godsend, and which (on my telling) "Holmes does not exist" instantiates and "The present king of France does not exist" does not. Retaining this intuition requires a view of quantification that restricts the values of bound variables to referring terms that have sense. Perhaps this would not be a well-motivated restriction generally, but it works well here. For here truth is primary and objects are nothing.

5.2 Contra a fictive modality

In §4.2.5, we noted that in Meinongian contexts, it is hard to see what the semantic import of T^F might be. We went so far as to suggest that in such contexts T^F is "semantically inert", thereby leaving the impression that this was something that told against the Meinongian analysis of fiction. As we now see, although this may be a consequence that Meinongians would be prepared to accept, for the rest of us it is a disaster. T^F is needed to mark the fact that for any sentence in the closure of any set of sentences containing a fictive sentence is false, and yet true in the story. One of the attractions of this is compatability with the T-schema. If the T-schema is adequate for sentences about the world, it is also adequate for the sentences of fiction, except where contra-indicated by its fictive sentences. Accordingly, we have it that

"Holmes is Watson's friend" is true iff Holmes is Watson's friend.

In other words, "Holmes is Watson's friend" is false. What is not false is that "Holmes is Watson's friend" is true-in-the story. "Holmes is Watson's friend" is true-in-the story iff it is a member of the story's maximal account M. "But that's not truth", some will complain. The reply to make is: *Of course* it is not truth, and this is nothing to complain of. If it is true that $T^F(S)$, then $T^F(S)$. But we do not have it that if $T^F(S)$ then S.

T^F is a way of keeping our assertions contradiction-free. More generally, it is a way of keeping our assertions falsity-free. In uttering $\ulcorner T^F(S)(\wedge \sim S) \urcorner$ I leave the law of noncontradiction untrifled with. This gives us no occasion to apply emergency measures from dialetheic logic. $\ulcorner T^F(S \wedge \sim S) \urcorner$ is true if $\ulcorner S \wedge \sim S \urcorner \varepsilon M$.

There remains the question of the place of $\ulcorner S \wedge \sim S \urcorner$ in fiction, concerning which a certain caution is wise counsel indeed. In "The Mischief of Ricardo Bosque", its author da Bloo provides that every sentence is true. A good part of the story involves an attempt to depict Ricardo's day-to-day reaction to the storied fact of absolute inconsistency. "The Mischief" is not, I think, a very satisfactory story on literary grounds, but it gives no offence on the score of what it obliges its readers to count as true in it. Since, every sentence S is true in the story, we must allow that for every sentence S, $T^F(S)$, where F is "The Mischief of Ricardo Bosque". However, there is nothing to indicate that Bradbury's story is one in which everything is true. If this is right, there are two options to consider.

Option (1). Allow the propositional closure of *A Sound of Thunder* to be as classical as you please; in which case, we concede that everything whatever follows from "Keith was elected President in 2055 $\wedge \sim$ (Keith was elected President in 2055)". Restrict the inferential closure (and accordingly, the maximal account) dialetheically, in the manner, say, of Priest's *LP* [Priest, 1979].

Option (2). Subject the propositional and the inferential closures to the same dialetheic constraint.

It is interesting to note that neither from the point of view of what readers must concede to or from the point of view of what a story's characters must attest to is there the slightest difference between option (1) and option (2). As far as we are concerned, all that is true in *A Sound of Thunder* are the sentences in its M. From the point of view of Keith and his ilk all that is true is in the inferential closure of what they know of themselves and their situations. In more generalized contexts, there might be differential advantages in keeping one's options open, or in plumping for one or the other. But this is not something that concerns us here.

All this has a bearing on the advisability of construing T^F as a sentential modal operator. No doubt one of the attractions of so doing is that there exist well-understood semantic theories for the modals. In §4.2.4 I attempted to show that possible worlds' semantics leave the logic of fiction in a conceptually underdetermined shape. Far and away, the best to be said of a possible worlds (or a fictional worlds) approach to fiction is that we have a fairly good command of worlds when considered as abstract mathematical structures. One senses here the presence of *Make Do*. Dropping the pretense that a semantics of worlds offers conceptual elucidations of the semantic dimension of fiction, deprives the T^F-as modal-operator assumption of much of its attractiveness. For if a modal operator requires a possible worlds semantics, and a possible worlds semantics tells us nothing (conceptually) about fiction, what can a modal operator tell us about fiction?

We would be better advised to conjure up a role for T^F that more closely comports with actual practice. We should aim for a construal that allows for the propositional identity of the S that the story makes true, and the S that the reader accedes to. But it is also necessary to pay close attention to variations in truth-attribution. So while my utterance of "Keith was elected President in 2055 $\wedge$ ~ (Keith was elected President in 2055)" has the same propositional content that it has in the maximal account of Bradbury's story, it is essential that what is true there not be confused with what is true here. These objectives do not require the postulation of modalities. *Labels* will do.

Although labels have only recently been studied in a systematic way,[59] they are a far from unfamiliar device. Among logicians, labels are most commonly used in recording the derivation histories of lines in proofs, and in marking the roles played by formulas not introduced by derivation from prior lines, as in axiomatic, conditional, indirect and reductio proofs. Then, too, we saw in our discussion of the S-model of §4 that truth by stipulation gives rise to hyphenation. If a theorist stipulates the truth of S in his theory T, then all else being well, S is true-in-T. Another abundant source is conjecture. Every time a theorist completes an abductive inference, he does two things. For some proposition H, he conjectures that H is true (knowing that he does not know that it is); and, secondly, he releases H for inferential duty in the domain of enquiry within which the conjecture has arisen. In each of these cases — the theoretical stipulation case and the scientific conjecture case — the proposition in question may in time find itself wholly integrated into some or other body of *knowledge*. When that happens, H's ancestry is overlooked. But until it does happen, it is essential that its ancestry *not* be overlooked. When Planck made the momentous conjecture of quanta in 1900, he released the quantum hypothesis for further work in the physics of light. It proved a transformation of physics. Large classes of

---

[59][Gabbay, 1996]. For a brief informal survey, see [Gabbay and Woods, 2003, chapter 13].

sentences were now derivable with the aid of the quantum hypothesis, and each of them retained the conjectural status of the hypothesis that abetted them until such time as independent experimental corroboration became available. Prior to that, it had to be kept in mind that all of this new physics was itself conjectural. Hence the importance of labels. Labels are an idealization of the more or less settled informal practice of not taking the experimentally unconfirmed propositions of fledgling quantum physics as demonstrably true in the world, rather than demonstrably true-in-quantum theory. Quantum theory is pretty wild conceptually, but it is not fiction. There were good reasons to want to integrate quanta into established science. When it happened, science was considerably enriched by it. With the creations of fiction, on the other hand there is nothing for them to integrate into (except, in limited cases, each other.).

We saw T^F as a sentence operator that converts a falsehood to a modal truth, and for this to be true, we took it as given that a modal semantics would have to be dreamed up for T^F. Of course, I now see that as a mistake. T^F is not a semantically loaded modality. It is a label. This is as it should be. There is nothing semantic about the fact that whereas S is false, $T^F(S)$. S is false precisely because it is not the case that S. That is a semantic fact about S. $T^F(S)$ precisely because $S \, \varepsilon \, M$. That is not a semantic fact about S. Again, if $T^F(S)$, it does not follow, and in large classes of cases it is false, that S.

5.3 An advantage of mathematical stipulationism?

In [Woods and Alward, 2002] much ado was made about a problem that is fundamental to fiction and only contingently an issue for mathematics. This, we suggested, was an asymmetry of sufficient import to tip the scales in favour of mathematical fictions rather than literary fictions as offering up the more generic or canonical model, thus ending the career of *The Literary Primacy Thesis*. The putative asymmetry arises from the fact that by and large literary fictions are rivals of the world, that what they make true the world has already made false. It is true that on occasion a mathematician's stipulations will contradict some antecedently preferred theorem or definition, but by and large mathematical stipulations go where others have not yet gone.

There is a further reason to question the importance we attempted to give the asymmetry between literary and mathematical fictions. For consider all those creative stipulations in mathematics for which there was no antecedently available claim that it contradicts. Mathematics is the natural home of negation-as-failure. Any S yet to find a home in mathematics is such that $\ulcorner \sim S \urcorner$ holds by default. Accordingly, any fresh stipulation will contradict an existing default. No one thinks that a default should be impervious to contradicting demonstrations. But removal by stipulation is another matter. So we have it that the asymmetry all but vanishes. For many sentences of fiction, there is an antecedently existing fact to the contrary. For most sentences of stipulative mathematics there is a presumptively antecedent fact to the contrary. This presents us with something quite close to a level playing field when it comes to handling those contradictions. It is not a problem. We handle them with labels.

5.4 The transfictive

There is as yet no place in this analysis for transfictive truths, such as that Holmes was admired by Agatha Christie. This is a sentence that could not have been true in the absence of truths in the maximal accounts of the Holmes stories. Like certain of the sentences in the maximal accounts, transfictive sentences depend on the fictional, but with a difference. These latter are true in fiction but not in the world, whereas transfictive truths are true in the world but not in fiction. So the dependency is different.

The paradigm of a transfictive truth is

2. Reader R knows who Holmes is and what he did.

All else is variation — Christie's admiration, King's appropriation, and Brett's dramatic representation. One of the attractions of the S-model is that it suffices to know who Holmes is to know the reference of "Holmes". This is done via *Sinn*, the individuating sentences of the maximal account. A reader's knowledge of who Holmes is is a matter of his knowing with respect to those sentences S that $T^F(S)$ is true. He knows that $T^F(S)$ is true if he knows that $S \varepsilon M$. Similarly, someone knows what Holmes did when he knows who Holmes is and knows with respect to those sentences S that give the action of the story that $T^F(S)$ is likewise true. Here, too, one knows that $T^F(S)$ is true if one knows that $S \varepsilon M$.

Knowing who Holmes is different from knowing Holmes. The same is true of Saul A. Kripke. Knowing Kripke demands acquaintance with an object. Knowing who he is requires acquaintance with 'Saul A. Kripke''s *Sinn*. With 'Holmes' this is all we get. There is no object for us to acquire acquaintance of. Knowing Holmes seems to require it to be true that

$\exists x$ (John knows x).

But this is false. It would also seem that admiring Holmes is like this too, requiring that it be true that

$\exists x$ (Christie admires x)

But this too is false. How, then, can it be that Christie's admiring Holmes is modeled on her knowing who Holmes is. The answer is that it suffices for Christie to admire Holmes that she finds Holmes to be admirable; and it suffices for this that she thinks that T^F(Holmes is admirable). It is much the same way with King's appropriation of Holmes in her own *A Monstrous Regiment of Women*, and of Brett's capturing nuances of Holmes' personality. In the one case, the Holmes of Doyle's telling is the Holmes of King's. In the Doyle stories "There exists an x such that x is denoted by 'Holmes'" is true. In the King stories, "There exists an y such that y is denoted by 'Holmes'" is also true. In King's story but not Doyle's $y = x$. So some of the sentences true in King's story are not so in Doyle's.

Brett's fidelity to Holmes' personality is similarly dealt with. Two conditions need to be met. One is that Brett must know what Holmes is like. The other is that he must be able to capture these features in the way that he plays Holmes on television. Knowing what Holmes is like is knowing the requisite propositions in the form $\ulcorner T^F(K \text{ (Holmes)})\urcorner$. And knowing how to capture K-ness is simply a matter of the actor's trade-craft.

Perhaps it will not have escaped notice that each of our intuitive axioms makes a transfictive claim. If it cannot accommodate the intuitive axioms, that will be reason to doubt the our present account. We said earlier that we should prepare ourselves for the eventuality that our intuitions will prove to have been misconceived. Certainly such was the lesson of the inconsistency that brought down intuitive set theory. It is quite true that these might have to be given up, but they should not be given up cavalierly.

Axiom A tells us that we refer to fictional beings even though they do not exist. We have already seen that the S-model accommodates a view of reference according to which one can know the reference of "Sherlock Holmes" without its having a referent. We have also seen that in combination with substitutional quantification we may give such reference *de re* formulation in the manner of $\ulcorner \exists x T^F$ ('r' denotes $x)\urcorner$.

Axiom B tells us that there are true sentences about the fictional. Again, we have seen that the S-model allows us to say that the only truth in a story are those that are true independently of it. All else is untrue. Yet everything in a story's maximal account is true-in-the story. T^F preserves all that is desirable in B if we are also going to allow that the truths of stories leave no metaphysical footprints.

Axiom C is about inference. I have already said my piece about inference in the earlier discussion of maximal accounts. The rough rule of thumb is that inference within fiction be as near as like inference in the world as the fictive sentences permit. In the particular case of $\ulcorner S \wedge \sim S \urcorner$ occurring in a story, the surrounding sentences of the maximal account will serve as context. In a story such as "The Mischief", one infers that everything is true in the story. In a story such as *A Sound of Thunder*, inference is paraconsistent — indeed dialetheic. A further tip: anything inferred from a sentence, labeled 'T^F' is itself labeled 'T^F'. Storied truths don't achieve cheap or unfettered *entré* to the world.

Axiom D provides that a story's fictive truths and those in their inferential closures are made true by the author. The truth is that they are made true in the story by the author. In some versions, D also has it that the author provides an ontology for his stories, a realm of nonexistent objects and happenings. There is a version of the S-model that allows for this; but not every variation does. In its purely instrumental form, all we can say (or would want to) is that authors provide ontologies in their stories — objects and events that are real in the stories, our acknowledgement of which is protected by the label 'T^F'.

Finally, E reminds us that real entities may be borrowed for guest appearances in fiction. This is true, but it is a truth of an appropriately distinctive form. For example,

$$\exists x \, (x = \text{London} \wedge T^F(\ldots(\text{London})).$$

Accordingly, whereas it is possible that

$$\exists x (x = \text{London} \wedge T^F(\ldots(\text{London}))$$

is part of the *Sinn* of 'London', nothing in the form of '$T^F (\ldots (\text{London}))$' is part of it.

One of the virtues of the S-model is that it preserves the flavour of the intuitive axioms while at the same time allowing for refinements driven by the foundational fact that the fictional leaves no metaphysical footprints. A further virtue is that it leaves more or less standard approaches to reference, truth and inference intact, taking care of needed qualifications by way of labels. What this helps us see is how close to a logic of non-fictions a logic of fiction turns out to be. This is as it should be. Fiction is parasitical on the world, with which it achieves a kind of partnership. But it is an arrangement in which it is very much the case that the world is the senior partner.

When we say that fiction leaves no metaphysical footprints, we nominalize the fictional, that is, we drift towards a nominalistic account of it. One of the difficulties thrown up by nominalism is that of integrating its nominalities with the tough customers of the real world. Such integration comprehends drawings of the real by the merely nominal, which is ludicrous on its face. Attempts to minimize this difficulty which trade-off ontic integration for predictive yield gets a kind of instrumentalism up and running. But, as we have tried to show, there is no virtue in this for fiction. Not only do the nominalia of fiction not trade blows with the denizens of the world, there is absolutely no predictive gain in integrating their truths. What is wanted is a form of stipulationism in which the truths of fiction leave no metaphysical footprints and no predictive ones either.

The S-model provides that the objects of fiction are a *façon de parler*. Given the way that natural languages are constructed, given that they deeply embed the realist stance, it is only natural that we see our relationships with Holmes and his ilk on the model of our relationships with Saul A. Kripke and his ilk. Perhaps this is a place at which to revisit the previously derided idea of fiction as pretense, although not with a view to recanting my earlier criticism. In our untutored and pre-theoretical moments we report our experience of Holmes objectually. But no one is in any doubt that such reports are a *façon de parler*. Readers of "The Hound of the Baskervilles" do not lose sight of the fact that none of this actually happened. And yet, in some cases — looking for it in the Doyle oeuvre might not be the best place — we are deeply moved by what we read. This is *not a façon de parler*. We are not pretending to be deeply moved, or playing at it or making-believe that we are. What is remarkable is that knowing that the denotation of "Ophelia" is a *façon de parler* we are greatly moved by her death. It is a trick, of course, a lovely gift of a trick. We are able to be moved by what we know isn't there. Our understanding of such things is double-aspected.[60]

The proposition that we are able to be moved by what we know isn't there gives great offence to philosophers of many stripes, who are moved to back-pedal with a certain earnestness. So we postulate (or borrow) nonexistent but otherwise wholly legitimate objects — the objects of Meinong's jungle, the objects of possible worlds, the objects of fictional worlds the objects of idealist stipulations. At every turn, these are rehabilitations induced by the objectural biases in-built to language and experience. By and large, these are biases that serve us well, but in the matter of our experience of fiction they lead us into error.

There are logicians galore for whom this is the right way of proceeding. But it is not the right way of proceeding for fiction, as I have been trying to show. Truth in fiction is not a matter of relations between fictional sentences and various kinds of set-theoretic structures (jungles, worlds, whatever). Truth in fiction is a matter entirely of membership

---

[60] An astute analysis of affective responses to fiction is [Alward, forthcoming, chapter 2].

in M. Again, people will complain. "That is not real truth", they will say. They are entirely right. It is truth in fiction.

In recommending an instrumental stipulationism for literary fiction, we make a large investment in fiction's parasitical nature. Perhaps it is natural to read axiom D as heavily creative. Certainly, it is nothing but right to acknowledge the pivotal role of the author in stocking the M of his story with its enabling fictive sentences. But the great bulk of what is encompassed by M is furnished by the world. What stories are like draws heavily on what the world is like; and the passage of what the world is like into fiction is one in which the fictive operator is picked up in a largely honorific and book-keeping sense. In their stories, authors need the world to be a certain way in order that the action of the story might unfold as the author intends. The default position is that the world in the story is our world, save only as may be required by its fictive sentences. In this regard, understanding a story is like revising a set of beliefs in something like the manner of [Gabbay, Pigozzi and Woods]. Fictive sentences serve both as new inputs and modularity triggers. Someone who understands that *The Hound of the Baskervilles* is a story will not revise his belief set on the strength of the truth of "Sherlock Holmes waved our strange visitor into a chair", but rather on the strength of that fact that T^F(Sherlock Holmes waved our strange visitor into a chair). But he will produce his version of the maximal account in reverse, with "Sherlock Holmes waved our strange visitor into a chair" making the cut and "T^F(Sherlock Holmes waved our strange visitor into a chair" not. The fact remains that most of what goes into it is already in the world. A great deal of what would occasion the revision of my beliefs also requires membership in a story's M. When this happens, the author borrows the world for a guest appearance in his story.

Fiction hasn't the slightest prospect of being integrated with our knowledge of the world. Equipping its stipulations with features designed to ease such integration is worse that a waste of time; is also a mistake. It encourages the idea that, in creating stories, authors create objects. In so saying, we learn a useful lesson about "in". It is true in Japan that one drives on the left. From this it follows that "One drives on the left" is a sentence contingently true in the world. In the Holmes stories, Holmes is a bit of a prig. But it is not the case that "Holmes is a prig" is contingently true of the world. "Holmes is a prig" is true-in-fiction, but true nowhere. Fiction leaves no metaphysical footprints.

6 ACKNOWLEDGEMENTS

For astute and helpful comments, I am indebted to conversations with Dale Jacquette, Kendall Walton, Nicholas Griffin, Dov Gabbay, Matthew McKeon, Hartley Slater, Peter Alward, Mohan Matthen and Ori Simchen. I thank the Engineering and Physical Sciences Research Council of the United Kingdom for financial support, and Carol Woods and Jane Spurr for technical assistance.

BIBLIOGRAPHY

[Adams et al., 1997] F. Adams, G. Fuller and R. Stecker. The semantics of fictional names, in *Pacific Philosophical Quarterly*, volume 78, pp. 128-148, 1997.

[Akiba, 2000] K. Akiba. Indefiniteness of mathematical objects, *Philosophia Mathematica* volume 3, pp. 26-46, 2000.
[Alward, to appear] P. Alward. *Attitudes Towards Fiction*, to appear.
[Åqvist, 2003] L. Åqvist. Some remarks on performatives in the law, *Artificial Intelligence and Law*, pp. 105-124, 2003.
[Armour-Garb, 2005] B. Armour-Garb. Wrestling with (and without) dialetheism, *Australasian Journal of Philosophy*, vol., 83, pp. 87-102, 2005.
[Austin, 1975] J.L. Austin. *How to Do Things with Words*, Cambridge, MA: Harvard University Press, 1975.
[Azzouni, 1994] J. Azzouni. *Mathematical Myths, Mathematical Practice*, Cambridge: Cambridge University Press, 1994.
[Azzouni, 2004] J. Azzouni. *Deflating Existential Consequence: A Case for Nominalism*, New York: Oxford University Press, 2004.
[Balaguer, 1996] M. Balaguer. A fictionalist account of the indispensable applications of mathematics, *Philosophical Studies*, volume 83, pp. 291-314, 1996.
[Batens, 2000] D. Batens. A survey of inconsistency-adaptive logics, edited by D. Batens, C. Mortenson, G. Priest and J.P. van Bendegem, *Frontiers of Paraconsistent Logic*, pp. 49-73, Baldock, UK: Research Studies Press, 2000.
[Benacerraf, 1973] P. Benacerraf, Mathematical truth, *Journal of Philosophy*, volume LXX, pp. 661-679, 1973.
[Bencivenga, 1980] E. Bencivenga. Free semantics for definite descriptions, *Logique et Analyse*, volume 92, pp. 393-405, 1980.
[Bencivenga, 1991] E. Bencivenga. Free semantics, in K. Lambert, editor, *Philosophical Applications of Free Logic*, New York: Oxford University Press, pp. 98-111, 1991.
[Blocker, 1974] H.G. Blocker. The truth about fictional entities, *Philosophical Quarterly*, volume 24, pp. 27-36, 1974.
[Brown, 2000] B. Brown. Simple natural deduction for weakly aggregative paraconsistent logics, in Dov M. Gabbay, editor, *Frontiers of Paraconsistent Logics*, Baldock, UK: Research Studies Press, 2000.
[Bunge, 1997] M. Bunge. Moderate mathematical fictionalism, in *Philosophy of Mathematics*, E. Agazzi and G. Darvas, editors, pp. 51-71, Dordrecht and Boston: Kluwer, 1997.
[Byrne, 1993] A. Byrne. Truth in fiction: the story continued, *Australasian Journal of Philosophy*, volume 71, pp. 24-35, 1993.
[Caldon and Ignjatović, 2005] P. Caldon and A. Ignjatović. On mathematical instrumentalism, *The Journal of Symbolic Logic*, pp. 778-794, 2005.
[Carlson and Pelletier, 1995] G. N. Carlson and F. J.Pelletier, editors. *The Generic Book*, Chicago: Chicago University Press, 1995.
[Cartwright, 1960] R. Cartwright, Negative Existentials, *Journal of Philosophy*, volume 57, pp. 629-639, 1960.
[Castaneda, 1979] H.-N. Castānada. Fiction and reality: Their fundamental connections, in *Formal Semantics and LiteraryTheory*, pp. 31-62, John Woods and Thomas Pavel, editors, a special issue of *Poetics*, volume 8, 1979.
[Coleman, 1973] F.X.J. Coleman. A few observations on fictional discourse, in *Aesthetics and Language*, edited by B.R. Tilghman, pp. 31-42, Lawrence: University of Kansas Press, 1973.
[Crittenden, 1973] C. Crittenden. Thinking about non-being, *Inquiry*, volume 16, pp. 290-312, 1973.
[Currie, 1990] G. Currie. *The Nature of Fiction*, Cambridge: Cambridge University Press, 1990.
[da Costa, 1998] N.C.A. da Costa. Paraconsistent logic, in *Stanisaw Jáskowski Memorial Symposium*, pp. 29-35, Department of Logic, Nicholas Copernicus University of Torun, 1998.
[Davis, 2000] M. Davis. *Engines of Logic: Mathematicians and the Origin of the Computer*, New York: Norton, 2000.
[de Kleer, 1986] J. de Kleer. An assumption-based TMS, *Artificial Intelligence*, 28, pp. 157-200, 1986.
[Deutsch, 1985] H. Deutsch. Fiction and fabrication, *Philosophical Studies*, volume 47, pp. 201-211, 1985.
[Devine, 1974] P.E. Devine. The logic of fiction, *Philosophical Studies*, volume 26, pp. 389-399, 1974.
[Doležel, 1979] L. Doležel. Extensional and intuitional narrative worlds, *Formal Semantics and Literary Theory*, pp. 193-211, editors, John Woods and Thomas Pavel, a special of *Poetics*, volume 8, 1979.
[Donnellan, 1966] K. Donnellan. Reference and definite descriptions, *Philosophical Review*, volume 77, pp. 281-304, 1966.
[Conan Doyle, 1981] A. Conan Doyle. *The Hound of the Baskervilles*, London: Penguin Books. Originally published in 1902 by George Newnes, 1981.
[Everett and Hofweber, 2000] A. Everett and T. Hofweber. editors, *Empty Names: Fiction and the Puzzles of Non-existence*, Stanford: CSLI Publications, 2000.
[Field, 1980] H. Field. *Science Without Numbers: A Defense of Nominalism*, Princeton: Princeton University Press, 1980.

[Frege, 1952] G. Frege. On sense and reference, *Translations from the Writings of Gottlob Frege*, pp. 56-78, Peter T. Geach and Max Black, editors, Oxford: Blackwell, 1952.
[Frege, 1967] G. Frege. Begriffsschrift ein der arithmeteschen nachgehildete Formelsprache des reinen Denkins, in *From Grege to Gödel*, Jean van Heijenoort, editor, Cambridge, MA: Harvard University Press, 1967.
[Gabbay, 1996] D. M. Gabbay. *Labelled Deductive Systems*, Oxford: Oxford University Press, 1996.
[Gabbay and Woods, 2003] D. M. Gabbay and John Woods. *Agenda Relevance: A Study in Formal Pragmatics*, Amsterdam: North-Holland, 2003.
[Gabbay and Woods, 2005] D. M. Gabbay and John Woods. *The Reach of Abduction: Insight and Trial*, Amsterdam: Elsevier, 2005.
[Gabriel, 1975] G. Gabriel. *Fiktion und Warheit*, Stuttgart: Fromman-Holzboog, 1975.
[Gabriel, 1979] G. Gabriel. Fiction — a semantic approach, in *Formal Semantics and Literary Theory*, John Woods and Thomas G. Pavel, editors, pp. 245-255, a special issue of *Poetics*, volume 8, Amsterdam: North-Holland, 1979.
[Gale, 1971] R.M. Gale. The fictive use of language, *Philosophy*, volume 46, pp. 324-340, 1971.
[Grice, 1989] P. Grice. *Studies in the Way of Words*, Cambridge, Mass: Harvard University Press, 1989.
[Griffin, 2005] N. Griffin. Through the Woods to Meinong's jungle, in *Mistakes of Reason: Essays in Honour of John Woods*, edited by Kent A. Peacock and Andrew D. Irvine, pp. 15-32, Toronto: University of Toronto Press, to appear in 2005.
[Hailperin and Leblanc, 1959] T. Hailperin and H. Leblanc. Nondesignating singular terms, *The Philosophical Review*, volume 68, pp. 239-243, 1959.
[Hanley, 2004] R. Hanley. As good as it gets: Lewis on truth in fiction, in *Lewisean Themes: The Philosophy of David K. Lewis*, pp. 113-129, Frank Jackson and Graham Priest, editors, New York: Oxford University Press, 2004.
[Heintz, 1979] J. Heintz. Reference and inference in fiction, pp. 85-89, in John Woods and Thomas Pavel, editors, *Formal Semantics and Literary Theory*, a special issue of *Poetics*, volume 8, 1979.
[Hintikka, 1959] J. Hintikka. Existential presuppositions and existential commitments, *The Journal of Philosophy*, pp. 125-137, volume 56, 1959.
[Hodes, 1984] H. T. Hodes. Logicism and the ontological commitments of arithmetic, *Journal of Philosophy*, pp. 123-149, volume 81, 1984.
[Hoffman, 1999] S. Hoffman. *Mathematics as Makebelieve: A Constructive Empiricist Account*, Ph.D Thesis, University of Alberta, 1999.
[Howell, 1974] R. Howell. The logical structure of pictorial representation, *Theoria*, pp. 76-109, volume 40, 1974.
[Howell, 1976] R. Howell. Review of John Woods: *The Logic of Fiction*, *The Journal of Aesthetics and Art Criticism*, pp. 354-355, volume 34, 1976.
[Howell, 1979] R. Howell. Fictional objects: How they are and how they aren't, in *Formal Semantics and Literary Theory*, pp. 50-72, John Woods and Thomas Pavel, editors, a special issue of *Poetics*, volume 8, Amsterdam: North-Holland, 1979.
[Howell, 1983] R. Howell. Review of *Non-Existent Objects*, *Journal of Philosophy*, pp. 163-173, volume 80, 1983.
[Ingarden, 1931] R. Ingarden. *Das literarische Kunstwerk. Eine Untersuchung aus dem Grenzgebiet der Ontologie, Logik und Literaturwissenschaft*, Halle: Neimeyer, 1931.
[Jacquette, 1996] D. Jacquette. *Meinongian Logic: The Semantics of Existence and Nonexistence*, Berlin: Walter de Gruyter, 1996.
[Jacquette, 1998] D. Jacquette. Paraconsistent logical consequence, *Journal of Applied Non-Classical Logics*, volume 8, pp. 337-351, 1998.
[Jacquette, 2001] D. Jacquette. Truth and fiction in David Lewis' critique of Meinongian semantics, *Metaphysica*, volume 2, pp. 73-106, 2001.
[Jacquette, to appear] D. Jacquette. Logic for Meinongian object theory semantics, in Dov M. Gabbay and John Woods, editors, *Handbook of the History of Logic*, volume 5, *Logic From Russell to Gentzen*, Amsterdam: Elsevier, to appear in 2006.
[Kaplan, 1973] D. Kaplan. Bob and Carol and Ted and Alice, in *Approaches to Natural Language*, edited by Jaakko Hintikka, J.M. Moravcsik and Patrick Suppes, pp. 490-518, Dordrecht: Reidel, 1973.
[Kivy, 1993] P. Kivy. *The Fine Art of Repetition: Essays in the Philosophy of Music*, New York: Cambridge University Press, 1993.
[Körner, 1967] S. Körner. On the relevance of post-Gödelian mathematics to philosophy, in *Problems in the Philosophy of Mathematics*, Imre Lakatos, editor, pp. 133-137, Amsterdam: North-Holland, 1967.
[Kripke, 1972] S. Kripke. Naming and necessity, in *Semantics and Natural Language*, edited by Donald Davidson and Gilbert Harman, pp. 253-355, 763-769, Dordrecht: Reidel, 1972.

[Kripke, 1973] S. Kripke. *Reference and Existence*, unpublished typescript. Presented as the John Locke Lectures, Oxford University, 1973.
[Kripke, 1979] S. Kripke. Speaker's reference and semantic reference, in *Contemporary Perspectives in the Philosophy of Language*, edited by Peter A. French, Theodore E. Uehling Jr., and Howard K. Wettstein, pp. 6-27, Minneapolis: University of Minnesota Press, 1979.
[Kripke, 1982] S. Kripke. *Wittgenstein's Private Language Argument*, Oxford: Blackwell, 1982.
[Landman, 1986] F.W. Landman. *Towards a Theory of Information: The Status of Partial Objects in Semantics*, Dordrecht: Foris, 1986.
[Larmarque and Olsen, 1994] P. Larmarque and S. Olsen. *Truth, Fiction and Literature, A Philosophical Perspective*, Oxford: Oxford University Press, 1994.
[Lambert, 1963a] K. Lambert. Notes on E!III: A theory of descriptions, *Philosophical Studies*, volume 13, pp. 51-59, 1963a.
[Lambert, 1963b] K. Lambert. Existential import revisited, *Notre Dame Journal of Formal Logic*, volume 4, pp. 288-292, 1963b.
[Lambert, 1964] K. Lambert. Notes on E!IV: A reduction in free quantification theory with identity and descriptions, *Philosophical Studies*, volume 15, pp. 85-88, 1964.
[le Poidevin, 1995] R. Le Poidevin. Worlds within worlds? The paradoxes of embedded fiction, *British Journal of Aesthetics*, volume 35, pp. 227-238, 1995.
[Lear, 1982] J. Lear. Aristotle's philosophy of mathematics, *Philosophical Review*, volume 91, pp. 161-192, 1982.
[Lejewski, 1954] C. Lejewski. Logic and existence, *British Journal for the Philosophy of Science*, volume 5, pp. 104-119, 1954.
[Levinson, 2000] S. C. Levinson. *Presumptive Meanings: The Theory of Generalized Conversational Implicature*, Cambridge, MA: MIT Press, 2000.
[Lewis, 1978] D. Lewis. Truth in fiction, *American Philosophical Quarterly*, volume 15, pp. 37-46, 1978.
[Lewis, 1983] D. Lewis. *Philosophical Papers*, volume 1, Oxford: Oxford University Press, 1983.
[Maddy, 2005] P. Maddy, Mathematical existence, *The Bulletin of Symbolic Logic*, volume 11, pp. 351-376, 2005.
[Martin and Schotch, 1974] R. Martin and P. Schotch. The meaning of fictional names, *Philosophical Studies*, volume 26, pp. 377-388, 1974.
[McKeon, 2005] M. McKeon. On the substitutional approach to logical consequence, in *Mistakes of Reason: Essays in Honour of John Woods*, edited by Kent A,. Peacock and Andrew D. Irvine, Toronto: University of Toronto Press, to appear in 2005.
[Meheus et al., forthcoming] J. Meheus, L. Verhoeven, M. Van Dyck and D. Provijn. Ampliative adaptive logics and the foundation of logic-based approaches to abduction, in *Logical and Computational Aspects of Model-Based Reasoning*, Lorenzo Magnani, Nancy J. Nersessian and Claudio Puzzi, editors, Dordrecht and Boston: Kluwer, forthcoming.
[Meinong, 1915] A. Meinong. *Über Möglichkeit und Warhscheinlichkeit*, Leipzig: Barth, 1915.
[Mooij, 1993] J.J.A. Mooij. *Fictional Realities: The Uses of Literary Imagination*, Amsterdam and Philadelphia: John Benjamins, 1993.
[Nash, 1950] J. Nash. Equilibrium, in the *Proceedings of the National Academy of Sciences*, volume 36, pp. 48-49, 1950.
[Neale, 1990] S. Neale. *Descriptions*, Cambridge, MA: MIT Press, 1990.
[Oversteegen, 1982] J.J. Oversteegen. *Beperkingen, Methodlogische recepten en andere vooronrdelen in de moderne literatuurwetenschap*, Utrecht: HES Uitgevers, 1982.
[Parsons, 1975] T. Parsons. A Meinongian analysis of fictional objects, *Grazer Philosophische Studien*, volume 1, pp. 73-86, 1975.
[Parsons, 1978] T. Parsons. Review of J. Woods' *The Logic of Fiction*, *Synthese*, volume 39, pp. 155-164, 1978.
[Parsons, 1980a] T. Parsons. *Non-Existent Objects*, New Haven, CT: Yale University Press, 1980a.
[Parsons, 1980b] T. Parsons. A prolegomenon to Meinongian semantics, *Journal of Philosophy*, volume 77, pp. 561-586, 1980b.
[Parsons, 1982] C. Parsons. Objects and logic, *The Monist*, volume 65, pp. 491-516, 1982.
[Pavel, 1975] T. Pavel. 'Possible worlds' in literary semantics, *The Journal of Aesthetics and Art Criticism*, volume 34, pp. 165-176, 1975.
[Pavel, 1986] T. Pavel. *Fictional Worlds*, Cambridge MA: Harvard University Press, 1986.
[Phillips, 1999] J. F. Phillips. Truth and inference in fiction, *Philosophical Studies*, volume 94, pp. 273-293, 1999.
[Plantinga, 1974] A. Plantinga. *The Nature of Necessity*, Oxford: Oxford University Press, 1974.

[Priest, 1979] G. Priest. The logic of paradox, *Journal of Philosophical Logic*, volume 8, pp. 219-241, 1979.
[Priest, 1987] G. Priest. *In Contradiction: A Study of the Transconsistent*, Dordrecht: Kluwer Academic, 1987.
[Priest, 1997] G. Priest. Sylvan's box: a short story and ten morals, *Notre Dame Journal of Formal Logic*, volume 38, pp. 573-582, 1997.
[Priest, 2001] G. Priest. *An Introduction to Non-Classical Logic*, Cambridge: Cambridge University Press, 2001.
[Quine, 1939] W.V. Quine. Designation and existence, *The Journal of Philosophy*, volume 36, pp. 701-709, 1939.
[Radford, 1975] C. Radford. How can we be moved by the fate of Anna Karenina? I, *The Aristotelian Society*, volume XLIX, pp. 67-80, Supplementary 1975.
[Rapaport, 1978] W. J. Rapaport. Meinongian theories and a Russellian paradox, *Noûs*, 12, pp. 153-158, 1978.
[Recanati, 1993] F. Recanati. *Direct Reference*, Oxford: Blackwell, 1993.
[Resnik, 1997] M. Resnik. *Mathematics as a Science of Patterns*, Oxford: Clarendon Press, 1997.
[Routley, 1966] R. Routley. Some things do not exist, *Notre Dame Journal of Formal Logic* volume 7, pp. 251-276, 1966.
[Routley and Routley, 1973] R. Routley and V. Routley. Rehabilitating Meinong's theory of objects, *Revue Internationale de Philosophie*, volume 27, pp. 224-254, 1973.
[Routley and Meyer, 1976] R. Routley and R. K. Meyer. Dialectical logic, classical logic and the consistency of the world, *Studies in Soviet Thought*, vol. 16, pp. 1-25, 1976.
[Routley, 1979] R. Routley. The semantic structure of fictional discourse, in *Formal Semantics and Literary Theory*, pp. 3-30, John Woods and Thomas Pavel, editors, a special issue of *Poetics*, volume 8, 1979.
[Routley, 1981] R. Routley. *Exploring Meinong's Jungle and Beyond: An Investigation of Noneism and the Theory of Items*, Canberra: Australian National University, 1981.
[Russell, 1937] B. Russell. *The Principles of Mathematics*, London: George Allen and Unwin, 1903. Second edition published in 1937.
[Salmon, 1998] N. Salmon. Nonexistence, *Noûs*, volume 32, pp. 277-319, 1998.
[Schotch and Jennings, 1989] P. Schotch and R. Jennings. On detonating, in Graham Priest, Richard Routley, Jean Norman, editors, *Paraconsistent Logic: Essays on the Inconsistent*, pp. 306-327, Munich: Philosophia Verlag, 1989.
[Scruton, 1974] R. Scruton. *Art and Imagination: A Study in the Philosophy of Mind*, New York: Barnes and Noble, 1974.
[Searle, 1970] J. Searle. *Speech Acts: An Essay in the Philosophy of Language*, Cambridge: Cambridge University Press, 1970.
[Searle, 1975] J. Searle. The logical status of fictional discourse, *New Literary History*, volume 6 pp. 319-332, 1975.
[Simons, 1999] P. Simons. On what there isn't: The Meinong-Russell dispute, in *Bertrand Russell: Critical Assessments*, Andrew Irvine, editor, volume III of *Language, Knowledge and the World*, pp. 69-100, London: Routledge, 1999.
[Slater, 1987] H. Slater. Fictions, *British Journal of Aesthetics*, volume 27, pp. 143-155, 1987.
[Slater, 1993] H. Slater. The incoherence of the aesthetic response, *British Journal of Aesthetics*, volume 33, pp. 168-172, 1993.
[Slater, 2002] H. Slater. *Logic Reformed*, Bern: Peter Lang, 2002.
[Smiley, 1960] T. Smiley. Sense without denotation, *Analysis*, volume 20, pp. 125-135, 1960.
[Herrnstein Smith, 1978] B. Herrnstein Smith. *On the Margins of Discourse*, Chicago: University of Chicago Press, 1978.
[Stone, 1937] W.H. Stone. Applications of the theory of Boolean rings to general topology, *Transactions of the American Mathematical Society*, volume 41, pp. 375-481, 1937.
[Stove, 1999] D. Stove. Cole Porterism: The jazz age in the philosophy of science, *Against the Idols of the Age*, edited by Roger Kimball, pp. 3-32 New Brunswick NJ: Transaction Publishers, 1999.
[Strawson, 1950] P.F. Strawson. On referring, *Mind*, volume 59, pp. 320-344, 1950.
[Suppes, 1962] P. Suppes. Models of data, in Ernest Nagel, Patrick Suppes and Alfred Tarski (eds.), *Logic, Methodology and Philosophy of Science*, Stanford: Stanford University Press pp. 287-301, 1962.
[Tait, 1981] W.A. Tait. Finitism, *Journal of Philosophy*, volume 78, pp. 524-546, 1981.
[Taylor, 2000] K. Taylor. Emptiness without compromise, in *Empty Names: Fictions and the Puzzles on Nonexistence*, edited by Anthony Everett and Thomas Hofweber, pp. 17-36, Stanford: CSLI Publications, 2000.
[Tharp, 1989] L. Tharp. Myth and mathematics: A conceptualistic philosophy of mathematics I, *Synthese*, volume 81, pp. 167-201, 1989.
[Thomas, 2000] R.S.D. Thomas. Mathematics and fiction I: Identification, *Logique et Analyse*, volume 43, pp. 301-340, 2000.

[Thomas, 2005] R.S.D. Thomas. Mathematics and fiction II: Analogy, *Logique et Analyse*, volume 45, pp. 185-228, 2005.
[Thomasson, 1998] A. Thomasson. *Fiction and Metaphysics*, Cambridge: Cambridge University Press 1998.
[Tiles, 1988] M. Tiles. Scientific dreamspace: Symbolic forms and scientific theories, *International Studies in Philosophy of Science*, volume 2, pp. 189-204, 1988.
[Torretti, 1981] R. Torretti. Three kinds of mathematical fictionalism, in *Scientific Philosophy*, Joseph Agassi and Robert S. Cohen, editors, pp. 399-414, Dordrecht and Boston: Reidel, 1981.
[Toulmin, 1953] S. Toulmin. *The Philosophy of Science: An Introduction*, London: Hutchinson, 1953.
[Urmson, 1976] J.O. Urmson. Fiction, *American Philosophical Quarterly*, volume 13, pp. 153-157, 1976.
[Vaihinger, 1935] H. Vaihinger. *The Philosophy of 'As If': A System of the Theoretical Practical and Religious Fictions of Mankind*, 2nd edition. Translated by C.K. Ogden, London: Routledge and Kegan Paul, 1935.
[van Fraassen, 1966a] B. van Fraassen. The completeness of free logic, *Zeitschrift für Mathematische Logik und Grundlagen der Mathematik*, volume 12, pp. 219-234, 1966a.
[van Fraassen, 1966b] B. van Fraassen. Singular terms, truth-value gaps, and free logic, *The Journal of Philosophy*, volume 63, pp. 481-494, 1966b.
[van Inwagen, 2000] P. van Inwagen. Quantification and fictional discourse, *Empty Names: Fiction and the Puzzles of Non-existence*, Anthony Everett and Thomas Hofweber, editors, pp. 235-247, Stanford: CSLI Publications 2000.
[van Neumann and Morgenstern, 1944] J. van Neumann and O. Morgenstern. *Theory of Games and Economic Behavior*, Princeton: Princeton University Press, 1944.
[von Feytag-Löringhoff, 1951] B. von Freytag-Löringhoff. *Philosophical Problems of Mathematics*, translated by Amethe von Zeepelin, New York: Philosophical Library, 1951.
[Wagner, 1982] S. Wagner. Arithmetical fiction, *Pacific Philosophical Quarterly*, volume 63, pp. 255-269, 1982.
[Walton, 1987a] K. Walton. How remote are fictional worlds from the real world?, *The Journal of Aesthetics and Art Criticism*, volume 37, pp. 11-23, 1978a.
[Walton, 1978b] K. Walton. On fearing fictions, *Journal of Philosophy*, volume 75, pp. 5-27, 1978b.
[Walton, 1990] K. Walton. *Mimesis as Make-Believe*, Cambridge MA: Harvard University Press, 1990.
[Wang, 1986] H. Wang. *Beyond Analytic Philosophy*, Cambridge, MA: MIT Press, 1986.
[Wittgenstein, 1958] L. Wittgenstein. *Philosophical Investigations*, G.E.M. Anscombe, translator, New York: Macmillan, 1958.
[Woltersdorff, 1976] N. Woltersdorff. Worlds of works of art, *The Journal of Aesthetics and Art Criticism*, volume 35, pp. 121-142, 1976.
[Woods, 1969] J. Woods. Fictionality and the logic of relations, *The Southern Journal of Philosophy*, volume 7, pp. 51-64, 1969.
[Woods, 1974] J. Woods. *The Logic of Fiction: Philosophical Soundings of Deviant Logic*, The Hague and Paris: Mouton, 1974.
[Woods and Pavel, 1979] J. Woods and T. G. Pavel. editors, *Formal Semantics and Literary Theory*. A special issue of *Poetics*, volume 8, Amsterdam: North-Holland, 1979.
[Woods, 1986] J. Woods. God, genidentity and existential parity, *Grazer Philosophische Studien*, 25-26, pp. 181-196, 1986.
[Woods, 2005] J. Woods. Dialectical considerations on the logic of contradiction I, *Logic Journal of the IGPL*, volume 8, pp. 231-260, 2005.
[Woods, forthcoming] J. Woods. Probability in the law, forthcoming.
[Zalta, 1983] E. N. Zalta. *Abstract Objects: An Introduction to Axiomatic Metaphysics*, Dordrecht and Boston: Reidel, 1983.
[Zalta, 2000] E. N. Zalta. The road between pretense theory and abstract object theory, in *Empty Names: Fiction and the Puzzles of Non-existence*, Anthony Everett and Thomas Hofweber, editors, pp. 117-147, Stanford: CSLI Publications, 2000.